THE LEGEND OF

YORK

INTERNATIONAL

THE LEGEND OF

YORK

INTERNATIONAL

JEFFREY L. RODENGEN

For Jean Dorgambide,
who has always kept us cool.

Also by Jeff Rodengen

The Legend of Chris-Craft

IRON FIST: *The Lives
of Carl Kiekhaefer*

*Evinrude-Johnson and
The Legend of OMC*

*Serving The Silent Service:
The Legend of Electric Boat*

The Legend of Dr Pepper/Seven-Up

The Legend of Honeywell

The Legend of Briggs & Stratton

The Legend of Ingersoll-Rand

*The Legend of Stanley:
150 Years of The Stanley Works*

The MicroAge Way

The Legend of Halliburton

The Legend of Nucor Corporation

The Legend of AMP

*The Legend of Goodyear:
The First 100 Years*

The Legend of Cessna

The Legend of Echlin

The Legend of AMD

The Legend of Amdahl

*Applied Materials:
Pioneering the Information Age*

The Legend of Pfizer

Publisher's Cataloging in Publication
Prepared by Quality Books Inc.

Rodengen, Jeffrey L.
    The legend of York / Jeffrey L. Rodengen.
    p. cm.
    Includes bibliographical references and index.
    ISBN 0-945903-17-0

    1. York International (Firm) 2. Heating and ventilation
industry. I. Title

HD9683.A2R64 1996   338.7'697
                                  QBI96-40367

Write Stuff Syndicate, Inc.

1515 Southeast 4th Avenue • Fort Lauderdale, FL 33316
1-800-900-Book (1-800-900-2665) • (954) 462-6657

Library of Congress Catalog Card Number 96-062225
ISBN 0-945903-17-0

Completely produced in the United States of America
10 9 8 7 6 5 4 3 2

TABLE OF CONTENTS

INTRODUCTION

WITHOUT A DOUBT, air conditioning makes our lives more comfortable. But even more importantly, without the technology of refrigeration, food would spoil and diseases would spread rapidly. For nearly 125 years, the pioneering work of York International has made the world both safer and more comfortable.

Developing this new industry required a combination of lofty visionaries and practical businessmen. York had both, and in time would become the world's largest independent supplier of heating, ventilation air conditioning and refrigeration.

York began modestly in 1874, when six investors founded the York Manufacturing Company to provide washing machines and water wheels for a nation in the midst of the Industrial Revolution. Within a short time, the company became a driving force behind the development of artificial ice and ultimately air conditioning systems.

Artificial ice in the late 1800s was slow to catch on. Who needed a machine that made "artificial" ice when "natural" ice was plentiful and easily harvested from frozen ponds? At one point, it

appeared that the enterprise would fold completely. Then, in 1890, the United States experienced an unusually warm winter. The supply of natural ice dwindled, stored food spoiled, and thousands of people fell ill. The market for ice-making machines suddenly went through the roof, and the York Manufacturing Company struggled to meet the demand.

Since then, York has established itself as a leader in the refrigeration industry, committed to quality and innovation. From the very beginning, the leadership of the company adhered to a few key values: integrity in business, skilled workmanship and good materials. They treated employees well, and generations of families joined the ranks of York employees. Thomas Shipley, a pioneer in the rapidly-changing refrigeration industry, laid the foundations for success when he took control of York in 1897, proclaiming,

"In every industry the products of one manufacturer stand out as the standard because of certain built-in qualities of excellence that defy competition. Thus it must always be with York products."

York's engineers and management have continuously developed products that both improve and save lives. York's refrigeration machines were deployed everywhere, from such prestigious locations as the Waldorf-Astoria Hotel in Manhattan to the humblest orphanages in Pennsylvania. During World War I, the company's outstanding reputation earned it important contracts to supply refrigeration for fighting ships and army camps, as well as powder and chemical plants.

In the 1920s, the company began to pioneer the new concept of providing air conditioning for human comfort. Thanks to York equipment, the San Joaquin Light & Power Corporation headquarters became the first air-conditioned office building in the world. York was soon air-conditioning movie theaters, shopping malls and places of worship. High-profile contracts included the United States Capitol and the Library of Congress Annex. Though sales suffered during the Great Depression, the company's survival was never in doubt.

World War II gave York, by then known as the York Corporation, another opportunity to serve its nation. York's FlakIce Machines provided ice to troops fighting in tropical climates throughout the world. Its refrigerators preserved food. Its air conditioners cooled industrial plants, naval bases, army camps, and ships for both the Navy and the Merchant Marine.

The company's leaders developed the York Plan, which increased wartime efficiency by encouraging companies to pool their resources and temporarily set aside competition. A central registry of the resources available from the community's 264 manufacturing concerns was created. Thomas Shipley's younger brother, William, was a leading organizer of the York Plan, widely imitated across the nation. Committed to teamwork, York became famous for its "Can-Do" attitude.

This philosophy helped the company win such high-stakes and sensitive assignments as the Manhattan Project, the frantic race to develop the atomic bomb that would end World War II. York's wartime contributions were recognized when it earned the coveted Army-Navy "E" Award.

The company's postwar success was fueled by the standard of built-in excellence that Thomas Shipley had first articulated. But the company's leadership in the refrigeration and air-conditioning fields meant that its fortunes ebbed and flowed with the changing seasons. Company officials decided to join forces with a larger firm that could balance these seasonal swings. In 1956, York became part of the Borg-Warner Corporation, a predominantly automotive industry holding company that had been established in 1928.

Whether under Borg-Warner or independent, as it was following the 1986 spin-off, York gradually recognized what has become its fastest growing market: the international arena. Trade barriers were falling and the standard of living was rising for emerging markets. Today, 45 percent of York's business is conducted with overseas partners. This is expected to increase to more than 50 percent by the year 2000, fueled largely by the huge potential within nations such as China. York officials predict that China will become the third largest market for air conditioners in the world, after the United States and Japan.

With revenues exceeding $3 billion, York International continues to enjoy steady growth. More importantly, it has done so while staying faithful to the tenets of excellence established by Thomas Shipley 100 years ago.

ACKNOWLEDGMENTS

RESEARCHING, writing and publishing *The Legend of York* would not have been possible without the cooperation and assistance of many people.

The development of historical timelines and a large portion of the archival research was accomplished by two hard-working and resourceful research assistants, Marilyn Coffron and Willis Shirk, Jr. Both sifted through thousands of documents, including many that were piled haphazardly in a dusty warehouse, to piece together the events in York's long history. Their careful research made it possible to publish much new and fascinating information about the origins and evolution of this unique organization.

The candid insights of York executives, both current and retired, were of particular importance to the project. I am especially grateful to Chairman, Chief Executive Officer and President Robert N. Pokelwaldt for sharing so much of his valuable time with me.

Many top executives took time away from their busy schedules to meet with me. These include: Scott Boxer, former president of the Unitary Products Group; Victor McCloskey, vice president of Corporate Development; Mark Fallek, vice president of Global Product Marketing; Kenneth E. Hickman, vice president of engineering for the Applied Systems Division; Dennis Kloster, vice president of North American Marketing for the Unitary Products Group; Helen Marsteller, director of Investor Relations; Joseph D. Smith, vice president and general manager of Airside Products Group; Peter Spellar, president of the Applied Systems Division; and Thomas Washburne, former president of the International Business Group.

Other York executives who contributed valuable insights include: Mark Bodell, principal engineer; Terry Bowman, director of purchasing for the Unitary Products Group; Robert Dolheimer, engineering manager for the Applied Systems Division; Bill Eastman, product manager for the Applied Systems Division; John McDonald, product manager for the Applied Systems Division; Bob Napp, manager of field service for the Unitary Products Group; Chuck O'Neal, executive sales engineer for the Applied Systems Division; Bob Schmitt, marketing manager for the Applied Systems Group; Woody Spangler, publications manager for the Unitary Products Group; James

Stambaugh, product manager for the Airside Products Group; and Bill Stewart, product manager for the Applied Systems Division.

Retired executives who were particularly helpful include: Bob Berger, G.E. Buchanan, Austin Diehl, Milton Garland, Jim Harnish, J.D. Johnson, Raymond Lecates, Jack Schultz and John Walsh.

A special debt of gratitude belongs to Rick Burt, director of Corporate Marketing and Communications, for providing assistance and support throughout the life of the project. Eunice Luckenbaugh, supervisor of Corporate Marketing Services, was always cheerful and helpful.

The employees and volunteers at the library of the Historical Society of York County were always helpful, especially in providing information about the men who founded and developed York.

Finally, a very special word of thanks to the staff at Write Stuff Syndicate, Inc., including Project Coordinator Karine N. Rodengen, Executive Assistant Bonnie Bratton, Executive Editor Karen Nitkin, Associate Editor Alex Lieber, Creative Director Kyle Newton, Art Director Sandy Cruz, Marketing and Sales Manager Christopher J. Frosch, Bookkeeper and Office Manager Marianne Roberts, and Logistics Specialist Rafael Santiago.

The original Penn Street location of the York Manufacturing Building, photographed in 1874, the company's first year in business.

CHAPTER ONE

LAND OF OPPORTUNITY

1874-1885

"Natural ice for cooling purposes is generally gathered from stagnant pools and ponds, impure canals and rivers, and when it melts it necessarily fouls the air and leaves a deposit of filth."

— 1884 York Manufacturing Company catalog[1]

PENNSYLVANIA'S FERTILE south central territory was first populated by the Susquehannocks, a branch of the Iroquois tribe that relied on the Susquehanna River for fishing and travel. In 1741, Thomas and Richard Penn, the heirs of Pennsylvania founder William Penn, sent a surveyor to create a town named for York, England. This community, populated by German immigrants, soon became the county seat, bustling with farms and other businesses. Located on the west side of the Susquehanna River, York was the last place westward-bound pioneers could buy supplies before heading into the untamed frontier.

Farmers grew corn, rye, wheat and barley, so it was natural for them to try their luck at brewing beer and distilling whiskey, selling the results to friends and neighbors. Over time, the recipes were fine-tuned and York's reputation for producing alcoholic drinks spread. York County farmers began exporting the alcoholic beverages to Baltimore and other nearby towns. By the time of the Revolutionary War, York County had 353 distilleries.[2]

York became a haven for the Continental Congress between September 27, 1777 and June 27, 1778. With the Susquehanna River serving as a barrier to British troops during the Revolutionary War, the Founding Fathers created the first constitution of the United States, the Articles of the Confederation. They also issued a proclamation making Thanksgiving a national holiday.

After America won independence, York emerged as a regional hub, with canals and railroads connecting it to Baltimore, Pittsburgh and Philadelphia. Many years later, following the Civil War, York County industries shifted from war production to the manufacture of similar items for civilian use. Most Americans recognized that it was the northern states' capacity to manufacture the tools of war that had helped preserve the union. Tired of wartime sacrifice, former soldiers became vigorous entrepreneurs. So it was for six men who pooled their resources in 1874 to form the York Manufacturing Company. This company eventually became the York International Corporation — a world-leader in air conditioning and refrigeration.

Stephen Morgan Smith

One of the six men to establish the company was Stephen Morgan Smith, who later would become a successful pioneer in the develop-

Stephen Morgan Smith, the first president of the York Manufacturing Company.

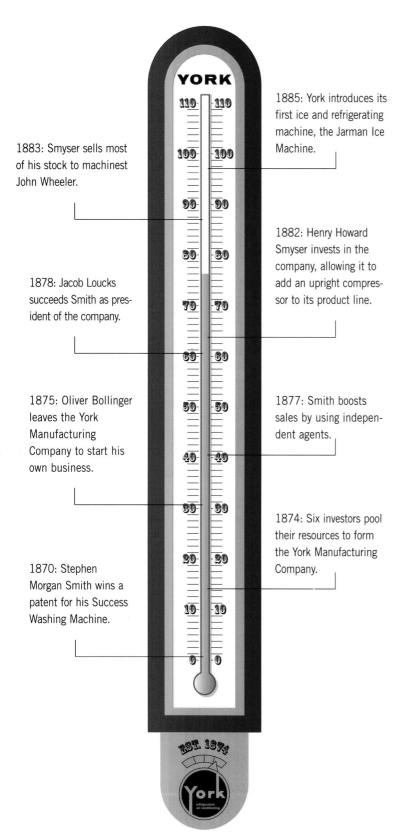

1883: Smyser sells most of his stock to machinest John Wheeler.

1878: Jacob Loucks succeeds Smith as president of the company.

1875: Oliver Bollinger leaves the York Manufacturing Company to start his own business.

1870: Stephen Morgan Smith wins a patent for his Success Washing Machine.

1885: York introduces its first ice and refrigerating machine, the Jarman Ice Machine.

1882: Henry Howard Smyser invests in the company, allowing it to add an upright compressor to its product line.

1877: Smith boosts sales by using independent agents.

1874: Six investors pool their resources to form the York Manufacturing Company.

ment of hydraulic turbines. Smith was born in 1839 in Farmington, North Carolina, to John W. and Sarah Purden (Beauchamp) Smith. He lived on his family's farm until he was 18, when he enrolled in Moravian College in Bethlehem, Pennsylvania, intending to pursue the ministry. When he graduated in 1861, his home state of North Carolina had joined the rebellious Confederacy fighting to secede from the union. Instead of joining his two brothers in the Confederate Army, Smith secured a position with the Moravian Church in York, where he lived in relative peace while the war raged on. In 1862, Smith married the church's organist, York County native Emma Fahs.[3]

This relative peace was shattered on June 28, 1863, as York was invaded by Confederate troops. The following is an account of the incident by Confederate General John B. Gordon:

"The church bells were ringing and the streets were filled with well-dressed people. The appearance of these churchgoing men, women and children, in their Sunday attire, strangely contrasted with that of my marching soldiers. Begrimed as we were from head to foot with the impalpable gray powder that rose in dense columns from macadamized pikes and settled in sheets on men, horses and wagons, it is no wonder that many of York's inhabitants were terror-stricken as they looked upon us."[4]

York County residents were torn between their loyalty to nation and their loyalty to friends and family in the South. At first, they seemed to ally with the South. Before the week was over, more than 10,000 Confederate soldiers had been fed and clothed by residents of York. The rebels planned to use the city as a base of operations while they invaded more of Pennsylvania, but this plan was abandoned when the soldiers were suddenly dispatched to Gettysburg by General Robert E. Lee.[5] Before the soldiers left York, they took food, supplies and about 1,000 horses from local stables and farms. Some of these men returned to York within three days to be cared for by residents again — this time as wounded prisoners of war.[6]

The invasion of York marked a turning point in the sentiments of many Southern

transplants, including Stephen Morgan Smith. Inspired by the Union cause, he joined the Two Hundredth Pennsylvania Volunteers, serving as a Union chaplain until the war ended two years later.

On April 21, 1865, a train on one of the tracks that cut through York carried the body of Abraham Lincoln, on its way to Illinois for burial. The citizens of York mourned his assassination with the rest of the nation and draped the slain president's burial train with a wreath of red, white and blue flowers.

Smith left York in 1866 to become a pastor of the Moravian Church in Dover, Ohio. Unfortunately, he developed a throat ailment that made it impossible for him to preach, and he reluctantly stepped down from the pulpit.[7] While regaining his health, Smith observed his wife in

the daily tasks associated with rearing children and housekeeping. He began to think of ways to ease her burden, and soon drew up plans for a mechanical clothes washing device. His informal sketch led in 1870 to a United States patent for the Success Washing Machine.[8]

Smith returned to York, hoping to sell his machine through the network of friends he had established as a preacher. He earned a modest income for his efforts, and soon developed a clothes wringer to speed the drying of washed clothes. However, by the time Smith earned his

Employees of the York Manufacturing Company, including many Civil War veterans, gather at the Gettysburg battlefield monument during a company outing around the turn of the century.

second patent, the Success Clothes Wringer, a national panic in 1873 had created a postwar depression.[9] Labor-saving devices, particularly for women, were considered luxuries that most Americans could no longer afford.

Undaunted by the continuing economic woes of the country, Smith became more determined than ever to realize his dream. He convinced five other York men — Jacob Loucks, Henry H. LaMotte, Oliver J. Bollinger, George Buck and Robert Shetter — to join him in establishing the York Manufacturing Company. Smith contributed his two patents for the Success machines, valued at $20,000.[10]

Jacob Loucks and Phillip Glatfelter

Businessman Jacob Loucks provided cash for the venture. In 1857, as a young man, Loucks had been a partner in the Loucks & Hoffman Mill, a paper manufacturer in Baltimore County, Maryland. Realizing that the Confederacy would be defeated, Loucks sold his share of the business in 1863 and moved his family north to York County, where much of his family lived. In the apparent safety of Spring Grove, he leased a paper mill and started a business. He also met Mary E. Hauer, the daughter of the mill's late owner, Jacob Hauer.

In the next few months, the Civil War battles of Hanover and Gettysburg raged dangerously near Spring Grove, so Loucks persuaded Mary Hauer to sell off her inherited property through an Orphans' Court Sale. He then loaned a former employee of the Loucks & Hoffman Mill $14,000 to buy the property. Phillip H. Glatfelter, who was married to Loucks' sister, purchased the property July 2, 1864.[11]

Loucks was wed to Mary Hauer and moved to York, where he joined the state's volunteer army supporting the Union. Meanwhile, Glatfelter built the small paper mill into a thriving company. When the war ended, Loucks began searching for another business in which to invest. Knowing this, Smith approached him in 1874 and convinced him to invest in his manufacturing company. Loucks took a chance and invested $10,000.

Oliver J. Bollinger

Smith's search for partners next led to a fellow patent-holder, Oliver J. Bollinger. Oliver had been born in 1827 in Adams County, Pennsylvania, the only child of Matthias and Elizabeth (Eckert) Bollinger. In 1838, he moved with his family to a farm near Spring Grove,

The Success Washing Machine, invented by Stephen Morgan Smith in 1870, was the first product offered by the York Manufacturing Company.

and was educated in the local schools. When he turned 18, Bollinger began learning the millwright trade as apprentice to his father, and eventually came to control his family's small manufacturing business.[12]

When his shop began manufacturing the Jonvial Turbine Water Wheel, Bollinger considered ways in which to improve the device. In 1870, he patented the Bollinger Turbine Water Wheel.[13]

Bollinger shared the rights to his invention with three investors: George H. Buck, Robert L. Shetter and H.H. LaMotte. When Smith persuaded Bollinger to join his new manufacturing business, the three investors joined as well. Bollinger, Buck, Shetter and LaMotte contributed the patent for the turbine water wheel for a stock share of $4,500, divided four ways. Bollinger also persuaded his cousin, H.H. LaMotte, to give the company his machine shop, located on the first floor of a brick two-story factory building in the heart of York. LaMotte leased the second floor to a cigar manufacturer. For $7,000, LaMotte conveyed the shop and its "lathes, line shafting, pulleys, belts and belting, vises and benches" to the new enterprise.[14]

The York Manufacturing Company

At the first stockholders meeting of the York Manufacturing Company, on September 7, 1874, Stephen Morgan Smith was elected president and Jacob Loucks was elected secretary. Smith earned $1,200 and Loucks earned $1,000 per year, "provided in each case the profits realized be 6 percent per annum on the capital of $50,000."[15] Bollinger, the company's mechanical engineer, was paid $2 a day to serve as the foreman in charge of 14 employees. The total daily payroll came to $69.50, with each man working about 60 hours a week. A post-war depression had created high unemployment in the area, and as a result the employees were exceptionally skilled machinists, pattern makers and millwrights.[16]

The York Manufacturing Company advertised the manufacture of the Bollinger Turbine Water Wheel, the Success Washing Machine and Wringer, a corn planter and cultivator, shaft pulleys and hangers. Most of the company's income was derived from repairs rather than sales, as few people could afford to purchase new equipment.

After less than a year, Bollinger resigned from the York Manufacturing Company and went into business for himself. He had improved his patented water wheel, and on June 1, 1875 he was awarded a patent for the New Bollinger Turbine Water Wheel.[17] Once Bollinger left the firm, Smith took a greater interest in the company's patent for the original Bollinger Turbine Wheel. He leased additional property behind the

Oliver Bollinger, the company's first engineer, contributed his patented water wheel to the venture.

company's building on Penn Street, and used the extra space for storage and research of turbine water wheels.[18]

Smith purchased prototypes for a number of successful turbine water wheels from other firms, and compared both effective and poor designs. Meanwhile, several stockholders, fearing that the young company would go bankrupt, made the financial situation worse by cashing in their stock.[19]

Smith knew he needed to take decisive action. He risked nearly all he owned to hire gifted machinist George Baugher, and put him in charge of the Turbine Water Wheel redesign.[20] In 1877, he boosted sales by recruiting independent agents to sell the Success Washing Machines at reduced prices. Smith also purchased another building behind the main facility for $260 and 20 percent of the company's proceeds.

Smith was unable to pay Baugher for his work, and sold him the company's patent for the Bollinger Water Wheel on July 26, 1878.[21]

York Manufacturing Company

YORK, PENN'A,

In June 1878, Loucks became president of the company. Two years later, Smith left, walking out the door with a note for $1,411.77 — his share of the company profits. With these funds, Smith continued his development of turbine wheels, independent of York Manufacturing Company. He patented the Success Turbine Water Wheel, and then contracted with the York Manufacturing Company to build it.

Smith earned enough profits from sales of his new turbine water wheel to form his own business, the S. Morgan Smith Company, in 1890. Over the next few years, he found ways to improve the speed and power of his turbines. Believing that the York Manufacturing Company had tried to accomplish too much at once, he focused on the improvement and sale of only one type of machine. Smith eventually built one of the world's largest companies devoted solely to turbine hydraulics.[22]

The nation was in the midst of the Industrial Revolution, and technological advances were taking place with breathtaking speed. In 1880, thousands of people flocked to Wabash, Indiana, to witness the first lighting of the city's new electric arc lamps invented by Thomas Edison.[23] The manufacture of agricultural implements, still the most important component of York's economy, was modernizing. Jacob Loucks, by this time president of the York Manufacturing Company, added steam engines and boilers to the catalog of items produced, and brought his son, George W. S. Loucks, into the company as secretary.

Steam Engines

Within one year, the company expanded its line to include side and center crank vertical engines. It offered several sizes of water wheels to serve the needs of the paper, flour and lumber mills owned by Loucks' relatives.[24] By 1882, the York Manufacturing Company was a respected industrial concern, and its success attracted the notice of Henry Howard Smyser, the eldest son of a wealthy Spring Grove businessman. His interest in the York Manufacturing Company was partially due to increased demand for steam engines, and partially to distant connections between the Loucks and Smyser families through marriage.[25]

Smyser's subsequent investment allowed the York Manufacturing Company to add marine engines, including an upright motor for small yachts, to its product line. It also allowed the company to lease the second floor of its building for use as a pattern shop and office area. The upgrade and expansion of the facility attracted Oliver Bollinger, whose improved turbine water wheel was enjoying tremendous success in Europe and the United States. To meet increasing demand, Bollinger contracted with York Manufacturing Company to manufacture his wheel. Loucks and Smyser constructed a foundry on the lots leased by Smith. According to George Motter, who was hired to manage the boiler department, the owners wanted to make their own steel and iron castings for machine components, previously subcontracted to local firms, including one previously owned by Motter.[26]

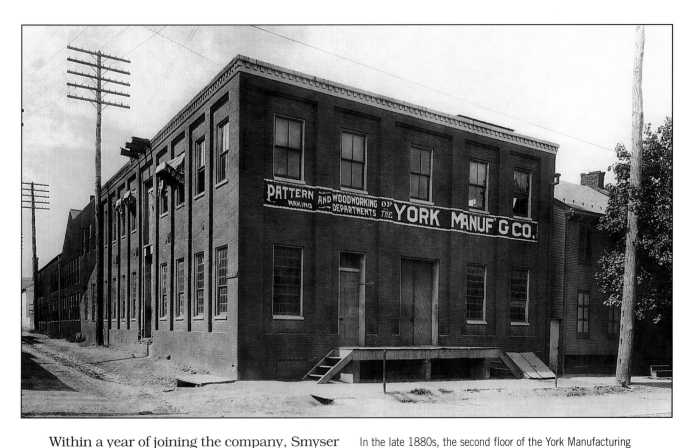

In the late 1880s, the second floor of the York Manufacturing Company was leased for use as a pattern shop and office area.

Within a year of joining the company, Smyser came into an inheritance from his grandparents.[27] With the unexpected windfall, Smyser became partners with a relative who ran a hardware store at 739 West Philadelphia Street and within ten years became a prominent businessman in the city.[28] Smyser sold most of his York Machinery Company stock to John Wheeler, a machinist with the firm.

When Wheeler became a partner in the company, he took over the plant's operations as general manager, freeing Loucks to explore various improvements to the steam engine.[29] Made of iron, steel and decorative brass, these engines were fitted with steam vacuum pumps, which were a profitable accessory.[30] York also began combining the engine, boiler and pumps on a single cast-iron base, creating conveniently packaged power for a large variety of uses.[31]

The company then developed a semi-portable engine that featured wooden wheels with iron hubs and heavy rubber tires. This engine, designed for use in tanneries and mills, featured a safety valve, steam gauge, glass gauge, water column, blow-off valve, spark arrester and steam whistle.[32] The steam whistle was originally used by machine operators to inform workers that more coal was needed. In paper mills, where there was quite a distance from one end of a machine to the other, the whistle also warned workers when the machine was about to start. Over time, the whistle came to signal the start and end of the work day and lunch break.[33]

York soon began manufacturing engines to drive compressors. The basic similarity of compressor and steam engines allowed the two machines to be mounted with a common crankshaft. In 1883, Loucks' interest focused on a related machine — one used for making ice.

A Brief History of Ice-Making

Nearly 50 years earlier, in 1834, Jacob Perkins of New England obtained a British patent on an ice-making machine that worked by compressing and condensing volatile liquids in a closed cycle. John Gorrie, a physician who was caring for sailors in Florida, became interested in the ice-making process when he discovered that cooler air halted the spread of malaria. His research led to an ice-production system that worked by compressing air in an open cycle.[34]

In 1853, Alexander C. Twining of the Cuyahoga Ice Works in Cleveland, Ohio, was awarded a patent for a refrigerating device that utilized ether instead of air. His was the first machine to produce commercial ice through vapor compression, but it still could not compete with the natural ice produced in the nearby Great Lakes.

In Australia, engineer James Harrison studied these refrigeration machines, hoping to find a way to freeze Australia's abundant meat supply and ship it overseas to sell in Europe. To gain support for his idea, he built several ice machines in 1859 and 1860 for breweries in Sydney and Melbourne, using sulfuric ether as a refrigerant. He was the first to use refrigeration for a brewery, an idea that would spread throughout the world in the coming decades. From this success, Harrison gained the support of several investors, and outfitted a ship sailing for England with a refrigerating machine. The trial failed, however, when the ship's refrigerating machine broke down and Harrison became a laughingstock.

In the United States, most people didn't see a pressing need to manufacture what was known as artificial ice. Natural ice was easily harvested from frozen lakes in the winters and could be stored in ice houses insulated with straw. In 1861, however, the Civil War disrupted the shipment of natural ice to the South. A single hospital equipped with the compressor designed by John Gorrie was the sole institution that could adequately care for malaria patients. The French smuggled two small refrigerating machines through a Union blockade for use in other Confederate hospitals. These machines had been invented by Frenchman Ferdinand Carre, who used aqua-ammonia as the refrigerant in his absorption system.[35] Eventually, the need for such machines was recognized, and after the war, improvements on Carre's refrigeration patent were developed.

Despite enhancements, the machines still operated on the same basic principal. They were belt-driven by a steam engine, with the refrigerating effect coming from frozen condensation on exposed iron and steel pipes. The pipes were defrosted at intervals by running warm refrigerant through them and then beating off the accumulated ice with wooden clubs. Many people feared that this early ice was unsanitary because it had a milky appearance caused by air that had been trapped during the freezing process. Their fears were somewhat justified, since artificial ice, which was simply skimmed from the top of the water as it froze, was usually contaminated with lubricating oil.[36]

Daniel L. Holden finally produced clear ice in the mid 1870s by using distilled water within a compressor system, powered by the horizontal steam engine that had been invented by George Corliss in 1849. The machine, though not popular for decades, was safer and more economical than machines that relied on exotic chemical compounds.[37] Meanwhile, manufacturers continued to use the ammonia absorption system and soon discovered that agitating non-distilled water while it froze prevented air pockets and also produced clear ice.

By the 1880s, the United States had established leadership in the field of ice making, especially for breweries and meat packers. International engineering expositions recognized ice and refrigeration machine inventors with high honors. Scientific journals contradicted popular belief by expounding the merits of artificial ice over "impure" natural ice.[38]

The Jarman Compressor

Loucks and Wheeler invested most of the company's funds in this new field. They hired

---

WHAT IS A TON?

A ton is the unit of refrigeration representing the absorption of heat equivalent to the production of one ton of ice in 24 hours. Since it takes 144 British Thermal Units to convert one pound of water to ice, one ton of refrigeration would use 200 BTUs per minute.

George Jarman, who had designed an easy-to-operate single-valve refrigerating machine that used anhydrous ammonia as its cooling agent. To manufacture these machines, the York Manufacturing Company factory was expanded to include a punching and rolling department, construction room and boiler department. The move into the "new ice age" represented a significant risk for Loucks and Wheeler, and nearly depleted their funds. To stimulate sales, they produced an illustrated catalog with descriptions of the company's engines, boilers, ice-makers and refrigerating machinery.[39] For those still skeptical about the benefits of artificial ice, the catalog noted that ice scraped off a frozen pond might not be as pure as it seems.

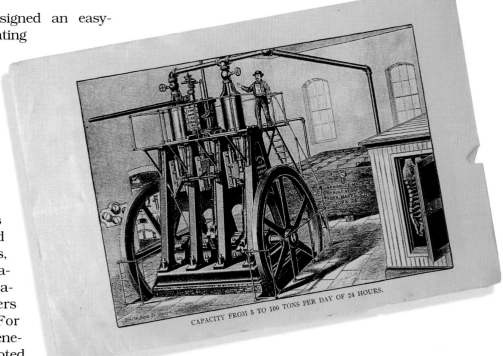

"Natural ice for cooling purposes is generally gathered from stagnant pools and ponds, impure canals and rivers, and when it melts it necessarily fouls the air and leaves a deposit of filth. This foul air impregnates and rots all the wood it comes in contact with, and in case of open casks must contaminate their contents. It speedily injures floors and joists and lessens their durability, and often has a deleterious effect on beer, even when made of the best ingredients."[40]

Brewers and packers were reminded that the brine or ammonia cooling agent apparatus could be located in a room, isolated from the area to be cooled. Operation of the Jarman Ice Machines required a day engineer, a night engineer, a day fireman and a night fireman. Two tons of coal produced 25 tons of refrigeration. The machine was guaranteed to operate satisfactorily and permanently with its manu-facture and installation supervised by George Jarman personally.[41]

Catalogs were distributed throughout the United States, with an emphasis on the southern Gulf states. Jarman Ice Machines were offered in a variety of sizes, capable of producing anywhere from one ton to fifty tons of ice in 24 hours. The first machine, with the capacity to produce eight tons of refrigeration, was sold in 1885 to the Water Valley Ice and Cold Storage Company in Water Valley, Mississippi.[42]

But in spite of these efforts, a decline in the economy led some of the stockholders of the York Manufacturing Company to sell their shares. Loucks and Wheeler, undaunted by the downturn, elected to hold on.

The first ice and refrigerating machine produced by York was the 1885 Jarman Ice Machine.

A York Manufacturing worker labors to clean flanges in the company pipe shop around 1890.

CHAPTER TWO

REFRIGERATION MACHINES

1886-1894

"Employ nothing but the best labor. Pay nothing but the highest wages. Do all work upon the day system. Use the best and highest grade labor-saving tools. Use nothing but the best material. Guess at nothing but TEST EVERYTHING. Guarantee our work as second to none in the country. Charge only fair prices for good work. Challenge the world to produce, either in design, workmanship or combination, a better machine, or one giving better results."

— Company catalog, 1892[1]

JACOB LOUCKS AND John Wheeler were confident that the York Manufacturing Company could successfully compete with other refrigeration businesses throughout the nation. In 1886, the company became a limited partnership, owned by Loucks & Wheeler, proprietors of the York Manufacturing Company.[2] Steam engines, compressors and boilers continued to make up the bulk of the business, although two ice machines, representing 16 total tons of refrigeration, were sold that year. Among the company's 40 employees was John C. Ruby, a skilled machinist who had taken charge of the new refrigeration department.[3]

Despite extensive advertising and marketing, the company could not win contracts to supply refrigeration to the shipping, packing and brewing industries.[4] Searching for another sales angle, Loucks and Wheeler suggested that their machines would be ideal for making ice to cool drinks. They also suggested that refrigeration could be employed in hotels, wine cellars and bars. Adopting the motto, "We cannot afford to have a customer dissatisfied," Loucks and Wheeler declared in their product catalog, "Perfect control of temperature can only be had by mechanical means."[5]

A Powerful Rival

But the York Manufacturing Company lacked the status enjoyed by its larger competitors. Its rivals included the Frick Company of nearby Waynesboro, Pennsylvania, which had a well-deserved reputation for excellence. Already renowned for its use of the Corliss Steam Engine, Frick hired refrigeration engineer Edgar Penney to adapt the engine for use in refrigeration machines. Penney was assisted by Thomas Shipley, a young mechanical engineer and designer who also specialized in the science of refrigeration.[6] The result was a best-selling refrigeration machine that garnered awards in prestigious scientific expositions throughout the world. It included such advanced features as twin vertical cylinders for smooth operation, and single-acting pistons for efficiency of compression. By 1888, the Frick Company had sold 14 of these refrigerating machines to breweries and packing houses.[7]

Meanwhile, the York Manufacturing Company had sold only seven machines, not enough to pay the debt that Loucks and Wheeler had incurred

An 1892 York Manufacturing two- to three-ton compressor.

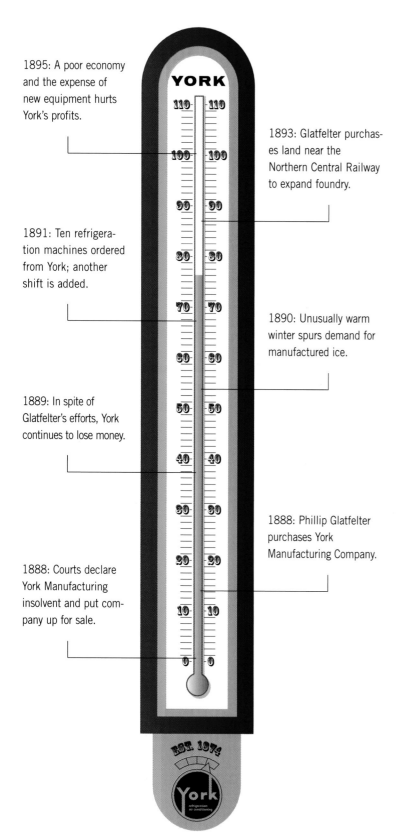

1895: A poor economy and the expense of new equipment hurts York's profits.

1893: Glatfelter purchases land near the Northern Central Railway to expand foundry.

1891: Ten refrigeration machines ordered from York; another shift is added.

1890: Unusually warm winter spurs demand for manufactured ice.

1889: In spite of Glatfelter's efforts, York continues to lose money.

1888: Phillip Glatfelter purchases York Manufacturing Company.

1888: Courts declare York Manufacturing insolvent and put company up for sale.

for new buildings, machinery and advertising. The high price of steel and iron made the products too expensive for most customers, so it became an accepted practice to offer a line of credit to customers. Despite the risk, Loucks and Wheeler began accepting notes that promised payment for merchandise.[8]

The risk backfired. Loucks and Wheeler struggled to make customers pay their notes. When the First National Bank of York demanded payment of their notes in 1888, Loucks and Wheeler were unable to pay. The courts declared the York Manufacturing Company insolvent, and the company was put up for sale. It probably would have folded altogether if not for Phillip Henry Glatfelter. Glatfelter was Loucks' brother-in-law as well as president of the First National Bank of York. The courts appointed him as the estate's assignee, which meant that he was required to pay off the notes owed to the bank through the sale of the company.[9] Glatfelter instead paid the full $15,000 debt himself. As the new owner of the York Manufacturing Company, Glatfelter assumed control of operations as the new president.

Phillip Henry Glatfelter

Phillip Henry Glatfelter had been born in 1837 to Charles and Louisa in North Codorus Township. For generations, his family had been farmers, but Glatfelter enjoyed mechanics and expressed a desire to go into business. When he was 23, Glatfelter was offered a job as apprentice under Jacob Loucks, co-owner of a paper mill in Maryland. For three years, Glatfelter worked without pay, receiving only room and board in exchange for on-the-job training. When Glatfelter finished his apprenticeship, Loucks offered him a job at the mill. While there, Glatfelter met Jacob's sister, Amanda Loucks, and married her in 1861.

In 1863, Glatfelter borrowed money from his friends to buy a paper mill of his own. It was old, small and falling apart. His discipline, business skills and technical abilities soon turned the mill into a prosperous enterprise, and Glatfelter built a second factory. Glatfelter eventually had seven children, six girls and a boy. His son, William

Above: Phillip Henry Glatfelter at the time he took over the York Manufacturing Company.

Right: Edson gauges, which allowed managers to know immediately of any problems in the system, were offered by York as an option.

a Knight Templar in the Masonic Order and a member of the International Order of Odd Fellows. As York historian George Prowell wrote in 1907, "In social and political circles, no man in the community enjoys a wider popularity than George W. S. Loucks."[11]

Glatfelter's son, William, became treasurer and a director. A graduate of the College of Gettysburg and Eastman's Business College in New York, William had joined his father's Spring Grove paper mill in 1887, the year he married Katherine Hollinger, of Abbottstown, Pennsylvania. William's friends described him as a quiet man with deep convictions. His hard work and good business sense helped him to become a wealthy, well-respected businessman. A man who lived by the Bible, he was also a generous philanthropist.[12]

In addition to family members, Phillip Glatfelter hired Stuart St. Clair, a specialist in refrigeration machinery. St. Clair joined York in 1889 as general manager, head engineer and designer. Meanwhile, Jacob Loucks and John Wheeler quietly faded into retirement.[13]

Glatfelter's paternalistic, uncompromising and authoritarian manner instilled confidence in his 40 employees. His prominently displayed "Rules of This Establishment" reflected his strong convictions and values.

Lincoln Glatfelter, would one day join his father at York Manufacturing. Glatfelter eventually became one of the wealthiest men in the area. In 1879, he hired his brother Edward to assume the company's day-to-day management, allowing himself the time to explore new business opportunities, such as the acquisition of the York Manufacturing Company.[10]

The New Executives

Glatfelter enjoyed working with family members and hired his nephew, George Loucks, as secretary. George Loucks had been an apprentice at Glatfelter's paper mill in Spring Grove. He was

A Health Crisis

Despite Glatfelter's enthusiasm, no refrigerating machines were sold in 1889.[14] Then, in 1890, fate intervened in the form of an unusually warm winter. The ice harvest was about half its usual size. By the following July, the ice houses were down to their last blocks of ice, and those were melting fast. Food began to spoil, but people continued to eat it anyway. That summer, thousands of people fell victim to food poisoning. The ice houses scrambled to order ice-making machines, and a shortage soon developed.

RULES OF THIS ESTABLISHMENT

Employees working here shall dust the furniture, clean their desks and sweep the floor daily.

All windows shall be cleaned once a week.

Each employee shall bring his own bucket of water and scuttle of coal for the day's work.

Lamps shall be trimmed and chimneys shall be cleaned daily.

Working hours shall be seven a.m. to eight p.m. every evening but the Sabbath.

On the Sabbath, everyone is expected to be in the Lord's house.

Employees are expected to trim their own pen nibs to suit themselves.

It is expected that each employee shall participate in the activities of the church and contribute liberally to the Lord's work.

All employees must show themselves worthy of their hire.

All employees are expected to be in bed by ten p.m. except male employees may be given one evening a week for courting purposes and two evenings a week in the Lord's House.

After an employee has been with our firm for five years, he shall receive an added payment of five cents per day, providing the firm prospered in a manner to make it possible.

It is the bounden (sic) duty of each employee to put away at least ten percent of his wages for his declining years, so that he will not become a burden upon the charity of his betters.

Any employee who is shaven in public parlors, frequents pool rooms or uses tobacco shall be brought before management to give reasons why he should be continued in employment.[1]

The public realized it could not rely on the weather for a dependable supply of ice. Orders for ice machines increased, and Glatfelter boosted his workforce to fifty. The Commonwealth of Pennsylvania granted the company a limited partnership in 1891, with the co-owners listed as Phillip H. Glatfelter, George W.S. Loucks, William L. Glatfelter and John C. Ruby.[15]

The partners attributed their success to integrity in business, skilled workmanship and good materials. The company paid good wages for the best workers, and guaranteed all products. In its 1892 catalog, York proudly listed "some of the things we do."

"Employ nothing but the best labor. Pay nothing but the highest wages. Do all work upon the day system. Use the best and highest grade labor-saving tools. Use nothing but the best material. Guess at nothing but TEST EVERYTHING. Guarantee our work as second to none in the country. Charge only fair prices for good work. Challenge the world to produce, either in design, workmanship or combination, a better machine, or one giving better results."[16]

York's refrigeration machines relied on mechanical compression. The latest model at the time was the Single-Acting Vertical Compound No-Oil System. The York Manufacturing Company claimed that the oil system was a crutch for a bad design, which required lubrication to keep ill-fitting parts in service. According to the company's engineers, the oil in competitive systems polluted the refrigerating coils and slowed down piston speed, which, in turn, increased fuel consumption.[17]

Even as double-acting pumps were becoming the industry standard, York engineers stubbornly insisted that single-acting pumps were more efficient. They asserted that the change was taking place with an "entire disregard for mechanics and only to make the almighty dollar. ... We can build you double-acting machines as good as our neighbor's, but we would not, for we know they fall far short in efficiency. It would cost us much less money for the same machine, but it would cost you more money to operate."[18]

By the spring of 1891, 10 refrigeration machines had been ordered from York, and a night shift was established to meet the demand. In 1892, the company received orders for 13 St. Clair Compound machines, with a total capacity of 289 tons. The following year, St. Clair's machine incorporated a high-pressure steam engine-driven compressor that compressed ammonia gas without the need for condensing or using a vacuum pump, due to the incorporation of an atmospheric exhaust. The result was a smaller, more efficient compressor and engine.

The appearance of the ice was also important. Impurities such as minerals or gases in water are the last to freeze, and they form in the core of the frozen ice mass, creating an unattractive, cloudy appearance. Ice without a discolored core could be produced from water that had been heated at high enough temperatures to decompose all organic matter. When the resulting vapor was frozen,

An 1892 catalog of York Manufacturing Company products. The catalog was designed to educate the public and promote company products.

the ice was clear. "The refrigerating machine is not just a compressor, but the harmonious blending of all parts," Stuart St. Clair insisted.[19]

The price of St. Clair's machine was lower than that of competitors, and customers were expected to pay cash. Glatfelter had no intention of allowing the York Manufacturing Company to fall into bankruptcy again, and he refused to repeat the mistakes of the company's former owners by issuing loans or lines of credit. Orders for refrigerating and ice making machines continued to arrive, and customers were elated with the product, as shown by this testimonial from the Greenfield Ice Company, manufacturers of "pure crystal ice."

"We have about 200 tons of ice in our house now, that we will put against any ice in the State for transparency and purity. Our machine has run steady since starting, and our bill for repairs has been just 25 cents. We consider the York Ice machine the best machine on the market today for durability and simplicity of construction, and honest workmanship."[20]

The company even installed two refrigeration machines for ice skating rinks. In 1893, the company sold fewer, but larger machines, resulting in even more profits. By then, the York Manufacturing Company had more than $150,000 in assets, and broke ground to build a new machine shop, boiler shop and foundry.[21]

A Time of Expansion

In 1893, George Loucks resigned from the company to serve as mayor of York. Meanwhile, Glatfelter decided to buy additional land to expand the factory and modernize production methods. He chose a site in west York, near the Northern Central Railway. The previous owner, Edison Electric Light Company, left buildings that could be used as the shell of a new foundry.[22]

Even though the nation had plunged into a deep recession, Glatfelter went ahead with the expansion. He had a personal reason for expanding the refrigeration business. Typhoid had claimed the lives of three of his children, and new evidence was linking the disease to ice harvested from ponds. Determined to speed production of life-saving ice machines, Glatfelter hired the architectural firm of J.A. Dempwolf in York to design the buildings. Dempwolf had previously designed the spacious Victorian mansion in Spring Grove where Glatfelter, his wife Amanda, and their surviving two daughters lived. Once the plans were ready, however, Glatfelter realized he couldn't afford to build. Consequently, he incorporated in March 1895, opening the door to outside investment. With a fresh infusion of capital, he contracted with the Wrought Iron Bridge Company of Canton, Ohio to begin fram-

Left: The York and St. Clair 10 Ton Ice Machine. The York catalog confidently proclaimed the machine as the "best machine on the market."

Center: A cross-section of the Compound machine. Advertisements stated that the Compound compressor saved at least 18 percent of energy.

ing the factory. The completed structure was built between July 13, 1895, and July 29, 1896.

A dispute between the Wrought Iron Bridge Company and the York Manufacturing Company resulted in a suit filed against York to collect unpaid debt. A lien was placed on the property until the Court of Common Pleas rendered an opinion. In 1897, the court ruled in favor of the York Manufacturing Company.[23] It was decided that York should not pay the machinist bill of $32,315, which included more than $2,000 for the cost of a mechanical engineer and supervisor. York's attorney argued that the company would never have paid for a mechanical engineer since it had plenty of engineers of its own.

While the new factory was under construction, Stuart St. Clair became mired in debt and faced additional legal challenges as well.[24] He was replaced by George Major, a machinist in the company's refrigeration department.

Major took the opportunity to persuade stockholders that Corliss engines should be used in the larger refrigerating machines. This change, he argued, would bring the company's products up to date and make them more efficient. Major also insisted that the company offer horizontal double-acting machines, which were popular with customers who were limited by ceiling height. This proposed strategy was designed so that the compressor worked in tandem with the steam engine, with the piston rods of each machine directly connected to one another. This design produced less friction, required fewer parts and improved access to the valves.[25] Major also encouraged the development of machines to produce plate ice. Plate ice was more clear than the block ice formed in cans. The stockholders approved Major's recommendations, and a new catalog listed the new products and improvements.

The expense of new buildings and equipment, located on what is now Roosevelt Avenue, and the low price of ice machines combined to create a new cash-flow crisis.[26] In desperation, Glatfelter lured a respected refrigeration engineer and manager away from a major competitor to take over operations at York in 1897.

Completed in 1896, the new York Manufacturing plant, which was located on what is now Roosevelt Avenue, almost broke the back of the struggling company.

These enormous blocks of ice were used to preserve meat and produce during transportation and storage.

CHAPTER THREE

A NEW INDUSTRY STANDARD

1895-1905

"I believe in being an expert in one line, and not a general practitioner. ... You can succeed in any line if you are an expert, but if you are only a dabbler, you'll be brushed aside."

— Thomas Shipley, 1897[1]

IN 1895, PHILLIP H. Glatfelter celebrated his 58th birthday, and was ready to turn over his business interests to a new generation. He hired Michael Kelly to manage his successful paper mill, then spread across five acres and valued at $1 million.[2] He named his son William president of the Hanover Wirecloth Company and he helped his son-in-law, Charles Moule, start the Hanover Match Company.

But the York Manufacturing Company remained financially insecure. In 1896, the nation was slogging through the worst depression on record, and the York Manufacturing Company was struggling to survive. Contributing to the national uncertainty was the fact that workers and management were locked in bitter battles throughout the country, reflected in the presidential race that year. William McKinley, the Republican nominee, was an advocate of protective tariffs and the gold standard of currency, two measures intended to protect American businesses. Meanwhile, most workers in the manufacturing facilities of York County supported Democrat William Jennings Bryan, who favored the unlimited coinage of both silver and gold, which he argued would improve the quality of life for laborers.

Glatfelter feared that a Bryan victory would devalue the nation's currency and cause further economic chaos, so he delayed plans to make improvements to the York Manufacturing Company until following the national elections. Meanwhile, the company continued to lose money, selling only seven ice machines in 1896, barely enough revenue to meet the payroll. Between 1885 and 1897, the company had sold exactly 100 ice machines — not enough to justify continuing in this line of business.

To supplement its income, the York Manufacturing Company in 1896 took on contracts to manufacture materials for other firms, including riveted pipe, plate work and specialized castings.[3] Glatfelter refused to give up the company as a lost cause and, after McKinley won the presidency, he increased his investment and activity in the enterprise. Convinced that the ice and refrigeration business had limitless potential, Glatfelter decided the company needed someone with a solid record of achievement to pull the business out of its financial doldrums.

Metal gauge boards measured steam and ammonia pressures in York's ice machines.

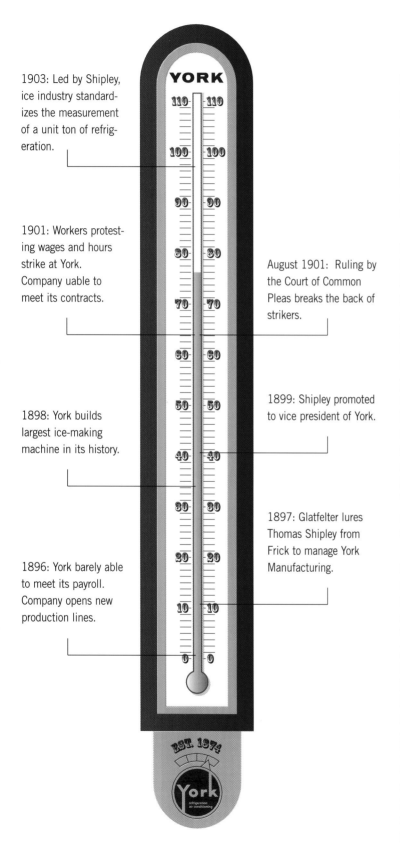

1903: Led by Shipley, ice industry standardizes the measurement of a unit ton of refrigeration.

1901: Workers protesting wages and hours strike at York. Company uable to meet its contracts.

August 1901: Ruling by the Court of Common Pleas breaks the back of strikers.

1899: Shipley promoted to vice president of York.

1898: York builds largest ice-making machine in its history.

1897: Glatfelter lures Thomas Shipley from Frick to manage York Manufacturing.

1896: York barely able to meet its payroll. Company opens new production lines.

Thomas Shipley

In 1897, Glatfelter located the ideal person at the Frick Company. In brazen fashion, Glatfelter captured Frick's manager, Thomas Shipley, by doubling his salary and offering him a four percent interest in York. He also promised the 38-year-old Shipley a free hand to make the York Manufacturing Company profitable.[4] Shipley's ideas and enthusiasm would change the ice and refrigeration industry, while proving worthy of Glatfelter's confidence many times over.

Shipley had already established a fine reputation for himself in the industry. In 1886, Shipley had joined the Frick Company, where he helped adapt the Corliss steam engine to the ice machine.[5] Prior to that, Shipley had been part-owner of a small but successful engineering firm. Shipley combined intelligence and commercial insight with an incredible capacity for work. Growing up in Jersey City, New Jersey, he supported his family and himself while going to school, graduating from the Cooper Institute of New York in 1881. A born innovator, Shipley had chafed under Frick Company's conservative business practices. He jumped at Glatfelter's offer, even though most in the ice industry believed Shipley was making a fatal career mistake. The York Manufacturing Company, with its 50 employees and old-fashioned designs, appeared to have no future.[6]

Upon his arrival, Shipley immediately began modernizing both the organization and equipment of the York Manufacturing Company. His first task was to redesign the factory buildings and modernize the production line. Shipley set up the West York plant on the corner of Hartley and Roosevelt streets to include his office, a malleable-iron foundry, a gray-iron foundry for small castings, annealing ovens and a gray-iron foundry for large castings. It also contained machine shops for tooling and erecting, a pipe and fitting shop, plus a loading crane in the yard. The old facility on Penn Street housed a pattern shop, woodworking department, blacksmith shop, sheet metal department and boiler shop. With the new factory configurations, Shipley achieved a harmonious organization that improved the quality of the machines, noted the 1901 catalog.

"Good results can only be obtained when the different parts of the [machines] are manufactured under the one management, so that every part can be tested and proved, not only in respect to its individual qualities, but also in relation to the other parts of the system in connection with which it is to be operated."[7]

Along with Shipley, Glatfelter recruited several more of Frick's top engineers. Shipley put this cadre of Frick expatriates to work on a new ice-making machine. The unit featured twin vertical cylinders containing single action pistons that compressed ammonia, driven by a steam engine. Shipley had worked on this design at Frick Company, but corporate leaders there had deemed it too expensive for commercial success. The design, though, was unusually simple for a customer to maintain and repair, while at the same time offering greater productivity.

The machine that Shipley eventually manufactured for York needed only two bearings for the crank shaft, with the flywheel located between. Parts were readily accessible for adjustment, as discharge and suction valves could be inspected by simply removing the compressor head. The machine was offered in various sizes and shapes. Smaller capacity designs featured engines with balanced piston valves, while larger ones employed a Corliss-type engine.[8]

Shipley knew he had to repair York's damaged image, so he sought to offer premier quality machines only, even if higher prices meant lost sales. In the 1901 product catalog, he criticized competitors who offered less-expensive machines. "We claim that the only reason a manufacturer builds double-

acting machines is to meet competition by cheapening his product."[9]

Cracking the Ice Market

Shipley eliminated the company's other product lines, concentrating solely on the production of ice and refrigeration machinery with its accessory equipment. "I believe in being an expert in one line, and not a general practitioner," he said. "You can succeed in any line if you are an expert, but if you are only a dabbler, you'll be brushed aside."[10] Shipley recruited a corps of good salesmen to promote the single-action ice-making compressor and defend the company's reputation. Shipley knew that destroying the competitor's reputation was a common sales tactic. His old employer, Frick, had been trying to discredit York's good name for years.

Shipley opened up sales offices in New York City and Cincinnati in December 1897 and hired his younger brother, Samuel, as sales representative.[11] The company targeted customers with great need of ice or refrigeration machines. In 1898, York opened offices in Houston and Pittsburgh, adding Atlanta the following year. Shipley hired salesmen with engineering backgrounds, so they would have the expertise to alter the machine's design to fit the specific requirements of customers.

In 1898, the York Manufacturing Company built the largest ice-making machine

An older Thomas Shipley. Shipley joined York at the age of 38, and transformed the struggling company into an industry leader.

to date. The machine featured 30-inch-by-48-inch ammonia compressors, driven by a 30-inch-by-58-inch-by-49-inch cross-compound Corliss engine. This behemoth was sold to the Packing House of Armour & Company in Kansas City, Missouri, where it remained in operation for more than 20 years.[12]

In the first three years of Shipley's employment, York sold 210 ice-making and refrigeration machines, more than the company had sold during the previous 13 years.[13] The York Manufacturing Company had grown to become one of the area's largest businesses, no small feat since the area could boast more than 800 different manufacturing concerns. Glatfelter was ecstatic with the York Manufacturing Company's new success. In 1899, he promoted Shipley to vice president of the company. Unfortunately, a growing labor unrest would put a temporary freeze on the company's growth.

The Strike of 1901

Shipley had hired aggressively in 1897 as part of his reorganization efforts, and the payroll of the York Manufacturing Company quickly mushroomed from 50 workers to more than 200.[14] Even with the additional workforce, workers struggled to keep up with a production schedule that seemed to grow more demanding each day. The men laboring in the factory were expected to do whatever was necessary to meet these schedules, even if it meant working 12 hours a day, six days a week. Even apprentices as young as 14 years old adhered to this difficult schedule.

Most of the machinists, mechanics, molders and other laborers at the York Manufacturing

The headquarters and factory of the York Manufacturing Company, depicted in the 1901 catalog.

Company belonged to either the International Association of Machinists or the Iron Molders' Union of North America. On May 1, 1901, 11 men representing both unions entered the superintendent's office and demanded higher wages for mechanics, apprentices and working men, and threatened to keep other workers away from the factories. The union leaders hoped the combination of adverse publicity and business loss would force Glatfelter and Shipley to meet their terms. Machinist Charles Oberdick, a local union officer, vowed to strike until the union demands were acknowledged. If not, he said, the unions would "prevent the smoke from coming out of the York Manufacturing Company smokestack."[15]

Glatfelter and Shipley decided to ignore the demands and hire replacement workers.[16] When the decision was announced on May 20, about 150 apprentices and workers — three-quarters of the workforce — abruptly walked out of the factory. They gathered in front of the factory's entrances to discourage others from working at the company and to publicize their struggle. The strikers, led by state and local union leaders, including ones from other cities, picketed the streets near the factory day and night.[17] They surrounded the homes of workers who chose to continue working for the company, harassing and threatening their families. Strikers intercepted prospective employees at the railway station and

told them if they took a job at York, it would be the last place they worked.

On May 24, several striking members of the molders' union assembled on the sidewalk to block Tom Shipley as he walked to work. They menaced Shipley to such an extent that, "although a man of courage, he walked off the sidewalk and around them to avoid a collision," said an account in a local paper.[18] That was the last straw. After arriving at his office, Shipley immediately fired all employees who were members of the molders' union and subcontracted work to other manufacturing shops in the area, preferring to take a loss than to submit to the workers.

He contacted S. Morgan Smith & Sons; Hench & Dromgold; York Safe and Lock Company; Baugher, Kurtz & Company; and

Above: York workers constructing the base of an ice machine.

Left: Brewers' thermometers, offered in the 1903 catalog, are valuable for making and storing beer.

George F. Motter & Sons. Some of the businesses refused because they didn't want to get mixed up in York's labor battles. Union members in other companies refused to work on any York Manufacturing Company contract, defying their bosses and often losing well-paying jobs. By July, many manufacturers in the city were refusing to take on the company's contracts because of the trouble it caused within their ranks.[19]

By August, the company could not deliver the orders as promised. The York Manufacturing Company was losing sales, but Glatfelter and Shipley continued to hold out against the strikers and fought back through the courts. They claimed union members had joined forces to ruin their business, in violation of the Sherman

Antitrust Act. The act, passed in 1890, was meant to encourage competition by making it illegal to form a trust that restrained trade. Glatfelter's brother, William, acting as the company's secretary, wrote a deposition requesting relief from the Court of Common Pleas of York County.

"By threats of personal harm and injury, and by loud, insulting and angry words and tones and violent and abusive conduct and gestures, [union members] attempted to prevent, intimidate and deter, and have succeeded in preventing, intimidating and deterring certain employees from remaining in the employment of the [company]."[20]

The courts ruled in favor of the York Manufacturing Company. Union members were prohibited from gathering at or near the York Manufacturing Company or interfering in its business in any way. Union members appealed, but they were denied a hearing. Strikers who violated the court order were fined $25 per violation.[21] The court ruling ended resistance to the York Manufacturing Company.

Working Together

Although the strike disrupted the company's production schedule, its sales force continued to branch out across the nation. By 1904, the company staffed offices in Chicago, Memphis,

Above: An ammonia gauge from the 1903 catalog.

Left: The Engineering Department, photographed in 1902. First row, left to right: [?] Hantz, George B. Wantz, Harold Morgan, Alfred Hueter, Arnold Roth, Ralph J. Hilliker, W.W. Conner and Harry Kain. Second row, left to right: Otis B. Morse, E.R. Corridon, Harry Hamberger, George B. Eichelberger, Louis S. Morse, Gustave R. Brostrom and Robert A. Spangler.

Boston and San Francisco. York even began to sell its ice-making machines overseas, gaining a foothold in Japan.

The York Manufacturing Company needed to sell a more comprehensive line of equipment if it hoped to sustain growth. Shipley elected to manufacture more peripheral components such as valves and fittings that would allow customers to upgrade, expand or repair their ice-making machines. Shipley also established an outline of basic principles for the refrigeration and ice-making industry to follow. By standardizing the definition of a machine's capacity, customers could compare specifications more easily, and manufacturers could develop pricing strategies consistent with competitive initiatives. Shipley also argued for the formation of a professional organization to provide a forum for refrigeration experts to exchange ideas and defend their common interests.

Not surprisingly, Shipley's vision caught on slowly with other manufacturers. Fierce rivals were naturally reluctant to share ideas with their competition. Undaunted, Shipley brought his idea to a meeting of the American Society of Mechanical Engineers. The society rarely dealt with refrigeration topics, so the engineers had to huddle in corners during the meetings.[22] Though other engineers mocked them, the informal discussions led to the publication of several trade magazines that dealt solely with ice-making and refrigeration.

Slowly, rivals in the industry began to come together. In February 1903, a private meeting was held at the Gibson House in Cincinnati. York's most important competitors attended: James Raby and Ezra Frick from Frick Company; J.C. Hobart

Above: A sectional view of York's single-acting compressor, surrounded by its components. Numbered from one to seven: suction valve, discharge valve, ammonia pistons, compressor cover, compressor base and compressor cylinder. The gas enters at the bottom of the compressor where it is compressed and driven through the discharge valve by the upstroke of the piston.

Below: Some of the compressor fittings offered by York in 1901.

from Triumph Company; Theo Vilter from Vilter Company; and W.P. Eagan from the Fred Wolf Company. After listening to Shipley's arguments in favor of standardization, they agreed to set standards for the size, riveting, soldering and material for a variety of ice cans.

The group also discussed the parameters by which a unit ton of refrigeration should be measured. Shipley, who had studied the matter in the company's test laboratory, suggested the conditions should include an evaporating pressure of 15.67 pounds of pressure, corresponding to an ammonia temperature of zero degrees Fahrenheit. He also said it should provide for a condensing pressure of 185 pounds of pressure, corresponding to an

ammonia temperature of 95.5 degrees Fahrenheit. However, competitors at the meeting could not reach an agreement on these important criteria.[23]

Later in the year, the same group formed the Ice Machine Builders Association of the United States. More meetings followed in rapid succession, with engineers from leading manufacturers joining the association. Ultimately, Shipley persuaded the association to conduct exhaustive tests of a refrigeration unit at his laboratory so all could agree on the conditions under which a standard ton of refrigeration could be calculated. The issue was so important to him that he offered to build a suitable refrigerating test system and pay hotel expenses for all representatives. His offer was accepted, and on September 16 and 17, 1903, the first tests were run on a 40-ton-capacity machine.

A second set of tests ran for six continuous days commencing on October 21. At the conclusion of testing, the manufacturers agreed to a standard rating system for compressor capacity. An article announcing and summarizing the results appeared in the August 1904 issue of *Ice and Refrigeration* magazine.[24]

Further efforts to standardize ice and refrigeration machines were rejected by a majority of members who feared higher costs if too many restrictions were implemented at once. In 1904, Shipley helped to establish the American Society of

This cartoon of Thomas Shipley highlights his tireless leadership in the refrigeration industry. The cartoonist and original publication are not known.

through a suction valve in the piston and was compressed and driven out by the upstroke of the piston, through the discharge valve in the center of the safety head. The safety head prevented damage to the compressor, even in the event of a valve failure. The compressor also featured a water jacket to reduce block temperatures and to remove the heat of compression during operation.[26]

Glatfelter eventually directed Shipley to offer a horizontal double-acting machine to meet the lower-priced competition. Shipley was determined to prove that the vertical single-acting principle of compressor design with the suction valve in the piston was superior. Sales records in 1905 supported Shipley's argument that customers were willing to pay a premium for the single-acting machine. The company sold 132 vertical single-acting machines, and only two horizontal double-acting machines that year.

Refrigerating Engineers, an organization devoted to the science of sub-atmospheric temperatures.[25]

Single-Acting

Until 1904, the York Manufacturing Company built a vertical single-acting machine to the exclusion of all other designs. York's design featured a safety head compressor. The ammonia gas entered at the bottom of the compressor, passed up

Above: A horizontal compound double-acting compressor and Corliss engine on a common base, offered before the turn of the century.

Below: A vertical single-acting Corliss engine-driven compressor. Although the company offered both models, the single-acting machines were more popular.

The Assembly Department, housed within the Large Machine Section of the York Manufacturing Company. By 1911, York was repairing and reconditioning competitors' machines in its shops.

CHAPTER FOUR

SETTING THE STANDARD

1906-1914

*"The success [York Manufacturing Company] has achieved is largely
due to [Glatfelter's] personal efforts. He was bold, but cautious, and combined progress with conservatism with nicest discrimination."*

— 1907 York Stockholders' Resolution [1]

BY 1906, THE YORK Manufacturing
Company employed more than
1,000 people and had a capital stock
worth $1.5 million. Branch offices for the
company could be found in Atlanta,
Baltimore, Boston, Houston, New York,
Philadelphia, Pittsburgh, San Francisco
and St. Louis. Foreign sales were
increasing under the management of Sam
Shipley, Tom's brother, who by then administered
independent foreign sales offices for the company.
The General Western Office in Chicago continued to
grow through the efforts of P. W. Pilsbry, who managed the sales for the western territories in the
United States.

Around the globe, York's reputation spread
as the most progressive company exclusively concerned with the refrigeration business. In 1902,
with Glatfelter's encouragement, Tom Shipley
inaugurated a two-year "special college course"
for apprentices. His youngest brother, William,
enrolled in the course, which consisted of rotat-
ing work assignments and the installation of
machines throughout the world. [2]

Tom Shipley continued his investigation into
new designs, often facing ridicule from his peers
in an effort to advance the science of refrigeration.
Once the refrigeration industry accepted Shipley's
standards for a Unit Ton of Refrigeration, he conducted further trials, at a cost of $50,000, from
1903 to 1906. Shipley's research resulted in published data on the comparison of sin-
gle- and double-acting compression,
condensers and other refrigeration
components. The company also
invested in the development of an
absorption test facility to evaluate
the efficiency of components under a
variety of conditions. In a 1906 pre-
sentation to the American Society of
Refrigerating Engineers, Shipley said such testing
was crucial, despite the expense.

*"The conducting of tests of this nature is an
expensive proposition, yet it is only by such
means that a manufacturer can keep his machinery and apparatus up-to-date and be in a position to give his customers the machinery best
suited for his position at the lowest cost.
Experiments must be made if improvements are
to be gained, and we believe it is a better policy
to manage experiments at our works at our
expense, rather than at the expense of the pur-
chaser after a (machine) is delivered to him."* [3]

Equipped with a modern physical and
chemical laboratory, Shipley and his staff next

A 1911 right-hand vertical single-acting enclosed piston valve machine,
championed by Thomas Shipley as superior to double-acting machines.

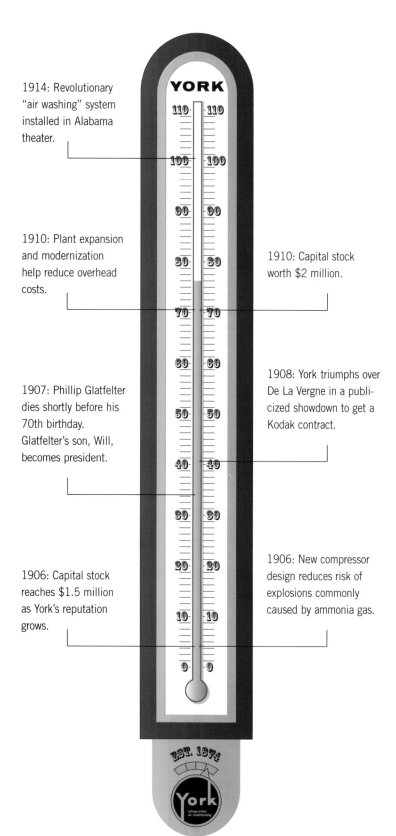

YORK

1914: Revolutionary "air washing" system installed in Alabama theater.

1910: Plant expansion and modernization help reduce overhead costs.

1907: Phillip Glatfelter dies shortly before his 70th birthday. Glatfelter's son, Will, becomes president.

1906: Capital stock reaches $1.5 million as York's reputation grows.

1910: Capital stock worth $2 million.

1908: York triumphs over De La Vergne in a publicized showdown to get a Kodak contract.

1906: New compressor design reduces risk of explosions commonly caused by ammonia gas.

EST. 1874

York

investigated the development of a standard for the horsepower required per one ton of refrigeration. The result was a table that would be used industry-wide.

Although the company offered double-acting machines, Shipley continued to advocate the single-acting vertical machine, a design that exceeded all other sales in the company. The majority of York's machines were sold to ice companies, with smaller numbers being delivered to cold storage and brewery companies. A few meat-packing businesses purchased the smaller, more expensive machines developed in York's test labs.[4] As a result of the company's continued willingness to invest significant resources into development of new products, York offered a complete line of standard valves and fittings for any make of refrigeration and ice-making machinery. The company promoted its new line of parts in cata-

York helped the industry evolve by continually improving its products. This steam-driven vertical pump, introduced in 1905, was more efficient than previous designs.

logs to solicit sales to competitors, even offering significant discounts.[5] York even repaired the broken machines of other makes, using its own line of parts, a service that would soon become extremely profitable for York.

Among the company's most significant accomplishments after 1906 was Shipley's work to refine the ammonia compression machine, an important component in the manufacture of ice. As a liquid, ammonia boils at a very cool 28.5 degrees below zero at atmospheric pressure. It is very efficient as a refrigerant because of the few pounds of ammonia that are needed to be compressed and circulated per ton of refrigeration. Early efforts at harnessing the effectiveness of ammonia, however, resulted in numerous deaths from explosions caused by misuse of the volatile substance.

York employed two different methods for making ice. The first was based on the production of distilled water from condensing the steam used in operating Corliss steam-driven ammonia compressors. Steam from the engine circulated through a condenser to a reboiler, heated by large steam coils to release any remaining oil in the water. This process ensured the elimination of white streaks radiating from the center of frozen ice, and resulted in the crystal clear product demanded by customers.[6]

In the second method, raw water passed through cooling pipes and then quartz and charcoal filters to remove remaining contaminants. From there, water was dumped to a "forecooler," which contained cooling coils filled with ammonia gas returning for re-compression from the freezing tank. The cooled water, with a temperature of 34 degrees, then passed through paper or cloth filters to the ice can fillers for final purification before freezing. The ice can filler extended to the bottom of the ice can so water would be less agitated, preventing the formation of bubbles.[7]

When the company began to sell a line of fittings, valves and other apparatus for refrigeration and ice-making machinery, it also offered to refurbish vertical double-acting machines for owners requiring greater refrigeration capacity. York promised to save businesses money by reconfiguring old horizontal machines to a vertical design and replacing double-acting compressors with the York Standard single-acting design. The company accomplished the work at low cost, and required payment only if the reconditioned machine worked to the customer's satisfaction. Shipley and Glatfelter knew they had to invest in superior service in order to build a list of satisfied customers who would turn to the York Manufacturing Company for additional equipment.[8]

The strategy worked. The Waldorf-Astoria Hotel in Manhattan replaced three of their De La Vergne double-acting compressors with York's single-acting models. "They are running perfectly in every respect and really do more than you guaranteed them to do, as two of them will really do more than the three De La Vergne (models)," wrote the hotel's chief engineer in a letter to York.[9]

As the company grew, Glatfelter became involved in the community's philanthropic efforts. A member of the community, George Prowell, said that Glatfelter was one of York's most benevolent and public-spirited men who was "always on the alert to second any measure tending toward the advancement and improvement" of his fellow residents of York County.[10]

Among his many gifts to the community, the temperance-minded Glatfelter built an alcohol-free hotel in Spring Grove. A strong advocate of public education, Glatfelter presented a lecture hall and other endowments to Gettysburg College and donated $20,000 to build a high school in Spring Grove from which his grandson, P.H. Glatfelter II graduated in 1905. In 1906, he donated $35,000 for the construction of the St. Paul Evangelical Lutheran Church, of which he was a member.[11]

This logo was adopted in 1901 and used throughout the decade.

Just before his 70th birthday on July 11, 1907, Glatfelter died in his Spring Grove home following a massive stroke.[12] Employees, customers and competitors alike mourned his passing. Glatfelter was "the best friend the York Manufacturing Company ever had," wrote Shipley. A resolution passed by the stockholders expressed their loss.

"The success [the company] has achieved is largely due to his personal efforts. He was bold, but cautious, and combined progress with conservatism with nicest discrimination. He had faith in his fellows, and in dealings with this company, men came to rely upon our president's word, as a absolute guarantee of good faith. He was courteous to his associates, considerate to the men, and kindly to all. The keynote of his character was a rugged honesty which attracted men to him, and endeared him to all his acquaintances."

Glatfelter's son, Will, assumed control of the company as its new president. Educated at the York County Academy, Gettysburg College and the Eastman Business College, Will had prepared himself to run his father's empire by becoming president of the Hanover Wire Cloth Company, president of the Spring Grove Bank, treasurer of the York Manufacturing Company, president of the Spring Grove School Board, treasurer of the Carroll Manufacturing Company, deacon of Saint Paul Evangelical Lutheran Church, chief burgess of Spring Grove and a prime organizer of the Lutheran Layman's Movement. He married Katharine Hollinger in 1887, and they had one son, Phillip Hollinger Glatfelter.[13]

Will inherited both the P.H. Glatfelter Company and York Manufacturing Company, and he became president of both. The titles were largely ceremonial, as his father had ensured the continued success of each company by installing capable general managers to operate the businesses. Will Glatfelter was content to let the managers run the businesses while he involved himself in philanthropic pursuits.[14]

The York Manufacturing Company was an important part of the community. Company departments were proud to march in local parades, such as this one held in 1909.

Tom Shipley remained vice president, while Bird Loucks, the youngest son of company founder Jacob, was elected to the role of secretary and treasurer. Other key positions were filled by Ambrose Strikler as sales manager, E. W. Gardner as purchasing agent and C.W. Vogel.[15]

After Glatfelter died Shipley's brother, Sam, formed his own sales company, Shipley and Company, with an office in New York City. The execution of contracts through the York office and the administration of sales through eleven branch offices was becoming unmanageable.[16] A decision was made to sell franchises to salesmen in a number of territories in order to establish independent construction and supply agencies to replace the existing sales organization.

The independent franchises were committed to promoting York Manufacturing products, and in return received funds for field engineering, sales, installation, service and fabrication. The first of these franchises was the Shipley Construction and Supply Company in New York, where Sam Shipley guided foreign sales as well as his local territory. With his brother's help, Sam also established the York Shipley Company of Shanghai, York Shipley, Ltd. in London, and the Canadian Ice Company in Canada. Within a year, 13 other franchises were formed throughout the United States.[17]

During this period, Tom Shipley continued to work in the chemical and test laboratories to research further advances in ammonia compressor efficiency and cost. In the 10 years since Shipley had arrived at the company, the stock had increased by more than $1 million, the facility's floor space had tripled, and the total refrigerating capacity of the machines sold exceeded that of all other manufacturers.[18]

Older firms, such as De La Vergne Machine Company of New York, continued to feign superiority over the more successful York Manufacturing Company. One tactic that raised the ire of this competitor was Shipley's strategy of replacing De La Vergne machine parts with York's own at cut rates.[19] A showdown between the two companies finally took place in 1908 over a large contract with the Eastman Kodak Company.[20]

A large user of refrigeration for industrial process work, Eastman Kodak planned to triple the capacity of its machines. Faced with the increased demands of a burgeoning motion picture industry, the company solicited bids. The news reached Sam Shipley, who headed up his newly formed Construction and Supply Company. Sam immediately offered to demonstrate the superiority of York's single-acting machine over De La Vergne's double-acting design.[21]

Kodak, York and De La Vergne all agreed that the winner of the demonstration would win the contract to build two 400-ton condensing systems. Winning the comparison test would also bring prestige and sales to the victor, since the contest was highly publicized. De La Vergne enjoyed the majority of the brewery and industrial refrigeration work, and so offered Kodak the

company's standard and popular double-acting compressor. Meanwhile, Sam claimed that York's single-acting machine would produce a ton of refrigeration using at least 10 percent less horsepower. After seven trials conducted in the New York office of Eastman Kodak, York won the competition — and the contract — hands down. The single-acting compressor used, on average, 10.25 percent less horsepower to produce a ton of refrigeration.[22] Shipley was confident of the result before the trials had begun because of his own comparative tests in the company's laboratory. The double-acting machine drew in gas at the center and discharged it at both ends of the cylinder so that hot gas passed over the same surfaces as cool gas, thus losing efficiency. The single-acting machine, on the other hand, pumped the gas in only one direction.

Following the Kodak competition, Charles E. Lucke published his analysis and presented it to the American Society of Refrigerating Engineers, while Shipley reported results to the first International Congress on Refrigeration, which was held in Paris in 1908.[23] Interest was raised throughout the industry, leading to further research. Shipley began to shift his research into other aspects of the machine, including low pressure systems and raw water ice-makers.[24]

The phenomenal growth of the business in 1908 led Shipley and his engineering staff to design a new machine and boiler shop to expand production. Construction of new buildings included the use of fireproof cork, abundant daylight and ventilation. It was an effective plan, demonstrated by reduced overhead cost in 1910 compared to 1908. The additions increased productivity to such a level that the output of 1,250 employees would be doubled by adding only 750 more workers.[25]

By 1910 the company's capital stock had increased to $2 million. Facilities covered 13 acres of land between West Philadelphia Street and West York Street, which included West Gas Alley, Manchester Street and Company Street. By this time, the company had earned a reputation for excellence in product research and design. It was a new beginning for the company, one of worldwide respect.[26]

By 1911, though the company continued to grow at a rapid pace, Shipley himself grew restless. He had enjoyed designing and supervising the construction of York's new facilities so much that he directed company employees to build a house of his own design on Linden Avenue. The new house was acclaimed as the epitome of modern living in several publications. Still restless, Shipley entered into a partnership with his younger brothers, Sam and William, to form a new company in Toronto, Canada. Naming the new enterprise the Kent Company, Ltd., the three Shipley brothers listed themselves as "Refrigerating Engineers," whose main business was distributing machin-

Left: The Pipe Shop Welding Department, photographed in 1909.

Right: A right-hand vertical single-action enclosed piston valve machine, introduced by York in 1912.

ery of the York Manufacturing Company, and cork insulation, pipe coverings and other products for the Armstrong Cork Company. However, the company was unsuccessful, and the Shipleys sold it to the York Manufacturing Company, the Shipley Construction and Supply Company and the Armstrong Cork Company for $50,000. It was a troubling period for Tom Shipley, who found himself in debt again. The Kent Company was eventually acquired completely by the Armstrong Cork Company in 1913.[27]

While Shipley was in Canada with his brothers, Will Glatfelter had assumed the management of the company and introduced a number of innovative concepts. He organized a "Publicity Committee" for the company, with Earl Gardner, Louis Morse and Robert Hilliker as members. Their job was to coordinate advertising and prepare text for a "Weekly Letter" to be distributed to salesmen and managers of the York Manufacturing Company.[28] Gardner had been in charge of advertising since his arrival at York with Shipley in 1897. The Weekly Letter disseminated company information every Saturday until 1919, when it was changed to a semi-monthly letter.

In addition, the publicity committee instituted an energetic publicity program that resulted in the preparation and circulation of special advertising bulletins, circulars and folders expounding the merits of the company, its facilities and products. Among the most notable examples of the committee's work were booklets for the Third

---

Left: The California Construction Company was one of many subsidiaries that marketed and installed York products.

Below: A shell and coil generator, showing the steam coils and internal analyzer outside the shell, from around 1913.

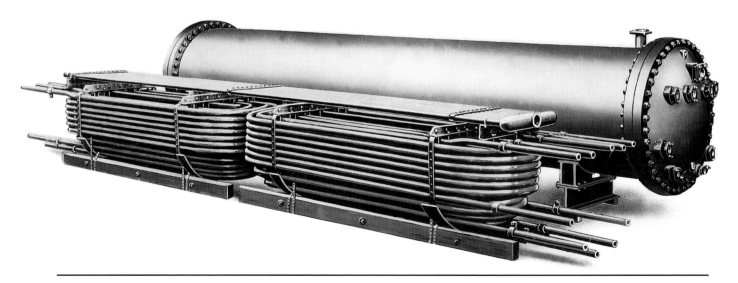

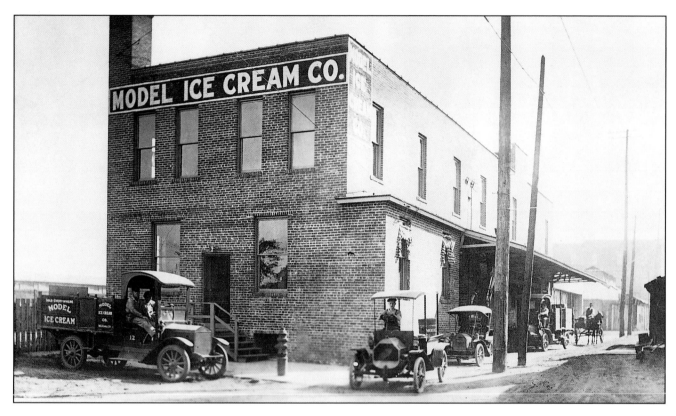

Above: The Model Ice Cream Company of Terre Haute, Indiana, manufactured 15,000 gallons of ice cream per month with the help of York refrigerating machines. The company's motto: Purity, Cleanliness and Mechanical Refrigeration.

Right: The ice cream company used this machine, with a capacity of 12 tons of refrigeration.

Below right: A view of the brine tanks where the ice cream was hardened.

International Congress of Refrigeration in Washington, D.C. and Chicago in 1913, and a booklet for the Panama-Pacific Exposition in San Francisco in 1915.

Following Shipley's return to York from his failed adventure in Canada, he once more immersed himself in productive research. His return to the labs resulted in a revolutionary comfort system which was installed in the Empire Theater in Montgomery, Alabama, in 1914. It was among the first installations of "air washing" and ventilation that came to be known as air conditioning.[29]

The Coca-Cola Bottling Co.

INCORPORATED

MEMPHIS, TENN. 3/19/19

RECEIVED
MAR 20 1919
PILSBRY-BECKER
Eng. & Supply Co.

Pilsbry/Becker Eng. & Supply Co.
St.Louis,Mo.

Gentlemen:

Replying to your favor of the 17th. will state that the work of your Mr. Rogers as far as we can see, is very satisfactory and we were particularly impressed with the disposition he showed to satisfy us and we have found that to be the case with all your representatives, who have called on us.

In discussing ice machines with prospective buyers I always emphasize the value of the service you sell with your machines and particularly the spirit of co-operation displayed by your men.

With best wishes, I am,

Yours very truly,

York's ice machines made the difference between a cold and refreshing soda and a disappointingly warm one.

CHAPTER FIVE

YEARS OF PROSPERITY

1913-1929

"Perhaps one of the most rapidly growing new applications of refrigeration is the cooling and air conditioning of the atmosphere in theatres, auditoriums and similar places of assembly. And if we may be permitted to make a prediction, it is that this application of Refrigeration will continue to grow rapidly, because it adds so much to the comfort of the public."

— York Semi-Monthly Letter, 1927[1]

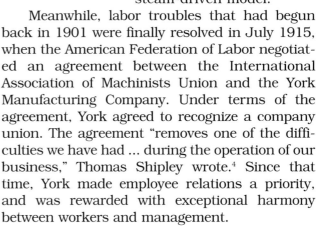

INNOVATION AND intensive research continued to characterize the York Manufacturing Company, two of the principal reasons for its continuing success. After four months of rigorous testing by Thomas Shipley and Louis Block, York introduced the Flooded Ammonia Condenser in 1913. The remarkably efficient 75-ton heat exchanger could accomplish in one square foot the same amount of condensing that required three to five square feet in competitive units. Shipley calculated that the lower condensing pressure of the machine saved operators 40 percent of the power required to drive the machine. Although Shipley patented the machine, he made the research public. "The result of this was to withdraw the cloak of mystery which had heretofore enveloped the production of cold by mechanical means," Shipley wrote in a letter to company stockholders.[2]

In 1914, York found another lucrative market when it began selling refrigerators to steamships transporting perishable goods. The first practical test of this new application was on the *Dochra*, a steamship that traveled 27 days from Buenos Aires to New York with a large supply of meat kept frozen or chilled by a York Ammonia Marine Type Machine.

Electric power was steadily gaining in popularity, and Thomas Shipley directed York engineers to determine if the new energy source could replace steam as the power for ice-making machines. As a result, York created a high-pressure air agitation system powered by electricity in 1915, and the new ice-maker quickly replaced the steam-driven model.[3]

Meanwhile, labor troubles that had begun back in 1901 were finally resolved in July 1915, when the American Federation of Labor negotiated an agreement between the International Association of Machinists Union and the York Manufacturing Company. Under terms of the agreement, York agreed to recognize a company union. The agreement "removes one of the difficulties we have had ... during the operation of our business," Thomas Shipley wrote.[4] Since that time, York made employee relations a priority, and was rewarded with exceptional harmony between workers and management.

Casualties caused by the volatile gases used in refrigeration machinery prompted York to develop the Absorbit Fume Mask in the late 1920s.

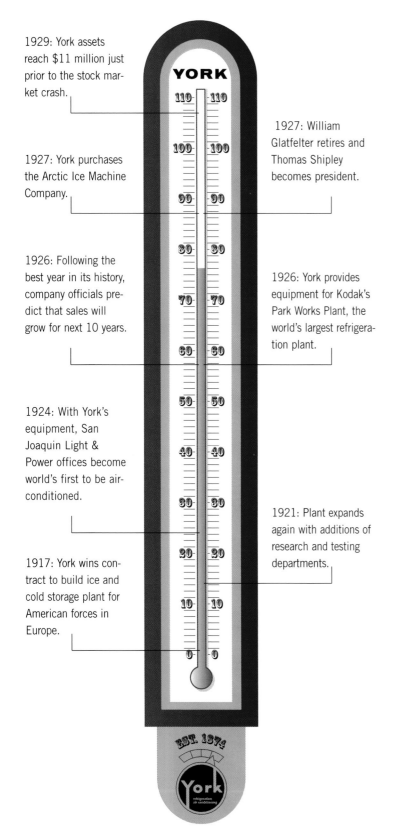

1929: York assets reach $11 million just prior to the stock market crash.

1927: York purchases the Arctic Ice Machine Company.

1926: Following the best year in its history, company officials predict that sales will grow for next 10 years.

1924: With York's equipment, San Joaquin Light & Power offices become world's first to be air-conditioned.

1917: York wins contract to build ice and cold storage plant for American forces in Europe.

1927: William Glatfelter retires and Thomas Shipley becomes president.

1926: York provides equipment for Kodak's Park Works Plant, the world's largest refrigeration plant.

1921: Plant expands again with additions of research and testing departments.

World War I

On June 28, 1914, a young member of a Serbian terrorist organization shot and killed the Archduke Francis Ferdinand and his wife Sophie. Ferdinand had been heir to the Austro-Hungarian imperial throne, and his assassination had a ripple effect in a complicated web of alliances throughout Europe. One by one, the nations joined what would soon become known as the "Great War," pitting the Central Powers (chiefly Germany and Austria-Hungary) against the Allied Powers (chiefly Great Britain, France and Russia).

President Woodrow Wilson, with the nation's approval, vowed to keep the United States neutral. But strong ties to the Allies propelled the United States closer to war. On February 3, 1917, an American merchant ship delivering goods to England was torpedoed by a German U-boat, and the United States severed diplomatic relations with the Central Powers. On May 7, 1915, the British steamship *Lusitania* was also torpedoed, with the loss of 1,198 lives, including those of 124 Americans. On April 2, 1917, after winning reelection on the slogan "He Kept Us Out of War," Wilson asked a special session of Congress to declare war against the Central Powers, and by April 6, America was officially at war.

A War Industries Board was formed to allocate scarce materials, standardize production and prices, and coordinate American and Allied purchasing. York Manufacturing halted production of machinery for domestic use and began operating on a 90 percent war production schedule.[5] The company's marine refrigeration business soon included battleships, cruisers and destroyers.

In July 1917, York won a government contract to build an ice and cold storage plant for the American Expeditionary Forces in Gieveres, France. The plant had a 500-ton refrigeration capacity, enough to preserve 5,000 pounds of beef. The York Manufacturing Company furnished skilled personnel as either commissioned officers or civilians to construct, operate and maintain the massive machine. Thomas Shipley's brother, Sam, was among several employees commissioned as a second lieutenant in the AEF to work as an engineer on the machine.[6] Will Glatfelter's son, P.H. Glatfelter II, spent 14

months in France as a second lieutenant in the Officers Reserve Corps of the AEF. Before returning home in 1919, he was promoted to captain in the Third Heavy Mobile Repair Shop.

York supplied refrigeration for fighting ships, army camps, powder plants and chemical plants, eventually supplying about 600 naval and cargo vessels with enclosed carbon dioxide compressors.[7] The company also contributed refrigerating coils that were used to cool the air aboard ships to make troops more comfortable. Still, York executives did not yet consider air conditioning an important market.

In 1917, York was credited with manufacturing almost half of all refrigeration machinery sold in the United States, with 5,000 employees engaged in the manufacture, sale and construction of its products.[8]

Tom Shipley's brother, 2nd Lt. Sam Shipley (far right) served as an assistant engineer during World War I, helping to operate and maintain a 500-ton capacity ice and cold storage plant used in France.

Postwar Prosperity

When the armistice was declared on November 11, 1918, American businesses were eager to return to peacetime activity. Mass production quickly resumed, fueled by pent-up demand. Consumers invested wartime savings in automobiles, housing and other goods that were previously in short supply.[9]

Following a brief period of raging unemployment and high inflation immediately after the war, America settled into a decade of economic growth that saw corporate profits soar and real per-capita income rise from $522 in 1921 to $716 by 1929.

During these years, the company added new product lines, expanded factories, consolidated businesses, and began exploring the new field of air conditioning. York found that refrigeration equipment was still in demand by the armed forces as well as commercial entities. The company continued to develop condensers, evaporators, freezing systems and self-contained units, focusing on the innovation of smaller refrigeration units for use in meat markets, confectionery stores, hotels, restaurants and other commercial establishments.

In 1920, York sold 1,752 machines with a total refrigeration capacity of 28,482 tons. The company's sales organization was the largest in the industry, with branch offices and agencies in 56 of the largest cities in the United States and Canada, plus several foreign countries. The sprawling factory in York covered 14 acres, with total floor space in the multi-storied buildings exceeding 33 acres. A total of 1,700 employees worked in the York plant and an additional 5,000 worked in the field, responsible for the manufacture, sale and installation of York's products.

In 1921, York purchased a three-story building adjoining the West York plant and converted it into a research department and testing facility. Another adjacent building was purchased and converted into a development plant and a hotel known as the Yorkco Club.

The enactment of Prohibition in 1920 had the indirect effect of increasing the consumption of ice cream, and York sold refrigerating equipment to the new ice cream factories that sprouted across the nation. As the decade unfolded, America's sweet tooth for ice cream, soda and candy exceeded York's expectations. It was not unusual to see 80 to 100 customers crowded around the long, narrow counters of ice cream and confectionery shops.[10]

York's growing market included the development of small self-contained units that could be easily transported from one location to another.[11] By responding quickly to the demands of its markets, York maintained its prominence as a leading manufacturer of refrigeration equipment. In 1922, York sold 2,500 machines, a 44 percent increase over the best previous year of 1920.[12] To cope with the rapid growth, the company in 1923 purchased 80 acres on Grantley Avenue, a mile south of the West York plant.

This ambitious expansion occurred during a period of buoyant optimism in America and within the city of York in particular. A 1922 information sheet, prepared for a meeting of York sales engineers, proclaimed that York, Pennsylvania, was the world leader in "the manufacture of refrigerating and ice making machinery, bank safes and vaults, artificial teeth, wall paper, automobile tire chains, baker's machinery and water turbines." The same document went on to boast that "York's labor force is almost 100 percent American. There is but little of the foreign ele-

Right: The bustling West York plant expanded in 1921 to include a three-story research department and a hotel, both adjacent to the manufacturing center.

Top: As ice cream became more popular across Prohibitionist America, York's refrigeration machines also spread, such as this 6X6 Y-12 Style belt-driven machine in the Hollywood Farm's Dairy Company, in Seattle, Washington.

ment to be found in our mills and factories and we have never been seriously affected by strikes and labor troubles."[13]

Industry observers credited Tom Shipley with the company's success. Shipley never abandoned the principles that he promoted: Know your business thoroughly; manufacture the best that can be made in your line of business; sell your product at a reasonable profit and on its merit without regard to the competitor's price; give customers an absolutely square deal; let employees share in the company's prosperity; and treat them square.[14]

The Air Conditioning Business

On July 7, 1923, the steamship *Naponset* docked in New York Harbor, having embarked from Seattle, Portland and San Francisco with 10,457 cases of refrigerated eggs. The Naponset was equipped with three York carbon dioxide refrigerating machines that delivered the delicate and highly perishable cargo to the destination in excellent condition. Temperatures during the transit through the Panama Canal were remarkably stable, ranging between 32 and 34 degrees.[15]

The company also branched into the realm of aeronautics. York provided refrigeration equipment to the National Bureau of Standards for use in developing modern aircraft engines, and to the Bureau of Mines for purifying helium for use in lighter-than-air aircraft. This was followed by an air conditioning contract from the U.S. Navy for testing airplane designs and power plants, as well as cooling systems for all of the Navy's aircraft carriers then in service.[16]

As York engineers developed refrigeration units for both ships and railroad cars, they began toying with the idea of providing air conditioning for human comfort. After all, if a room could be made comfortable for a crate of eggs, why could it not be made comfortable for human beings?

In 1924, York installed equipment that made the 10-story San Joaquin Light & Power Corporation headquarters in Fresno, California, the world's first air-conditioned office building. The first installations were large buildings, since the equipment was expensive. That same year, York engineers developed a line of complete factory-assembled "dry coil" air conditioning units, a packaged unit that was manufactured at York and easily adapted to individual locations. The duct work was still customized, but it was no longer necessary to build each system in the field from scratch. Two years later, the company began to develop an automatic temperature control system that would make it possible to regulate temperature by setting a dial.

In July 1924, the company replaced four Frigidaire household refrigeration units at St. Clara's Orphanage in Denver, Colorado, with a single one-ton fully automated unit that allowed the orphanage to expand the size of the refrigeration storage room and to also add an ice tank capable of freezing 200 pounds of ice a day.[17] Word of such conversions, which cut the orphanage's electric bill by roughly $20 a month, spread rapidly. In a matter of months, the nearby St. Vincent's Home converted from similar inadequate Frigidaire units to a York installation.

Following this work, York then directed its attention toward the dairy market. Milk carried bacteria from the teats, udder and body of the cow, or from dust in the milking stalls. However, 99 percent of the bacteria would be killed if the milk was heated between 145 and 185 degrees. Cooling the milk to below 50 degrees slowed the growth of remaining bacteria. In 1925, York refrigera-

Above: A typical farm cooling plant for milk, designed to retard the growth of dangerous bacteria that often caused sickness.

Left: The dairy market was extraordinarily profitable for York. A chart demonstrating household uses for milk shows how much milk was produced in the United States by 1922 and how it was used.

tion equipment found applications at several key stages of the milk handling operation. Small refrigeration units were used by farmers to chill the milk as soon as it was collected. Larger units were used along rail lines throughout the dairy regions, in the pasteurizing operation, and for the storage of butter, cheese, and other milk products. With nearly 30 million dairy cattle on 4.5 million farms, the market was enormous.[18]

Expansion

In 1925, a temporary oil shortage led to the breakdown of a number of York refrigeration units that had not been properly oiled. This crisis prompted York to construct a new plant to manufacture Yorkco Oils, adhering to the strict lubricating standards required for refrigeration compressors.[19] Seven varieties of Yorkco oils were designed for seven different applications: Yorkco Ammonia Compressor Oil; Yorkco Ammonia Compressor H.D.T., for high discharge temperatures; Yorkco Ammonia Compressor Oil L.S.P. for low suction pressure; Yorkco Ammonia Oils; Yorkco Carbon Dioxide Compressor Oil; Yorkco Electric Motor Bearing Oil; and Yorkco Air Compressor Oil.[20]

With all the new markets and products, York's sales were outgrowing the manufacturing capacity of the 19-acre west York plant. The company responded by purchasing 80 acres just southwest of the city limits. Bounded by Codorus Creek, Grantley Avenue, Richland Avenue and the main line of the Pennsylvania Railroad, this location became the site of what would be known as the Grantley Avenue Plant. Before construction could begin, the low spots of the site were filled in with more than 129,500 cubic yards of earth, stone and concrete. The first building at the Grantley Avenue site was the Sheet Metal Building, completed in September 1925. Can fabrication, moved from the West York Plant to the new facility, tripled from 500 to 1,500 cans a day.[21]

The woodworking shop and attached wood storage sheds were completed by May 1925, and the new York Oil & Chemical Company plant was ready for operation the following September. The plant was established to produce the vital Yorkco Oils for ammonia and carbon dioxide compressors. Groundbreaking for the Grantley Plant gate and office building took place March 1, 1926. The office housed the superintendent's office, architectural staff, emergency hospital, and nurse's office. The new boiler house, with two 200-horsepower boilers, was completed by the end of 1926, and the foundry, capable of turning out 16 tons of iron per hour, opened a short while later. The foundry was built with 2,000 tons of steel. Glass windows on all sides of the building ensured maximum light for the molders.[22] Although the building was called the Four-Acre Foundry, the total area under roof was only three and a half acres, though designed to accommodate future expansion.[23]

The York Oil and Chemical Company plant, completed in 1925, was the first company in the world established solely to manufacture lubrication oils.

In a lecture to York employees on March 14, 1927, Thomas Shipley explained that the improvements were part of a long-range plan.

"I want to impress upon your minds the fact that these improvements are not haphazard. Altogether we might slip up once awhile, but as before stated, every action that goes on around this institution is the result of some man's thought, some man's vision. Some man just like yourself, has an idea and brings it to the attention of those who have the authority to bring it into force wholly or in part. These ideas, especially of expansion, come almost entirely from business necessity, and business necessity is the incentive that drives us ahead." [24]

As the company expanded, high-profile contracts became increasingly common.

In 1926, York provided the refrigerating equipment for the largest refrigerating plant in the world — Eastman Kodak's Park Works Plant in Rochester, New York. Since 1908, York had been providing Kodak with refrigeration units ranging in size from two to 690 tons. [25]

The same year, York installed refrigeration systems on both the *Lexington* and the *Saratoga*, the two largest and fastest aircraft carriers in the world. Both ships were 888 feet long, large enough to carry 72 aircraft and 1,500 men. In order to provide sufficient refrigeration capacity, York installed two brine carbon dioxide cooling units in each vessel, one forward and one aft, "that could maintain cold storage room temperatures, cool drinking water, manufacture ice, condition air for certain confidential parts of the ship, as well as the photographic and other laboratories." [26] The conditioning of air for comfort was mentioned almost as an aside.

In July 1926, York announced that the Brooklyn Office of the Shipley Construction & Supply Company would install the cooling and ventilating system for the 4,060-seat State Theater auditorium in Hartford, Connecticut, an installation that required a 300-ton carbon dioxide refrigerating system. [27]

Also in 1926, York announced that the National Press Club headquarters at 14th and F streets, the largest office building then standing in Washington, D.C., would be equipped with a York air conditioning system. Other important company sales during the same period included installations at Carnegie Refining Company in Carnegie, Pennsylvania; Frank H. Bierman & Son of York, Pennsylvania; O.H. Hostetter of Hanover, Pennsylvania; Orange County Ice Company of Fullerton, California; and Petersburg Cold Storage Company of Petersburg, Alaska. [28]

Thomas Shipley becomes President

In 1927, W.L. Glatfelter retired and Thomas Shipley became president of the company. Though he was heavily involved in the day-to-day

As part of a string of prestigious contract awards for York, the Brooklyn-based Shipley Construction & Supply Company traveled to Hartford, Connecticut, to install a cooling and ventilation system in the 4,060-seat State Theater.

A touch of the exotic invades downtown York, as members of the Engineering Department, looking decidedly uncomfortable, march in the 1927 Halloween Parade.

activities of the company, Shipley still found time to write technical articles addressing serious engineering problems of the day. The central theme that runs through his writing is man's ability to influence his own destiny. Even the least senior plant laborer had a duty to inform his superior about any idea that might enhance the prospects of the company, and every salesman could speed the growth of the organization.

York Manufacturing was an important asset to the community in which it was located. The annual company Halloween parade, a tradition that started in 1897, became a city-wide event. Other manufacturing companies, merchants, and public service organizations eagerly participated in the contests and festivities. York Manufacturing always provided five prizes for the best floats or bands in addition to the five prizes offered by the city of York. The company also had a baseball team, which won the pennant in the

Industrial League in 1924 by shutting out a team fielded by Gulf Refining Company.

The Arctic Ice Machine Company

Sales for 1926 were 10 percent better than any previous year, and 1927 was expected to be even better, according to a company newspaper.

"The industry in which we are engaged is growing by leaps and bounds. To cite one phase, ten years ago the manufacture of raw water ice was in its infancy — now it is considered almost the only system considered practical to install. Last year was one of consolidations — a spirit of cooperation was apparent in all lines of industry, and it is apparent, since we have seen the accomplishments of these consolidations, that it will go on to the limit. That limit is the point where the greatest comfort and convenience is provided for the general public. ... Perhaps one of the most rapidly growing new applications of refrigeration is the cooling and air conditioning of the atmosphere in theatres, auditoriums and similar places of assembly. And if we may be permitted to make a predic-

tion, it is that this application of Refrigeration will continue to grow rapidly, because it adds so much to the comfort of the public. We believe the next 10 years will see every important auditorium in the Country equipped with Atmospheric Conditioning Apparatus.[29]

York embarked upon a series of strategic acquisitions and consolidations. One of the most important acquisitions was the Arctic Ice Machine Company of Canton, Ohio, purchased in 1927. The successful Arctic Ice Machine Company was most famous for the stationary can icemaking system invented by its president and general manager, Henry D. Pownall. According to Arctic's promotional literature, a typical 125-ton Arctic-Pownall freezing system might consist of 24 ice tanks, each containing 78 300-pound cans, and two brine cooling tanks, each with 12 ice tanks.[30]

To begin the freezing operation, a valve was opened to fill all 84 cans to a uniform water level and begin air agitation. Two levers on the brine valves were pulled to set the water freezing, while another lever on each tank permitted draining of core water from each can through a non-freezing zone at the bottom of the can. To harvest the ice, the cold brine supply was then shut off and two thaw valves and a mixing valve were opened. An ice puller would walk the length of the tank, pulling ice from each can. In a 35-ton plant, a tank of ice could be harvested every 8 hours, while a 300-ton plant could provide a harvest every hour.

THE ARCTIC ICE MACHINE COMPANY
CANTON·OHIO·U·S·A·
WE DO IT RIGHT

A bulletin issued to York's sales organization explained the advantages of Pownall's invention.

"We find that where it was believed that only a steam-driven distilled water plant could produce satisfactory ice from certain grades of water, that we are now able to motorize these plants with attendant economy in labor, maintenance, and power because the Arctic-Pownall System can freeze a very satisfactory grade of raw water ice. ... Nonetheless where a buyer is willing to pay a premium for a quality product, you can recommend the Arctic-Pownall System, unqualifiedly, and feel assured that the results will substantiate your recommendations."[31]

After the acquisition, Pownall retired to Santa Barbara, California, where he died several years later.[32] For York, the stationary ice can patents and the physical plant in Canton proved important assets during a period of aggressive corporate growth and reorganization.

H.D. Pownall (left), president of the Arctic ice Machine Company, found a method to produce ice that was "superior in appearance, quality and sanitation," according to company literature. York bought the company in 1927.

Consolidation and Reorganization

Until 1927, York marketed its products through a number of individual field companies with only loose contractual connection to the parent York Manufacturing Company. Each contractor had exclusive rights to market York's products in defined territories. Each company was given an exclusive region, and it supplied its own financial, engineering, sales and construction staffs. Though this system worked well for many years, inefficiencies developed as competing interests emerged in the organization.[33] Thomas Shipley and other company leaders gradually reached a consensus that the best solution was to "consolidate or merge the interests of all those involved, who were willing to join such a combination."[34]

Negotiations resulted in the merger of the York Manufacturing Company with seven of its eight sales companies, along with three companies that sold collateral products. The reorganized company was called the York Ice Machinery Corporation. It included the York Manufacturing Company, the Shipley Construction & Supply Company, the Cold Storage Door Company, the York Products Corporation of St. Louis, the Central Construction & Supply Company of Philadelphia, the Southern Construction & Supply Company of Atlanta, the Greenwood Construction & Supply Company of Pittsburgh, the York-Ohio Ice Machine Company of Cleveland, the Bay State Construction & Supply Company of Boston, the Arctic Ice Machine Company, and the York Oil & Chemical Company and York Milk Machinery Company, both of York, Pennsylvania.

The day-to-day business of the corporation was conducted under three groups. The York Group, under the leadership of Thomas Shipley, was responsible for all manufacturing activity. The Eastern Group, under Tom Shipley's youngest brother, W.S. Shipley, and the Western Group, under V.H. Becker, were each responsible for sales within their respective regions of the country.[35]

Two years later, the company also consolidated the independent construction companies that installed its products throughout the nation. These companies had been modifying products and prices as they learned about

William S. Shipley, youngest of Tom Shipley's brothers, assumed day-to-day control of the corporation's activities in the eastern sections of the United States in 1928.

York's refrigeration and ice-making engineering principles. With each company offering something slightly different, York was losing control of its products and reputation for reliability. In 1929, York officers acquired and merged a number of the construction companies and created standards that would apply to all York installations. Stuart Lauer, assistant to the president, agreed with Thomas Shipley about the importance of universal pricing, and explained what the consolidation accomplished.

"Standard pricing, the product of standard engineering, in our business, means that York

installations will be identical, and that establishes our identity in a manner not otherwise possible. This is especially true because of the individuality of York engineering, which engraves the name of 'York' across the entire installation. The small brass nameplate becomes merely a matter of form. Our salesmen carry to the trade in every territory exactly the same message. The standard Price Book can be laid down in front of any buyer, for we have nothing to hide — nothing to check up on. We need not resort to subterfuge. We can do business in an open-faced manner."[36]

WHAT IS BRINE?

Brine is a solution of salt and water that has a freezing point lower than water. Its freezing point depends upon the amount of salt dissolved in a given quantity of water. There are two kinds of brine used in mechanical refrigeration — salt brine, made by dissolving common salt (sodium chloride), and calcium brine, made by dissolving calcium chloride.

Salt brine is most commonly used in freezing tanks, although occasionally calcium brine is used for this purpose. Calcium brine is preferred for pipe circulating systems as it can be cooled lower than salt brine, it has a lower freezing point for the same density, has less corrosion effect on pipe, is cleaner and it leaves less sediment.

orders. Since York already possessed a large sales network, the company began acquiring related patents, and on April 1, 1927, York purchased the Union Insulating Company of Chicago, Illinois. In its first 14 months in the new business York shipped 1,305 cold storage doors.[38]

Other York products introduced in 1928 included the Yorkco Brine Testing Set for testing the chemical composition of brine, the York Milk Bottle Crate Transfer Truck, York Ice Cream Can and Cover Trucks, York Milk Bottle Crates, Surface Type Milk and Cream Coolers, Milk Pumps, York Plate Type Dairy Heat Exchangers, and York Pasteurizing and Holding Vats.[39]

York's ability to market and distribute products was enhanced by the consolidation. In 1928, York purchased the U.S. Freezer Corporation of Brooklyn, New York, a move that helped to complete its line of milk and ice-cream plant equipment. The company also announced the addition of several new product lines. The Yorkco Smoke or Ammonia Mask, manufactured by the Mine Safety Appliances Company in Pittsburgh exclusively for York and available only through Yorkco distributors, was the only mask on the market that provided protection against ammonia, acid gases, organic vapors and dust. The gas mask helped to reduce casualties caused by the poison gases.[37]

Another new product was the Yorkco Cold Storage Door. Many of York's contract companies had long been selling cold storage doors made by other suppliers, often of poor design and workmanship. The company studied the market and learned that most manufacturers sold the doors by mail or through jobbers, maintaining small sales organizations that concentrated only on obtaining large

Iceless Refrigerators

By 1928, York was paying close attention to an emerging market that was attracting government scrutiny. As a June 24, 1928 article in the *New York World* explained, "Building Experts Consider Iceless Refrigerator Code, Multiple Installation Chief Target of Attack."[40] New York City became the first municipality in the nation to implement a mechanical refrigeration code similar to those used to regulate gas and electrical installations.

During this period, sulfur dioxide was the preferred refrigerant for domestic installations. Even small leaks could prove extremely hazardous, and risks would naturally increase in apartment buildings where many refrigerators were operating. York took a leadership role in addressing this issue before government regulation intervened to dictate terms to the industry. York engineers concluded that sulfur dioxide should be prohibited as a refrigerant in dwellings and multiple installations.

"It is realized that such prohibition on the use of Sulfur Dioxide will prove inconvenient and costly to manufacturers employing it. There is little or no doubt, however, that eventually, it will be entirely outlawed or its use greatly restricted in the home. ... The importance to the industry as a whole for it to unite in the formulating of a sane code and the securing of its uniform adoption throughout the country with the least possible delay can scarcely be exaggerated."[41]

Employing an impressive array of charts and graphs in this campaign, York was attempting to reduce the dangers of sulfur dioxide installations in private homes. Industry sales figures for domestic mechanical refrigerators increased from 24,000 units in 1924 to 43,800 in 1928. There were most likely over 1,185,000 domestic units in service from all manufacturers by that year, more than the number of vacuum cleaners that had existed in 1918 or the number of washing machines in service by 1920. Based on such studies, York engineers predicted in 1928 that there would be more than 12 million iceless refrigerators in private homes by 1940. If each unit had an average life span of 10 years, then 10 percent might need replacement each year, and 10 percent of these units would experience some loss of refrigerant.

As the company approached the great stock market crash of 1929, the York Ice Machinery Corporation could claim assets of $11 million against liabilities of less than $1.3 million.[42] The building project was finally complete, and was paying off in the form of increased quality and efficiency. The 1929 Annual Report showed a 10 percent increase in gross sales and a 13 percent increase in profits. On the eve of the Great Depression, York was looking forward to continued high profits, low debt and booming sales.

Friends, neighbors and family of the York Manufacturing Company helped the company and each other weather the Depression.

CHAPTER SIX

SURVIVING IN STYLE

1930-1939

"We in America today are nearer the final triumph over poverty than ever before in the history of any land."

— Herbert Hoover, 1928[1]

IN 1930, AS THE national economy slid into a terrifying economic depression, a widening sense of panic and despair swept the nation. The national income declined from $81 billion dollars in 1929 to just $68 billion in 1930, while the ranks of the unemployed ballooned to a staggering 4 million. By 1932, 16 million Americans, a quarter of the working-age population, were out of work. Farmers let their produce rot in the fields as prices dropped so low that it was no longer worthwhile to bring it to market. Without income, the fortunate raided their savings accounts. As panic spread, 1,352 banks closed their doors in 1930. In 1932, 3,646 banks had gone out of business.

Industrial production in 1932 was only one-third of 1929 levels. Fortunately, the survival of the York Ice Machinery Corporation was never in doubt. Cost-cutting measures, combined with industry-defining advances in air conditioning, kept the company afloat even during the darkest days of the crisis.

In the years immediately following the stock market crash, management counseled employees to remain optimistic and to plan for future prosperity. The 1930 Annual Report reflected that York "is in a strong financial position. ... Current assets of almost $11 million and current liabilities of less than $1 million ... is an improvement over any Annual Report heretofore."[2]

Death of a Visionary

On January 22, 1930, Thomas Shipley died. For 33 years, Shipley had transformed York into the largest refrigeration equipment manufacturer in the nation. A memorial expressed the sense of loss felt by both management and employees.

"His many and lasting contributions to the science of refrigeration, due to his progressive spirit, are so well known to us that to recount them would be superfluous. Suffice it to say that the story of the early days of his career, the obstacles he overcame, of his reverses in his first business ventures, of his ability to turn defeat into experience and use it to achieve success, of how he assumed the leadership of this company in 1897 and built it to its present magnitude, is proof that here was a man in whom self-mastery, concentration, vision and common sense were blended in a fine figure. ... His life was an example of the truth that the strongest personalities are the

The York logo. After years of struggle, York became the bellwether of quality in the air conditioning and refrigeration industry.

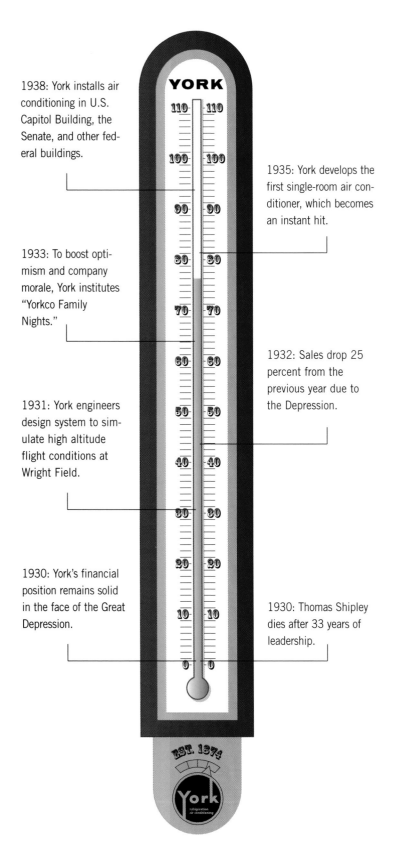

1938: York installs air conditioning in U.S. Capitol Building, the Senate, and other federal buildings.

1933: To boost optimism and company morale, York institutes "Yorkco Family Nights."

1931: York engineers design system to simulate high altitude flight conditions at Wright Field.

1930: York's financial position remains solid in the face of the Great Depression.

YORK

1935: York develops the first single-room air conditioner, which becomes an instant hit.

1932: Sales drop 25 percent from the previous year due to the Depression.

1930: Thomas Shipley dies after 33 years of leadership.

EST. 1874

York

result not so much of a desire for personal gain as of implicit faith in an ideal."[3]

On February 5, 1930 the board of directors formally elected Thomas Shipley's brother, then Vice President and General Sales Manager William S. Shipley, as president. Stewart E. Lauer was promoted from assistant to the president to general sales manager, and W.S. Stair was made assistant general sales manager with responsibility for advertising.[4] Among the objectives established by the new management team was an intention to evaluate the competition.

Sizing Up the Competition

In an address delivered on February 17, 1930, Philadelphia Branch Manager F.A. Weisenbach explained in detail the products and the sales strategies employed by York's competitors.[5] He divided the competition into two categories, those building large machines and those building smaller machines. The larger manufacturers included the De La Vergne Machine Company, Frick Company, Vilter Manufacturing Company, Carbondale Machine Company and Henry Vogt Company. Among the manufacturers of smaller refrigerating machines were Brunswick-Kroeschell of Brunswick, New Jersey; General Refrigeration Company (Lipman Machine) of Beloit, Wisconsin; Kelvinator Company of Detroit, Michigan; and Frigidaire Corporation of Dayton, Ohio. Weisenbach believed that the competitive pressures exerted by these organizations had been greatly reduced as a result of "the foresight of our own organization under the guidance of our late president, Thomas Shipley, in keeping at the forefront with new ideas, more advanced practices, very much more efficient equipment and probably a more active sales organization."[6]

De La Vergne, once an innovator in the field of icemaking, had been reduced to copying York designs. Weisenbach criticized York's longtime business nemesis, the Frick Company, for designing refrigerators and icemakers that were low-cost, low-quality imitations of York products. Frick was still considered a troublesome competitor in ammonia compressors and carbon dioxide compressors.

AIR WASHER Nº 2
DEHUMIDIFIER
& AIR COOLER

YORK

COLD WATER PUMP

Theaters quickly blossomed as a market for air conditioning such as the 1932 York air conditioning installation at Fox Theater in Spokane, Washington.

Other large machine competitors drew mostly technical comments from Weisenbach, as they were held in higher esteem.[7]

Of the small machine manufacturers, Frigidaire and Kelvinator had launched aggressive national advertising campaigns to establish a household name, and York considered them a serious threat in the small machine market.

Manufactured Weather

The company was experiencing success in its new lines of air conditioning products. By 1930, York air conditioning systems were keeping patrons cool in 47 theaters in 16 states.[8] Air conditioning continued to gain in popularity across a broad spectrum of industry. Letters of praise, such as this October 2, 1930 letter from T.E. Lapres, vice president of Fralinger's Original Salt Water Taffy, became common.

"The summer season is at an end and we would feel we were not doing our part if we did not write to tell you how pleased we have been with your Air Condition Units. We purchased the first one in July when the protracted heat spell made it absolutely impossible to handle chocolates in our packing department. Machine number one solved this problem immediately and perfectly. Then in August Machine Number Two gave us the much needed addition(al) refrigeration in our coating department. In fact, after this installation, we found it practical to altogether eliminate our old overhead refrigeration in this department. Both units have worked without interruption and without any need of adjustment or repairs since their installation. We are contemplating at this time some considerable alterations

and additions to our factory and we believe that when these are completed we will have need of several additional Air Conditioning Units."[9]

Once people experienced air conditioning, they couldn't live without it. The demand for indoor climate equipment steadily grew, and one trade journal modestly predicted that "air conditioning will soon be the greatest industry of civilized man. Compared with it, the automobile, the radio, and the motion picture industry combined will pale into insignificance. Why? Because air is the medium in which mankind exists. ... Because his health, comfort, and happiness, and his terrestrial span depend very largely upon his aerial environment."[10]

By the end of the October 1, 1930 fiscal year, York had sold 3,625 machines of all types, representing a 48 percent increase over the 1,747 machines shipped in 1920. But the competition was getting tougher. Fifteen companies had merged to create the Carrier-York Company, creating some confusion for York Ice Machinery, which was forced to spend time and money advertising the fact that it was not related in any way to Carrier-York.

In 1931, York's new coil-type air conditioner had emerged as a leading product. The coil types were built according to a standard design that ensured a high degree of reliability and low production costs.[11] The line allowed the company to exploit a new market — fur storage. Since moth larvae remain dormant at temperatures below 20 degrees, cold storage became a popular way to protect expensive fur coats, jackets and stoles. The coil was soon introduced throughout the nation and in England.[12]

In 1931, York engineers helped to advance the science of aviation, designing a refrigerating system to simulate the frigid temperatures of high altitude flight. The company entered into a contract with the United States Army Air Corps to install the system at Wright Field, in Dayton, Ohio. Because of York's expertise, scientists could predict how aircraft fared at 30,000 feet, where temperatures were minus 55 degrees.

Freon-12

Refrigerant-12 (dichlorodiflouromethane), commonly referred to by the DuPont trade name Freon-12, revolutionized the refrigeration and air conditioning industries when it was developed in 1930. Carbon dioxide, though non-irritating, non-toxic, non-flammable and non-explosive, was inefficient because it required high operating pressures and had a low critical temperature. Ammonia, the most efficient refrigerant at the time, was highly odoriferous and irritating to the skin and eyes. Methylene chloride, though odorless and comparatively non-toxic, was flammable. Freon-12 gradually replaced methylene chloride and carbon dioxide in all applications and replaced ammonia in all but industrial applications because it was less toxic and very efficient.

Developed through the cooperative research efforts of Frigidaire Corporation, General Motors Corporation and DuPont Corporation, Freon-12 met the goal of being safe to use in homes. Freon-12 was completely odorless, non-irritating, non-

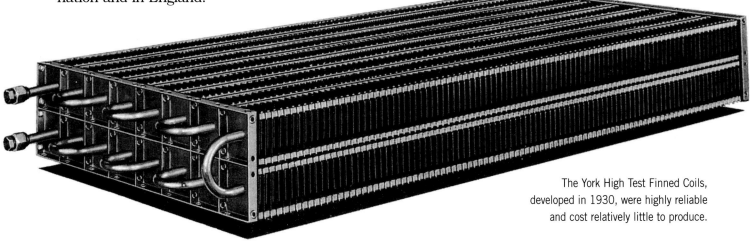

The York High Test Finned Coils, developed in 1930, were highly reliable and cost relatively little to produce.

flammable, non-toxic, non-explosive, non-poisonous and non-corrosive. Its extraordinarily low boiling point of minus 21.7 degrees at standard atmospheric pressure meant that it could be made to boil at a positive pressure.[13] Furthermore, it wouldn't decompose unless the gas came in contact with an open flame at temperatures above 1,000 degrees.

Milton Ward Garland, who was chief engineer for Frick at the time, recalled that the heated rivalry between the two Pennsylvania refrigeration manufacturers waned following the introduction of Freon-12. "Frick and York were no longer the real competitors that they had been. York primarily now concentrated on air conditioning, while the Frick Company concentrated on industrial work."[14]

With the introduction of the new refrigerant, the market for air conditioning exploded. In 1933, an air conditioning unit that relied on Freon-12 was installed at the historic Radio City Music Hall in New York City.[15] By 1938, more than 15,000 Freon-12 machines had been installed, with a combined capacity of 100,000 tons of refrigeration. Among the more important Freon-12 installations completed by 1938 were the Neils-Esperson Building in Houston, Texas; Kansas City Municipal Auditorium in Kansas City, Missouri; Hershey Chocolate Company's Windowless Office Building in Hershey, Pennsylvania; the Gimbel Brothers' Department Store in Pittsburgh, Pennsylvania; the United States Capitol Group in Washington, D.C.; as well as six Ford assembly plants, 97 F.W. Woolworth Company stores, and 250 First National banks.[16]

Fighting the Depression

Thanks in part to the invention of Freon-12, York surged ahead of its competitors to take the lead within the air conditioning industry. However, the Great Depression would still take its toll on the company. In the 1932 Annual Report, William Shipley acknowledged that sales had dropped 25 percent from the previous year, but reassured stockholders that "your corporation's sales appear to have held up equally as well as the general business of the country."[17] In response, the company instituted tight budget controls and reduced employee ranks. The company managed to avoid

deeper cuts by suspending the payment of a stock dividend payment for 1932. All things considered, Shipley mused, York fared well.

"We are passing through no ordinary times. Business in general throughout the world has been declining for the past three years and the present rate of activity is further below the estimated normal than at any previous period for which records are available. ... That the financial result will probably be disappointing to the stockholders is accepted. However, it must be recognized that performance under existing conditions is hardly comparable with what is possible under more normal years as they return. Adversity is a hard master but exerts a consistent urge to better standards, which in turn should have a telling effect on future income statements as business confidence returns and conditions improve."[18]

Optimism was an integral component of Shipley's strategy. He urged York's salesmen to refrain from talk of hard times in favor of "passing along honest information which will revive public confidence."[19] The *York Monthly Letter* contained upbeat columns entitled "Hopeful Signs" that consistently predicted better times.

In 1933, York introduced "Yorkco Family Nights" to spread optimism about the economy. By 1937, more than 100 York employees were involved in this annual event, held on four evenings every August.[20] Shipley explained that a sense of family was important during periods of difficulty.

"Unless it is possible to create a Yorkco Family, happy and contented, from the time we start work in the morning until we stop in the afternoon, I am not very anxious to continue in my position, for I consider this attainment a great measure in my success. Why should not this be possible with the sincere desire on the part of men and management? Those things which prevent it must be eliminated! If we are men it can be done."[21]

The Yorkco Family Nights offered leisure time to entire families because several generations often worked for the company. Marriages between employees were common, and children often followed their parents' — and grandpar-

Beginning in August 1933, Yorkco Family Nights were one tangible way York fought against the widening sense of despair and hopelessness caused by the Great Depression.

ents' — footsteps into York. Austin Diehl came to York as an engineer in 1933 and retired in 1974. He would be followed by James Stambaugh, his grandson, in 1972.

"Besides my grandfather, my uncle used to work here before he retired. I met my wife here, and we've been married 19 years. Her father still works here, and her grandfather retired from here sometime in 1973." [22]

"We lived right next door to York, on Philadelphia Street," remembered J. Duane Johnson, who first went to work for York in 1949 as a tester. "My father, Clayton A. Johnson, worked here for 22 years as a pipe fitter." At age 65, Johnson is still employed as senior training specialist. [23]

The Specialty Department

William Shipley was determined to do something to help the company's older employees. He refused to do away with the Specialty Department that provided light jobs for elderly employees, who were permitted to come and go as they liked. The department, which dated back to 1874, was losing money, but Shipley firmly believed that it provided a valuable service, as he explained in 1935.

"I have heard many good workers say they would like to spend their last years at leisure. But there is a difference between leisure and idleness, you know. Any workman enjoys the leisure hours when, tired from honest labor, he can rest and devote his evening hours or his day off to recreation. But to tell even an old man accustomed to work that he must keep his feet in the stove for days on end is heartless. And it is harder on the man in overalls than on the man with the white

collar. We must do all we can to take care of our own workers who have grown old in service."[24]

There was a practical benefit to the department: York did not lose its vast knowledge and experience to retirement. Employees in the department worked less strenuous hours, providing trouble-shooting ideas and service to both customers and company personnel. The practice of retaining this living resource continues. G.E. Buchanan became acquainted with York while in the U.S. Navy during World War II, and joined the company immediately following the war as a refrigeration technician. In 1996, at 71, he continued to work as a "temporary employee" since retirement in 1982.

"I'm handling consumer inquiries and complaints. Sometimes the consumer just doesn't know where to go for help. They need service or parts or they want to buy a new unit and we'll direct them to a distributor. Or they'll ask a simple question, like, what's the capacity on this model so-and-so. With a model and serial num-

ber, we can usually tell them that kind of thing right off the top of our heads."[25]

As the Depression lingered, company speeches and articles began to question how President Franklin D. Roosevelt and his New Dealers were handling the crisis. In one piece, the company decried the escalating public debt resulting from various "alphabet soup" projects and programs. Within the corporate newsletter and other forums, York officials stated their opposition to public works projects awarded for the sole purpose of providing jobs. "Eliminate federal loans to local governments and private enterprises," was the advice of a 1936 article. "Discontinue all federal grants or 'matching' allotments to the states. ... Discontinue the use of public funds to establish or conduct enterprises competing with private industry and labor."[26]

By 1937, net losses had accumulated to $1,420,205.[27] Yet, even through the worst years of the Depression, York continued to penetrate new markets and introduce important new products.

Universal Air Conditioning

In 1935, York produced the first successful single-room air conditioner in the United States. Housed in an attractive cabinet, it drew outdoor air through a window adapter fresh air inlet. This adapter also housed condenser-air suction and condenser-air discharge ducts. A fan circulated filtered room air over the cooling surface. Cooled, dehumidified and filtered air was discharged vertically through a vent on the top of the unit, diffusing it gently throughout the room. Moisture

Experience was and remains a resource retained by York. Workers who reached 25 years of service entered the Twenty-Five Year Club. The photo shows the club from 1932.

removed from the air condensed on evaporator surfaces, while the excess accumulated in a pan at the base of the conditioner to be diffused outdoors assisted by a rotary vaporizer in the condenser air stream. These units were also offered to stores, restaurants, beauty parlors and other small businesses.[28]

The company continued to secure major contracts for large commercial and office installations. In 1935, York provided air conditioning for the Abraham Strauss & Son Building in Brooklyn, the largest department store in all five boroughs of New York.[29] This system circulated 405,000 cubic feet of conditioned air per minute through 139 departments with a total of 355,000 square feet. That year, York accomplished 45 major installations in large public buildings, theaters, hotels, railroads and department stores, including the Franklin Institute and the Philadelphia General Hospital.[30]

Despite differences of opinion with the federal government, York undertook one of the most visible governmental air conditioning installations imaginable. In 1938, it installed air conditioning in the United States Capitol, the Senate building, and both the old and new House of Representatives. Other installations included the United States Archives and the Library of Congress Annex.

The company's annual sales had been growing since hitting bottom in 1933, and by 1937, the company reported sales of $18.7 million, an impressive 31 percent increase over the previous year. Almost 45 percent of orders were for air conditioning, while commercial and industrial refrigeration orders amounted to 39.4 percent of sales. For the first time in the company's history, distributor sales exceeded $1 million.[31]

In 1938, York improved the Yorkaire Conditioner Model BA-90 by adding such features as a rotary grill to better direct air diffusion throughout a room. An attractive new cabinet was designed by Walter Dorwin Teague, among the nation's top industrial designers. These cabinets featured a distinctive walnut finish and occupied just 4.3 square feet of floor space. Extra-large cooling coils reduced noise by allowing air to pass through at low velocities.[32]

In this same year, York introduced the York Air Conditioning System Oil-Burning Boiler, available either for domestic heating applications or as part of an integrated residential air conditioning system. The new boiler was available in steam, vapor, and hot water versions, while the burner unit was of the pressure-atomizing type that ensured quiet operation.[33] These new systems were sold under the newly-created Automatic Heating Division, headed by the late Edward Rob Walsh, Jr., a well-respected heating sales executive. In addition to heading the division, Walsh was father to another eventual York executive, Jack Walsh, who retired in 1990 after 30 years with the company. Other new product lines for 1938 included three Yorkaire Self-Contained Air Conditioning Units for commercial installations, such as the Yorkaire-275, Yorkaire-350, and Yorkaire-475 models which cooled as well as earlier units while occupying half the space. A new line of sectional air conditioners was also announced. These were designed to reduce the cost of large installations.

On January 1, 1939, York entered into a contract with Philco Radio and Television Corporation,

The first successful single-room air conditioner in the United States, developed by York in 1935, in the midst of the Great Depression.

to manufacture a line of single-room air conditioners exclusively for Philco's distribution.[34]

The Darkening Horizon

By 1939, the economy had begun to show signs of recovery. But on September 1, 1939, Germany invaded Poland, and a polarized Europe erupted into war. Two months later, the United States Congress approved the United States Neutrality Act. Though most Americans wanted to stay out of the war, the nation's leaders began to prepare for the worst. The Selective Service Act was enacted in 1940 to bolster the armed forces, and an Office of Production Management was established.

Mirroring the national recovery, York's sales and profits rebounded from their nadir of the Great Depression. As the new decade began to unfold, Stewart E. Lauer was elected president of the York Ice Machinery Corporation in 1940, succeeding Shipley. Shipley became chairman of the company's board of directors. At the 1940 Annual Employee's Picnic in Hershey, Pennsylvania, President Stewart E. Lauer explained that York was contributing to the nation's survival.

"I believe that the real urgency we are facing to prepare a Gibraltar-like defense, to protect our shores, our shops, our homes and our freedom, will create a unity of purpose between our government and its people that will wash away all barriers. You should know what your company is already contributing to the program of defense. We are equipping the fighting ships of the Navy which will protect our shores, with York refrigeration and air conditioning amounting to the stupendous sum of nearly a million and three-quar-

ter dollars. We are equipping with York refrigeration the first series of smokeless powder plants, which is located in Memphis, Tennessee. ... I pledge to you that the management group of your company will use every waking hour thinking and planning constructively how we can best serve our nation."[35]

New products and a plan for the future marked the York Conference and Exposition, as reported in the January 1938 edition of *York News.*

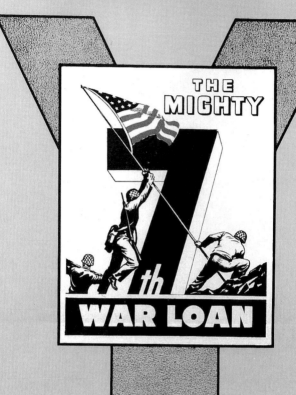

PUT YORKCO AHEAD IN THE 7th

THE MIGHTY 7th WAR LOAN

OUR GOAL—$415,000

This is our toughest objective yet — but Iwo Jima wasn't easy. Yorkco has never failed and can't fail now. To make this objective every Yorkco family, man and woman, must join the attack. We will raise our flag of victory on June 30th. It's up to you!

REMEMBER THE DATES MAY 14th to JUNE 30th

Even in the waning months of World War II, York exhorted its workers to contribute to the final victory in August 1945.

CHAPTER SEVEN

YORK "CAN DO" AS THE NATION GOES TO WAR

1940-1945

"We must rearrange our affairs so as to withstand the rigors of business under the conditions imposed by the most serious Emergency in our national history. Your Government needs your help and you need the help of your Government at this time. Only by working together to do the best within our ability for the benefit of all of us can we come through this as we should."

— The York Priority Business Plan[1]

AS WAR RAGED in Europe, America was rapidly mobilizing its forces and industrial might at home. In 1940, Congress passed the Selective Service Act, the nation's first peacetime conscription as industries began converting to wartime production. In late 1940 York received its first contracts from the National Defense Program to manufacture refrigeration and air conditioning equipment for windowless industrial plants, smokeless powder plants, factories, army camps, naval bases, and ships for both the Navy and the Merchant Marine.

Despite wartime damage and disruptions in overseas commerce, York's international business grew during 1940, especially through its London and Shanghai subsidiaries. The York Ice Machinery Corporation was ideally situated to meet expanding market demands. A bulletin issued October 13, 1941, reminded salesmen of the critical need for government contracts.

"Every day of the present National Emergency will add importance to the job of securing business that carries with it priority certificates ... because straight civilian business is now almost out of the picture. It is true that margins of profit on this Government business will not be as large as in civilian business, but we must rearrange our affairs so as to withstand the rigors of busi-

ness under the conditions imposed by the most serious Emergency in our national history. Your Government needs your help and you need the help of your Government at this time. Only by working together to do the best within our ability for the benefit of all of us can we come through this as we should. 'It can be done' is more than a mere possibility ... so let's make our slogan for the Priority Business Program strong and positive to the core, 'IT WILL BE DONE.'"[2]

In mid-1941, the York Ice Machinery Corporation collaborated with the United States Navy to inaugurate a school to instruct service personnel from the Atlantic and Pacific fleets on the proper operation, care and maintenance of air conditioning and refrigeration systems. The only school of its kind in the industry, it was praised in 24 newspapers and 14 magazines, including *Business Week* and the *New York Journal of Commerce and Steel.*[3]

The training provided by the school, and the patriotic fervor encouraged by York's leaders, would soon become vital. On December 7, 1941,

---

York's workers wore identification badges such as this during the war years for security.

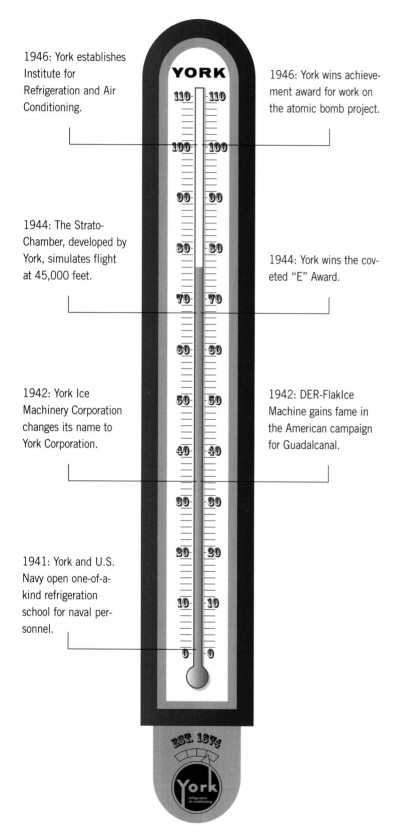

1946: York establishes Institute for Refrigeration and Air Conditioning.

1946: York wins achievement award for work on the atomic bomb project.

1944: The Strato-Chamber, developed by York, simulates flight at 45,000 feet.

1944: York wins the coveted "E" Award.

1942: York Ice Machinery Corporation changes its name to York Corporation.

1942: DER-FlakIce Machine gains fame in the American campaign for Guadalcanal.

1941: York and U.S. Navy open one-of-a-kind refrigeration school for naval personnel.

while the unsuspecting United States Pacific Fleet conducted its peacetime Sunday routine in Pearl Harbor, more than 360 Japanese warplanes screamed down from the clouds to attack Battleship Row. Five battleships were either sunk or heavily damaged, along with 14 other ships. More than 2,000 naval personnel and about 400 civilians were killed in the attack. Within four days, the United States declared war on Japan, Germany and Italy. America turned from isolationism and joined the fury of the world war.

"For the war effort, there was a great sense of urgency," recalled Raymond Lecates, who arrived at York in 1944 and designed eight-inch gun trails, cradles and saddles.[4]

Some of York's field inspectors were trapped on warships as the U.S. Navy scrambled to meet the enemy. Longtime York engineer Austin Diehl, who joined the company in 1933 and retired in 1974, remembered one man, while testing pipes and a refrigeration unit aboard a destroyer, ended up somewhere in the Pacific Ocean.

"He'd usually go out two or three weeks during the shakedown cruise on these ships. They'd test fire their guns and he'd look for leaks in the pipes. When the war broke out December 7, he happened to be out on a ship that was immediately called into duty. He'd try to find another ship on its way in and he'd get on that ship, and then that one would get called for duty. It took 14 months for him to get home."[5]

The FlakIce Machine

York had produced the first self-contained flake-ice machine in 1940, a novel device able to produce one ton of flaked ice per day. The machines produced ice in ribbons, a form that could be used by troops who fought under hot, tropical conditions. The machine inspired an almost magical reverence among beleaguered soldiers. One of York's first flake-ice machines was sent to Guadalcanal, site of one of the most dramatic battles in the Pacific.

Following a resounding American naval victory against the Japanese Navy at Midway Island, several thousand Marines captured an airfield on Guadalcanal in August 1942. The amphibious assault was hastily planned, and the resources allocated to the mission were so meager that soldiers dubbed the invasion "Operation Shoestring." The Japanese launched ferocious counterattacks. At one point during the campaign, the Marines were stranded with virtually no supplies other than what the Japanese had left at the airfield. For more than six months, Marines withstood wild banzai attacks, relentless shelling, malaria and torrential rains. Small creature comforts took on enormous importance. On Christmas Eve in 1942, York's DER-10 FlakIce Machine arrived. A company newsletter described the reaction.

Defense
IS OUR
Business

"That day a DER-10 FlakIce Machine had been set up on four aluminum kegs, and men labored in the hot night to get it working. A welcome yell indicated that something worthwhile had happened. Out there in the night, with its terrific heat, drama and great danger, FlakIce Frosty Ribbons flowed from the DER-10. Word passed with magical speed. As each precious pound of FlakIce Frosty Ribbons flowed, the hands of thirsty men reached eagerly forth. [One of the Marines] said that was one of the greatest thrills he ever experienced."[6]

York salesmen found it easy to market the machines to the public by citing the reliability they had provided overseas during the war. By 1941, military contracts helped to propel York's sales to $27.5 million, of which air conditioning and refrigeration comprised 90 percent. Net income was $1.2 million, double that of the previous year.[7]

The York Plan

In 1941, the Commonwealth of Pennsylvania passed the State Council Act to assist communi-

Left: Cherished by hot and hungry soldiers, the DER-10 FlakIce Machine provided a measure of relief from the hot tropical jungle.

Above: With the motto "Defense Is Our Business," York mobilized for war.

THE YORK PLAN

1. Utilize existing tools and manufacturing equipment.
2. Put idle equipment and manpower to work.
3. Make a survey of tools that might be available in plants outside the metals trades.
4. Determine the types of work that might be accomplished with the facilities currently available.
5. Publicize and sell the plan to the community at large.
6. Devise strategies for educating the new employees required to make the plan work.
7. Study local needs and devise a housing plan for the local community.
8. Make a study of workers' health needs.
9. Devise guidelines for defining the cost of subcontractors to the prime contractor on a given project.
10. Study ways to ensure that deliveries of materials from subcontractors will reach the prime contractors when needed.
11. Devise methods to ensure that the quality standards necessary for the final acceptance of assembled products under federal contracts are properly adhered to by all subcontractors.
12. Study and develop ways of coordinating demands on labor when operation of three full production shifts is required.
13. Make a study of the labor potential of the York area.
14. Devise strategies to supply optimal levels of manpower on a given project when and where required.
15. The Defense Committee is committed to becoming involved in all local activities that could have a bearing on meeting the demands in the present National Emergency.[9]

ties to meet the demands of war production. William Shipley, then chairman of the Manufacturers Association of York, was selected to chair the York Defense Committee. Known as the York Plan, a plan of cooperation among manufacturers was developed under his leadership that became a national model.

Shipley informed Washington authorities that he was developing a central registry of York's 264 companies to pool available labor skills, equipment and schedules to fill government contracts.[8] The goal was to "do more with less," so that manufacturers could minimize the cost of retooling for war production. The York Plan was defined by 15 objectives.

By 1942, 31 York factories were working to complete military contracts under the York Plan. Shipley also served on the Job Mobilization Committee, which helped match workers with jobs. By the end of the war, William Shipley's leadership during the war was a point of intense pride for both the company and the community.

The York Corporation

On June 29, 1942, the York Ice Machinery Corporation changed its name to the York Corporation, since ice machines were no longer the company's primary product line. As part of the name change, the company exchanged its outstanding preferred stock on the basis of 15 shares of common stock in the new company for one share of preferred stock in the old company. In 1942, York's sales totaled $22.5 million, a 14 percent increase over 1941 sales. Those numbers failed to describe the full scope of York's production that year, since many of its government contracts required a long period of planning and execution. Unfilled orders at the end of the fiscal year were worth $27.8 million, up from $10.3 million a year earlier. Roughly 73 percent of the new production volume was air conditioning and refrigeration equipment for the war effort.[10]

In the winter of 1942, York introduced *Cold Magic*, a magazine which reminded employees that they were "fighting together in the battle of production for ... Victory!"[11] Stewart Lauer launched the new publication with his comments.

"You and I, all of us, are in the toughest war in this country's history. The first vicious onslaught of the treacherous Japanese left us gasping for an instant but America is now aroused, and united as never before! We are in this war with both feet and we intend to see it through to the finish. ... Over the past eighteen months we have been building a defense manufacturing program which today places our corporation on a 60 percent 'war work' basis. We expect by the last half of 1942 to

This edition of Cold Magic magazine was almost ready to go to press when the Japanese attacked. It was quickly revised, but still ran a peacetime article about a Jai-Alai Palace in Manila, which had just fallen to Japanese forces.

be working on an 80 percent war work basis. The remaining 20 percent of our capacity will be held for essential civilian applications.

"For over a year we have had a staff of permanent Naval Inspectors in our shops — whose duty it is to check York equipment against Navy requirements before it is shipped from our plant. About a year ago also, because of the large amount of defense work handled here, the government asked us to put our plant under armed guard to protect against possible sabotage. ... A few months ago a large contract for Barbette gun carriages was awarded this company, and today there is a staff of resident Army Inspectors in our plant to assist us in carrying out this job. ... We are fighting the battle here at home just as surely as our brave lads are fighting the battle in the Pacific. We, at home, are fighting the 'battle of production' and we are fighting to win!"[12]

Also during 1942, York won a contract to provide gas compression and refrigerating equipment for the government's synthetic rubber and aviation gasoline production programs.[13] Under the terms of this high-priority project, York began delivering equipment in October 1942, completing most of the project no later than July 1943. Negotiations for the contract coincided with round-the-clock Allied air raids on Germany, which began with a 1,000-plane air raid on Cologne in May 1942 that disrupted German transportation and fuel reserves. As a result of such raids, much of the German Luftwaffe was grounded due to a lack of aviation fuel by the time of Operation Overlord, the invasion of Normandy in 1944. Among the key requirements for this eventual assault were rubber products and high-octane aviation gasoline, both of which required low temperatures for their manufacture. The War Production Board wanted to manufacture one million tons of synthetic rubber per year, and increase the production of aviation gasoline from 100,000 barrels per day to 250,000 barrels per day.[14]

While there were 29 varieties of synthetic rubber, only three were suitable for war production needs: Neoprene, Buna and Butyl. Neoprene

No Time for Stewing

York refrigeration is speeding up the manufacture of explosives. York men are fighting
the war in York plants today and every day.

KEEP ON FIGHTING

This graphic image served as a reminder to York employees of the importance of war production.

equipment also assisted in controlling material processing temperatures in industrial plants processing lubricating oils, manufacturing sensitive electronic components, and manufacturing delicate instruments such as range finders, theodolites and gun sights.

The demands of war inspired York engineers to find creative solutions to tough problems. One of these involved an important advance in producing the highly efficient finned evaporating coils used in refrigeration systems.[17] Previously, the softness of copper had limited the maximum length of finned coils to 72 inches, so that longer coils had to be assembled by running two copper coils in series. York engineers managed to fabricate single steel coils with a length of 107 inches. These 107-inch finned steel coils also offered 11 percent more surface area than two 48-inch-long copper coils.[18] For this seemingly simple innovation, York engineers had to solve a serious corrosion problem. Various oxides of carbon, sulfur and chloride caused steel coils to corrode. After being required by government contracts to discover a substitute for copper coils, York engineers realized they could make steel coils relatively resistant to corrosion by galvanizing them with a hot dip. Because most plants at the time did not have hot dip facilities, York was able to corner this particular market. By the spring of 1943, York had a backlog of 500 orders for steel fin air conditioning coils sealed by means of the new hot dip galvanizing process.[19]

York was constantly called upon to balance war production with essential civilian services required for hospitals, schools and other locations. The use of Freon-12 was forbidden for civilian use either in new systems or as a replacement in older systems, so methyl chloride was used instead.[20] The War Production Board also restricted construction of new buildings and additions to existing buildings.[21] In a letter to employees, President Stewart Lauer stressed the importance of remaining flexible.

"With only so much raw material available, the War Production Board must time its activities to front line needs, and must decide which contracts must be rushed to completion and which should be held back. ... The thing we should all

at the time was manufactured exclusively by DuPont Corporation. The DuPont plant at Deepwater, New Jersey manufactured 10,000 tons of Neoprene per year, while the Louisville, Kentucky plant, completed in 1943, had a capacity of 20,000 tons annually. Buna rubber was manufactured by government plants, while Butyl rubber was manufactured exclusively by Standard Oil.[15]

Another vital war contribution was industrial air conditioning, which was critical for quench-cooling during the fabrication of Duralumin rivets for aircraft. Unlike ferrous metals, Duralumin softens upon being cooled rather than heated. York provided a system that could chill billions of Duralumin rivets so that they could be driven more easily and grip more securely.[16] York

keep in mind, however, is the cause of these sudden changes. Remember that one reason for our existence these days is simply to back up our armed forces. If you think these changes are hard on you, think for a moment of the soldier who finds himself up against it because he doesn't have what he needs to keep on fighting. These orders from the War Production Board keep that from happening."[22]

The company established an annual contest to reward employees for suggestions that would boost productivity. In January 1943, Tool Room employee William S. Diehl won a $100 savings bond for his suggestion that a special tool maintenance crib be set up to speed the handling of templates and special fixtures for war production projects. Second prize of a $50 savings bond was awarded to Norman E. Warner of the Grantley

Maintenance Department. He suggested that the casting truck in the Sand Blast Department would be more efficient if it was equipped with a winch and wheels with heavier flanges to ensure that the truck moved more securely on its tracks. A $10 savings bond went to Richard E. Massam of the Inspection Department who suggested that the 7,500 gallons of oil sold each year for salvage should be reprocessed using equipment similar to that employed in the automotive industry.[23]

In 1944, the hard work of York employees was officially recognized when Brigadier General H.F. Safford, chief of the production service branch of the United States Army, presented York Corporation employees with the coveted Army-Navy "E" production award.[24]

The "E" pins were presented by Lt. Cmdr. B.P. Edmunds of the United States Naval Reserve and Corporal Robert Cherry, a veteran wounded in the Mediterranean theater, to a group of representative York employees. The group included V. Marie Slenker, who had served the company for 26 years; Robert Spangler, who had been at York 48 years and at 83 was the company's oldest employee; and Claude W. Baum, an employee of 25 years who had twin sons serving in the Army, one of whom was captured by the Japanese on the Bataan peninsula.

By 1944, the highest priority in York's machine shops was outfitting self-propelled landing barges (also called amphibious "ducks") and tank landing craft for the anticipated invasion of Europe. To prepare for the attack, roughly $75 million worth of landing craft were manufactured by 4,000 contractors and 20,000 subcontractors across the nation over a period of five months. The project was top-secret. A January 1944 article in the employee newspaper revealed only that: "Invasion has been on our lips ever since the first American doughboys set foot on English soil. Well, it is coming up now! We here at Yorkco have our part of that invasion mapped out for us. Anchors away!"[25]

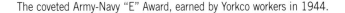

The coveted Army-Navy "E" Award, earned by Yorkco workers in 1944.

Bringing the Sky to Earth

Another important York contribution was the design and manufacture of a Stratospheric Test Chamber to simulate conditions encountered by pilots at altitudes between 35,000 and 40,000 feet. At this altitude, the average temperature was minus 67, and could fall below minus 120 degrees. These low temperatures are accompanied by extremely low air pressures and densities; at 40,000 feet, air pressure is only about 2.75 pounds per square inch, compared to 14.7 pounds per square inch at sea level.

Such conditions are extremely dangerous as aircraft hydraulic fluid would freeze at minus 50 degrees, and even gasoline will freeze at minus 90 degrees. Aircraft components made of rubber become as brittle as glass, and pilots must be protected by heated high-altitude flight suits, oxygen masks, or pressurized cabins.

The first test chambers were simply equipped with vacuum pumps to simulate pressure changes, along with small air conditioning units to lower temperatures. From these crude chambers, scientists learned that flight crews would lose efficiency above an altitude of 15,000 feet, and actually lose consciousness above 20,000 feet as a result of oxygen deprivation. They also discovered that a sudden reduction in air pressure resulted in aeroembolism, a condition known to deep-sea divers as the "bends." At altitudes above 42,000 feet, only a pressurized suit or pressurized cabin could protect a pilot from death. Early flight chambers failed to consider the extreme temperature conditions of the stratosphere.

The Canadian Ice Machine Company, Ltd. manufactured the first chamber that could simulate both pressure and temperature conditions for an altitude of 45,000 feet. However, the Canadian design could not reproduce the rapid changes in temperatures encountered by powerful fighter aircraft during steep climbing and diving maneuvers.

In 1944, this challenge was met by York engineers with the development of the York Strato-Chamber for physiological research. The York Strato-Chamber consisted of a lock approximately four feet in length and a main chamber of 18 feet. The main chamber was an insulated "climb" environment with space on one side for refrigerant coils which could be isolated from air inside the chamber. A company brochure describes how the chamber functioned.

"The climb chamber is opened to the refrigerated space with fans and refrigerating equipment operated for a sufficient length of time to pull all the heat out of the coils, shell, insulation, etc. This may take from 10 to 20 hours, depending upon the type and method of insulation. During the last several hours fans are not operated, and air

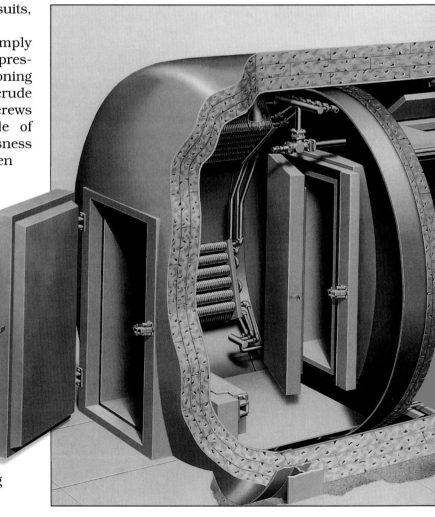

flows by gravity down through the coils and up through the climb chamber back to the coils. The coils, fan, shell, etc. are cooled to a temperature of -90 degrees to -100 degrees Fahrenheit, which is considerably below the final temperatures to be produced in the climb chamber. At the end of the preliminary cooling period, the climb chamber is isolated from the cooling circuit and heated up to normal atmospheric conditions by means of electric heaters. ... After the test subjects have been put into the climb chamber, the vacuum pumps and fans are started, and the dampers admitting cold air to the chamber are opened. A sufficient reservoir of refrigeration has been built up to reduce the temperature within the climb chamber to minus 70 degrees in 12 minutes or less."[26]

Similar test chambers specifically designed to test equipment were capable of simulating conditions found at altitudes of 60,000 feet.

In addition, York engineers provided expertise for the construction of an improved wind tunnel at Wright Field in Dayton, Ohio, to simulate extremely high altitude conditions for advanced aircraft designs. York provided a cooling capacity of 8,000 tons of refrigeration to produce temperatures as low as minus 67 degrees at the tunnel throat.[27]

Food for the Troops

Among the company's most important missions was to build refrigerators to preserve food for the nation's troops. An early contribution to the war effort was the Yorkaire 335 Air Conditioning Unit, a self-contained unit that was easy to place into immediate service anywhere in the world. All branches of the military relied on the Yorkaire, which could run 24 hours a day, seven days a week even in the most hot and humid tropical conditions. Such a product would normally have required a year of development, but under wartime pressure, the company managed to design and build four units in only 30 days. Hundreds more were ready for shipment

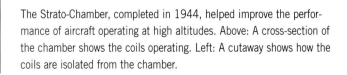

The Strato-Chamber, completed in 1944, helped improve the performance of aircraft operating at high altitudes. Above: A cross-section of the chamber shows the coils operating. Left: A cutaway shows how the coils are isolated from the chamber.

within a few months. The rugged steel cabinet of the Yorkaire 335 contained a York Balinseal compressor, air-cooled condenser, three-horsepower motor, recirculating fan and motor, evaporator, air filter, and controls. The Balinseal was the first of the mechanical seals to replace the earlier stuffing boxes. It was so named because the product was a balanced seal.

York also provided the Army and Marine Corps with a gas engine-driven plug-in refrigerating unit known as the Standard Sectional Demountable Walk-in Cold Storage Facility. York was the only manufacturer capable of meeting the Army's special requirements. The success of this product led to an Army contract to build the fully-automated York V-30 plug-in refrigeration unit. This unit was of critical importance, since it could keep food fresh at 35 degrees and frozen foods at 10 degrees, even when outside temperature reached 110 degrees at 85 percent relative humidity.[28]

The cold storage rooms to which these refrigerating units were attached were often located well behind the front lines, leading York to develop a refrigerated truck-trailer unit to transport food directly to hungry troops. Even at an outside temperature of 120 degrees, food inside the York

Trailer Unit V-45 would remain frozen at 10 degrees.

By the end of the war, York had made a substantial contribution to the effort, including 4,200 York Ammonia Refrigeration Systems, 29,318 York Freon-12 Refrigeration Systems, the Quartermaster Corps V-18AG Portable Frozen Food Refrigerator, the Marine Corps Model V-60 Mobile Self-Contained Air Dehumidifier, the Navy Self-Contained Ice Making Machine with a capacity of 400 pounds of ice daily, and the Engineer Corps Model V-50 Self-Contained Factory Assembled Ice Plants and Navy Model DER-10 Self-Contained FlakIce Units, each of which could produce a ton of ice daily.[29]

The Manhattan Project

The York Corporation participated in the Manhattan Project, the biggest, most expensive and most controversial American industrial project in history. The Manhattan Project produced the atomic bombs dropped on Japan in 1945 and ushered in the potentials and dangers of nuclear technology. Despite the protests of competitors,

Above: The Model V-60 Mobile Self-Contained Air Dehumidifier, built for the Marine Corps, helped keep food fresh for soldiers on the move.

Left: The V-30 refrigerator unit was similar to the V-60, which could quickly plug into portable cold storage rooms.

who insisted it couldn't be done, York installed the world's largest water-cooling system at the Atomic Energy facilities of the Hanford Engineering Works in Pasco, Washington. This system, which employed 10 centrifugal turbo compressors, was capable of cooling the equivalent of 15,000 tons of ice per day. York also installed a Gaseous Diffusion Plant at Oak Ridge, Tennessee.

In recognition of these two projects, the York Corporation won the Chemical Engineering Achievement Award in 1946 for significant scientific research and engineering contributions to the Manhattan Project. Lauer accepted the award at a dinner in New York City, where 117 corporations, universities, and research groups were similarly honored.[30] On August 6, 1945, the first atomic bomb was dropped on Hiroshima. That day, a bulletin was issued to the York sales force by Major General L.R. Groves, who commanded the mammoth project.

"ATOMIC BOMB SECURITY RULES STILL EFFECTIVE: While we are extremely anxious to tell the part York has played in the development of the amazing Atomic Bomb, we are prevented from doing so . ... Release by the President of the United States and the War Department of Information on certain phases of the military use of and our work on atomic energy will necessarily result in revision of security rules on the entire project of the Manhattan Engineer District. Pending receipt of further instructions which are now being issued all publicity must be cleared with my Washington office. ... I am asking you personally to continue the existing complete cooperation by your entire organization and by each of your subcontractors in the maintenance of national safety. Please so notify your subcontractors by telegraph — L.R. Groves, Major General, U.S.A."[31]

Three days later, a second bomb was dropped on Nagasaki. World War II was over.

Between 1941 and 1945, the company had supplied $132 million in production and services to the war effort. Of the total, fully $115 million represented refrigeration and air conditioning machinery for battleships, aircraft carriers, cruisers, destroyers, submarines, hospital ships, ammunition ships, landing craft, naval bases, laboratories and cargo vessels. The other $17 million represented other war matériel, including gun mounts. Another $69.5 million in air conditioning and refrigeration equipment was employed to help produce aircraft, chemicals, communication equipment, synthetic rubber, lubricants, gasoline, food, as well as the first atomic bombs.[32]

Between 1941 and 1945, York emerged as the nation's largest supplier of naval air conditioning and refrigeration equipment. The company provided 75 percent of refrigeration for submarines, and half of the refrigeration for the American merchant marine.

York's productivity also increased steadily during the war years. In 1943, sales were $32.4 million and earnings were $902,000.[33] In 1944, sales were $34.1 million though earnings dropped to $729,000.[32] And in 1945, sales surged to $38.4 million, with profits of $949,000.

The Aftermath of War

About 1,200 York employees were gradually released from the military. To assist returning workers, the York Corporation established the York Institute for Refrigeration and Air Conditioning. The first school of its kind in the nation, the institute provided programs ranging from a two-week "refresher" course for distributors, to a five-year engineering course conducted in cooperation with Pennsylvania State University.[34] The school offered training programs for boilermakers, draftsmen, electricians, heat treaters, machinists, molders, patternmakers, pipe fitters, plumbers, refrigeration service mechanics, sheet metal workers, tool designers and toolmakers. A factory management training program was also available.

The company was preparing its workers and itself for a peacetime economy, one that would boom with unprecedented strength and wealth.

A grateful York Corporation shows its appreciation for its engineers by hosting an Engineers' Banquet in 1946.

CHAPTER EIGHT

FROM WAR TO PEACE

1945-1949

"I have not heard anything but praise on the part of our church members and visitors for the comfort afforded by this air conditioning unit. ... We wish to express to you and your personnel our appreciation for the cooperation and efficient manner in which the job was handled."

— Letter to the York Corporation, 1948[1]

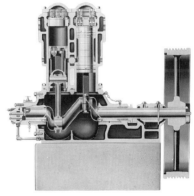

FOLLOWING THE war, American armed forces began the complicated yet welcome task of demobilization. Millions of soldiers, crowded aboard aircraft carriers, were whisked from Europe back to the United States as part of Operation Magic Carpet. American businesses hurried to retool from war production to peacetime industry.

The York Corporation's transition from war to peace was relatively easy because most of the company's war production had been devoted to refrigeration and air conditioning. In 1946, York manufactured fully half of all single- room air conditioning units produced in the United States.

FlakIce in Peacetime

The famous DER-10 FlakIce machine that had provided much-needed relief to hot and tired Marines found a ready market in the civilian market. Fishmongers, poultry shippers and sausage makers all began to rely on the ready supply of ice, and FlakIce machines were found in bakeries, cafeterias, restaurants, dairies, hospitals and hotels. The York sales force was quick to point out the machine's low-cost operation and boasted that it had survived combat in the tropical jungles of Guadalcanal.[2]

York executives were confident that only the surface of a huge potential market had been scratched.[3] Soon, the installation of air conditioning equipment in high-rise buildings usually included at least one York DER-10 FlakIce Machine as well.[4] Stewart & Company, the first air-conditioned department store in Baltimore, was also equipped with FlakIce machines. Other notable installations included the landmark Old Bookbinders Restaurant in Philadelphia[5] and the Sinai Hospital in Baltimore.[6]

In 1946, William S. Shipley was once again elected chairman of the board, while Stewart E. Lauer remained president.[7] A member of the American Society of Refrigerating Engineers for 30 years, Lauer had skillfully guided York's growth by investing in the research and development of refrigeration technology. He had earned his bachelor's degree in mechanical engineering from the University of Pennsylvania in 1911, joining York the same year. Lauer had been promoted to general manager in 1929 and president in 1940.

A cross section of the York Y-36 Ammonia Compressor.

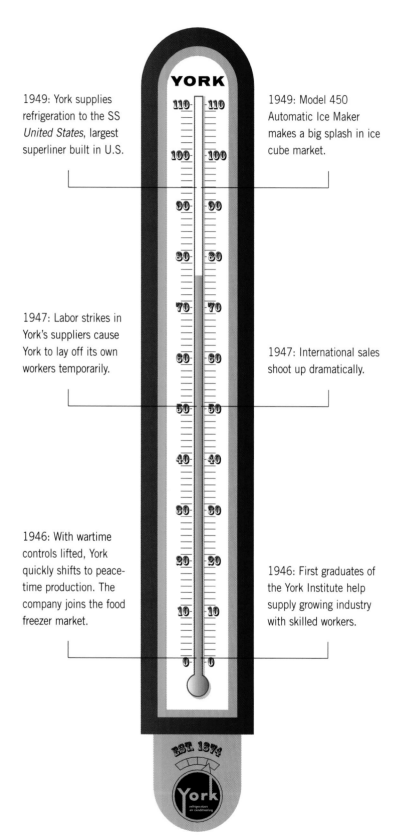

1949: York supplies refrigeration to the SS *United States*, largest superliner built in U.S.

1949: Model 450 Automatic Ice Maker makes a big splash in ice cube market.

1947: Labor strikes in York's suppliers cause York to lay off its own workers temporarily.

1947: International sales shoot up dramatically.

1946: With wartime controls lifted, York quickly shifts to peacetime production. The company joins the food freezer market.

1946: First graduates of the York Institute help supply growing industry with skilled workers.

With government restrictions on production finally lifted, orders from distributors poured in. At first, York could handle the increased work with relative ease because its factories remained geared up for wartime production. The high volume of DER-10 FlakIce machines produced during the war, for example, made it possible to take assembled units off the shelf and ship them directly to civilian customers.[8]

Improvements and Inventions

The line of Freon-12 compressors that York had developed in the thirties was dramatically refined during the forties. Among the company's early innovations was a patented "unloading port," a small hole drilled into the side of each piston above the top piston ring to equalize pressure above and below the piston when the compressor was shut off. These tiny holes were critical in reducing wear and stress on the motor when the compressor was turned on again soon after being turned off.

Another innovation, the patented York Balinseal, was designed to prevent the crankshaft of the compressor from flexing or distorting under operational loads, or when the compressor was idle for long periods of time. Its unique design also ensured a positive lubrication of bearing and seal surfaces.

The patented York Centriforce Oiler lubricated the rear bearing and shoulder of the crankshaft. Drilled holes arranged in an L-pattern in the shaft acted as channels which directed oil from a reservoir located behind the rear bearing. Centrifugal force generated by the rotation of the crankshaft forced a continuous stream of oil under pressure through the drilled passages to the oil groove in the shoulder of the crankshaft, thereby distributing a film of oil over the entire thrust surface of the crankshaft bearing.

Other important features offered on all York Balinseal compressors included simple and efficient steel disc Pressure Flex suction and discharge valves, double trunk-type pistons having larger bearing surfaces to promote even wear, and an especially rugged base designed to reduce vibration. These unique York features were heavily promoted in York sales literature and used to

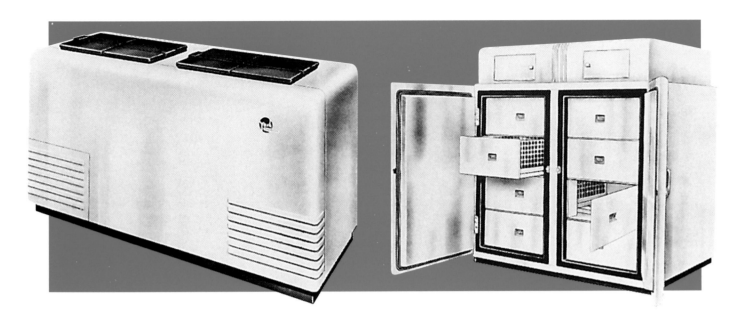

justify the higher prices often charged for York's products under the prevailing corporate policy that the customer is willing to pay more for a superior product.

Food Freezers

In 1946, York entered the food freezer market with the introduction of the York Model 165 Food Freezer, followed soon after by the York Model 350 Food Freezer. At 71 inches long, 29 inches deep and 36 inches high, the 165 Food Freezer could hold 600 pounds in the main storage compartment. An additional three cubic feet of storage space was available for instant use. The larger 350 freezer measured five feet in length, six feet high and 34 inches in depth. It could hold 1,300 pounds of frozen food in the storage compartment while providing 8 additional cubic feet for immediate use. The rounded corners and shiny white baked enamel surfaces of these machines marked York's move toward modern postwar designs.[9]

The Model 350 freezer was extremely popular with restaurants, and orders soon exceeded York's ability to manufacture the machine. Within six months of the freezer's introduction, Lauer announced that York would spend $1 million to expand its production capabilities. Two new buildings were planned, and additions would be made to three existing buildings at the Grantley Avenue

Plant. At the West York plant, the company planned to increase the square footage of one building and completely renovate several others. The project would add 113,000 square feet of floor space, a 10 percent increase overall.[10]

To equip the renovated plants, York invested an additional $3 million in modern production tools. The goal was to increase the dollar value of production per square foot by four times the number achieved during the best years of war production.

Company officials predicted that employment at its factories would grow by 20 percent in coming years.[11] The entire refrigeration and air conditioning industry cried out for trained workers, service mechanics and salesmen, and the York Institute of Air Conditioning and Refrigeration helped supply York and its distributors with the necessary workforce. In 1946, after one year of operation, about 140 graduates of both the sales engineering, and maintenance and service courses were employed by 118 domestic distributors and five export distributors.[12] William P. Emley, a foreman for Electric Products Company in Jersey City, New Jersey, reported his satisfaction with employees trained in the York program.

The model 165 Food Freezer (left) was York's first entry into the freezer market. The larger Model 350 Food Freezer followed quickly.

District commercial sales managers took time to inspect the famed York Institute of Refrigeration and Air Conditioning, which graduated highly competent and sought-after workers.

"The men who have completed training at the York Service School have noticeably changed from the type who pull machines apart locating the trouble to the type who use their head and figure out what is wrong — then use their tools to correct the trouble. The school has further helped to give the service mechanic a sense of assurance, which naturally helps when the serviceman is subject to customer scrutiny."[13]

The success of the program encouraged York officers to continue to improve the institute's curriculum. In February 1947, York established a minimum entrance requirement of 10 years of formal schooling for the service program, including at least two years of high school or a satisfactory grade on an aptitude test administered by the company.[14] At the time, this was considered a significant amount of schooling, particularly for rural Pennsylvania.

Nationwide Labor Unrest

The years immediately following the war were marked by national labor unrest. Unions throughout the country demanded higher pay and improved benefits. Strikes paralyzed important segments of the economy, including the automotive, steel, mine, petroleum and railroad industries.[15]

Labor relations remained positive at York, but the corporation's suppliers were plagued by strikes that upset production schedules, delayed shipment of orders and caused several temporary layoffs. A strike at a parts supplier for York's line of frozen food cabinets cost York $1.1 million in lost production when customers canceled orders for equipment that could not be manufactured in time for the summer season. Another strike at a firm manufacturing fans for York air conditioners threatened to cause a temporary layoff at the Grantley Avenue plant, and a strike at a plant supplying air conditioner motors resulted in a temporary layoff in the Hench plant.

York President Stewart Lauer pressured his suppliers to resolve their disputes quickly. He also expressed support for the Taft-Hartley Bill, which would soon be passed by a Republican-controlled Congress over the veto of President Harry S. Truman. The bill weakened the power of unions by outlawing closed shops, and gave the President of the United States the power to order "cooling off" periods to interrupt strikes that threatened public safety or the national interest.

"My own confidence that these hardships will not continue in the long-range future lies in the hope that President Truman will accept labor legislation, which is now [June 1947] on his desk. Many people say the bill will be tough on labor. I don't believe these people understand the bill. I have studied this bill and am convinced that it protects every basic right that labor wants and needs. ... The right to bargain collectively, the right to picket — these rights are preserved. The bill, however, puts union leadership and the employer on an equal footing before the public in carrying out their responsibilities. There are definite means provided for breaking deadlocks which are tying up production in our plant and causing unemployment and cancellations."[16]

York Corporation newsletters and magazines addressed labor issues more openly than in the past and sought to separate what the company perceived as legitimate labor concerns from more radical demands. It was a time of growing paranoia about communism, and union philosophies were often perceived as dangerously un-American. In a December 1947 article, York's management warned of the dangers of excess.

"American labor is free and is keenly conscious of that freedom. This free labor which abhors regimentation and unwarranted interference stands as a bulwark between the free enterprise system and feudalism. Unlike the parlor pinks and pink professionals whose educations have brought knowledge but not understanding, labor has little time for the communist line. The man who drives trucks or lays bricks isn't the man who encourages by his presence those communist front groups with the patriotic American names."[17]

The same article quoted Labor's *Monthly Survey*, an official publication of the American Federation of Labor. After contrasting the wage and living standards of Russian and American workers, the survey concluded,

"Every Russian worker is bound by a compulsory labor system. He must accept the wages and conditions imposed by bureaucrats on pain of arrest if

The York Corporation's service fleet contained skilled mechanics trained in York's acclaimed service school.

Above: York rescued scientists and machinery in Purdue University's Physics Department from stifling and corrosive humidity, a side effect from the peacetime research of nuclear power.

he protests. He is tied to his job and may not quit or strike."[18]

Peacetime Nuclear Research

In spite of the general labor unrest, York continued to play an important role in the field of peacetime nuclear research. A Model 350 Yorkaire Conditioner helped fight humidity in the physics department of Purdue University in Indiana, where experiments were taking place in 1947. The humidity was the result of a water-cooled cyclotron, encased in steel tanks filled with water that protected personnel from the neutrons generated by the cyclotron. The warmth and moisture made the

men lethargic and the machines prone to breakdown. The air conditioner reduced the temperature by 15 degrees and dropped the humidity to 50 percent in the middle of the hot summer afternoon.[19]

In 1947, sales increased 35 percent over the previous year, to $43.4 million. Earnings after taxes totaled $2,242,733, or $2.18 per share of common stock, an increase of 81 cents over 1946.

Comfort for Body and Soul

Part of the increase in sales came as a result of finding faithful customers. Prior to 1945, houses of worship were places of comfort for the spirit but not the body. In the summer, temperatures would soar in the stuffy old buildings. Many churches and synagogues were forced to close down in the summer to protect the health of the congregations. York saw a perfect opportunity to tap a market of more than 175,000 buildings. One of the first churches to use the Model 1501 Yorkaire Conditioner was the First Christian Church of Macon, Georgia. The unit served

the main auditorium, readers' room, foyer and Sunday school room. In 1948, the church's treasurer, F.W. Clifton, wrote York with praise for the system.

"With the inception of summer weather, we have been most pleased with the effects. The interior of the building is cool and refreshing at all times when the unit is operating, and we are able to eliminate disturbing noises by keeping all doors and windows closed. I have not heard anything but praise on the part of our church members and visitors for the comfort afforded by this air conditioning unit. ... We wish to express to you and your personnel our appreciation for the cooperation and efficient manner in which the job was handled."[20]

Word of this success spread quickly, and air conditioners were soon cooling the congregations of the First Christian Church of Macon, Georgia, and the Urbandale Baptist Church in Dallas, Texas. Attendance and plate donations increased,

and churches were confident they could recoup the $3,750 expense in a few years.[21]

A Worldwide Presence

Following the war, York enjoyed a surge in international sales, particularly in China. York air-conditioning was installed in the Capitol Theater in Nanking, the Fish Freezing Corporation in Shanghai and the 265-foot-high Joint Savings Fund Society Building in Shanghai. During the same period, a modern York ice plant was constructed in Lahore, India.[22]

In 1948, York equipment was installed in the largest cold storage warehouse in the world, in Rio de Janeiro, Brazil. The building was 530 feet in length and three stories high, and could accommodate one million boxes of fruit per month, generally divided between 400,000 boxes of oranges for export, and 60,000 boxes of imported apples, pears, peaches and plums that were not indigenous to Brazil. The sale of this cold storage facility to Brazil enabled the United States to increase fruit and vegetable exports to Brazil by 1,200 percent. Construction began in 1942 and was not completed until 1946. During the war, several shipments of essential York components were lost at sea. When construction was nearly complete, a fire destroyed the top floor. The plant's $2 million price tag included $1 million for mechanical and refrigeration equipment.[23]

"Cubes with a Hole"

In 1948, York introduced a push-button automatic ice cube maker that could produce 500 pounds of clear "cubes with a hole" per day. Tom Breneman, standing in his famous Hollywood Restaurant, told the world about the new machine on his live television program. Even before full-scale production, a prototype drew a rave review from Jack M. Davis of the Hotel Marcy on Lake Placid, New York.

"No need for me to tell you that the demonstration of the York Automatic Ice Maker scored a bull's eye at the Hotel Show in New York. We have an acute need for an Ice Maker as we

Below: The First Christian Church of Macon, Georgia, was one of the first houses of worship to install air conditioning, which helped to boost church attendance.

inevitably run into trouble during our busy season in the matter of keeping supplied with ice for service in our Cocktail Lounge and Blue Room. As you know, Lake Placid is a world-famed mecca for the sports-minded. The name of our town is synonymous with skating, skiing, bobsledding, and other winter pastimes utilizing snow AND ICE."[24]

York officials promised Davis that two of the ice machines would be routed to Lake Placid within a month. A year after they were installed, Davis wrote again to express his delight.

"Here, in Lake Placid, world famed winter sports resort, we've come to take for granted the wonders that Mother Nature creates for us in the way of ice and snow. But, along came the York 450 Ice Maker and, for once, old Mother Nature had to take a back seat. For a year now, we've enjoyed a limitless supply of just about the clearest, purest ice cubes I've ever seen. Best of all, the savings over our previous method of storing ice will pay for the machine within two years. ... Yes, Lake Placid may

excel in ice and snow, but York is certainly tops in the man-made field."[25]

By 1949, five York Model 450 Automatic Ice Makers and one DER-10 FlakIce Machine were installed in the renowned Chalfont-Haddon Hall hotels on the Atlantic City Boardwalk. Two of the "cubers," as the Automatic Ice Makers came to be known, were installed in the Haddon Hall kitchen, one was positioned in the service room off the Derbyshire Cocktail Lounge, and the remaining two were in the Chalfont kitchen. Chalfont-Haddon Hall General Manager Joseph McDonnell praised the machines in a letter dated January 28, 1949.

"We want to let you know how pleased we are with the installation of one FlakIce Machine and five cubers, which were put in operation last summer. The FlakIce Machine more than takes care of our needs, and this form of ice has been very satisfactory. It saves considerable labor because it only has to be handled once. The cubers have been very well received by our guests, and our capacity is up to your estimate. Our only problem is whether to purchase more for our peak loads."[26]

York officials calculated that the FlakIce machine saved the hotel $1,735 per year, while the five cubers eliminated the need to purchase 7,926 bags of ice, saving the hotels another $3,011 per year.[27]

The popularity of the York "cubers" led to another high-visibility installation at Hackney's Sea Food Restaurant in Atlantic City. With a seating capacity of 3,000, Hackney's was the largest

Above, from top to bottom: The popular York window unit air conditioner, from the years 1947, 1948 and 1949.

Left: A York water cooling installation in the Pepsi-Cola Bottling Company in Los Angeles, utilizing a 6X6 Double Cylinder Ammonia Condensing System.

one-floor restaurant in the world, famous for allowing customers to choose their dinner from the crustaceans swimming in the Lobster Pool, then cooking it to order. Hackney's once served 14,000 meals in a single day, and during the summer 10,000-meal days were common. Both a FlakIce machine and a cuber were located next to the Lobster Pool, where thousands of patrons from across the country and around the world could see them.[28]

"Geared to Go"

York continued to pioneer technological advances. In 1948, the company introduced the first hermetically-sealed refrigeration circuits for single-room air conditioners. Such technological advance increased efficiency, safety and reliability, giving York confidence to establish a five-year customer protection plan that became an important promotional theme in the years ahead.

Sales in 1948 were $56.5 million, a 30 percent increase over the previous year. Earnings after taxes and dividends were $3.2 million, roughly equivalent to $3 per share of outstanding common stock. Thanks to recent factory expansion, York's production had increased 266 percent over prewar levels, and payroll reached a record $12.1 million.[29]

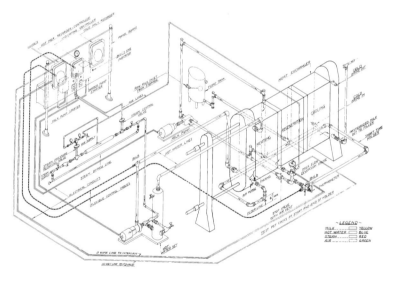

Top: An 8,000-pound-per-hour High Temperature Short Time Milk Pasteurizer, installed in the 1940s in the Harrisburg Dairies in Harrisburg, Pennsylvania.

Middle: A diagram showing the layout of the York High Temperature Short Time Milk Pasteurizer.

Left: A York Cabinet-Type Milk Cooler from sometime in the 1940s.

With the plant expansion finally complete in early 1949, the York Corporation shifted its attention to sales. The company launched its "Geared To Go" sales program with a series of eight two-day field meetings attended by 1,075 York distributors and dealers, plus members of the press and invited guests.

The theme was a return to creative specialty selling, a change from the company's recent emphasis on commodity sales. Two professional actors put on a little play featuring a veteran salesman giving advice to his son, who was just starting out. York salesman Dean Seitz followed up with specific suggestions. For condensing units, he advised, tell customers about features that protect bearings and save them money. For Yorkaire conditioners, men-

tion the increased output and recent 20 percent weight reduction of the units. Further suggestions were provided by salesmen Walt Landmesser and John Garceau.[30]

Shopping Malls and Superliners

In the prosperous postwar years, a new kind of community began to dot the American landscape. It was known as the suburbs, and for the first time, Americans could enjoy the best qualities of both city and country life. These leafy towns were generally close to cities, but they had their own banks, churches, movie theaters and shopping districts. Before long, the shopping mall was born, and another lucrative market was created for York air conditioners.

One of the first shopping malls air-conditioned by York was the City Line Shopping Center in Philadelphia. The complex had 23 stores, including a movie theater, supermarket, florist, bakery, drug

Christmas dinner in 1949 for York workers and their families.

store, hardware store, women's clothing store, men's clothing store, radio and television store, gift shop, stationary store, beauty parlor and barber shop. The parking lot had space for 3,500 cars. In 1949, York supplied 25 air conditioners, plus two 30-horsepower York Model 366E compressors to cool the 1,200-seat theater.[31]

In September 1949, York air-conditioned the largest private yacht in the world, the magnificent 136-foot four-masted *Sea Cloud*. Owned by former ambassador Joseph E. Davies, the yacht cost $1 million to build in 1931. It had an elegant master bedroom, with separate bathrooms for Mr. and Mrs. Davis, plus six guest cabins and quarters for the maids and valets. The yacht had a 72-man crew, which included 40 men just to raise all 29 sails within a one-hour time span. York also provided two 10-horsepower condensing units for food refrigeration.[32]

York also established itself as the air conditioning manufacturer of choice for superliners. In October 1949, the company announced that it had landed a contract through the Newport News

One of the largest superliners built in the United States, the SS *United States* was a model of comfort for passengers.

Shipbuilding and Dry Dock Company, to provide air conditioning for the SS *United States*, the largest American superliner ever built. This 950-foot superliner would be completed in three years and four months, at a cost of $67.4 million. It would be able to carry 2,000 passengers and 3,000 crew members. Mindful of the recent war, the ship was designed to allow easy conversion to a troop ship capable of carrying 12,000 troops.[33]

By 1949, the value of York's commercial and industrial businesses had risen to $639 million, up from $232 million in 1945 and $163 million in 1938.[34] York was positioned for continued growth in all of the markets in which it had developed and nurtured — home and commercial air conditioning, FlakIce, cubed ice, marine refrigeration, industrial refrigeration, shopping malls, aircraft testing facilities and nuclear research facilities.

By 1948, York could provide stylized "cubes with a hole" to customers who wanted to spruce up their drinks.

CHAPTER NINE

THE COLD WAR

1950-1956

"The need for civilian defense on a national scale ... brings up potential business of terrific magnitude."

— John Hertzler, 1950[1]

THE FEELING OF relief following the end of World War II quickly gave way to the tension of Cold War. In 1945, mere hours after the first atomic bomb had been dropped on Hiroshima, the War Department somewhat arbitrarily chose the 38th parallel as the dividing line between Soviet-occupied North Korea and U.S.-backed South Korea. The uneasy peace was shattered on June 25, 1950, when North Korean troops invaded South Korea. The large-scale invasion took the world by surprise as North Korean troops quickly overran the capital city of Seoul. President Harry S. Truman declared a state of emergency in the United States, imploring all citizens to unite their efforts to combat "communist imperialism." The United Nations declared North Korea the aggressor, and Truman immediately sent air and sea forces as part of an international coalition to defend South Korea. He also called for a "mighty production effort" to rebuild American military might.

York Corporation's post-war optimism quickly turned into cautious conservatism. Yorkco President and CEO Stewart Lauer wrote letters to several newspapers urging protection of the "American Way of Life," which he believed was threatened by the nation's emerging social programs. He predicted that American industries would suffer "a slow death under the pressure of the social planners. And when social planning finally brings about the collapse of the economy which it has carefully planned for, then the great horde of experts in communism rush in and make the final kill — smother the last breath of free life from every individual who is not lucky enough to capture one of the big jobs."[2]

Yorkco executives became involved in nationwide Republican congressional campaigns in 1950, fearing that President Harry S. Truman's policies would damage the nation's economy. Lauer led the company in joining with the National Manufacturers Association in its anti-Truman and anti-socialism campaign. He also started a campaign among York County businesses in an attempt to prevent the enactment of Truman's "socialist ideas." Truman had pushed for an Economic Bill of Rights, calling for broader civil rights guarantees, a higher minimum wage, new regional conservation and several public power projects. The bill meant more power to segments of the federal government. In a note to York

---

The entrance to the York Corporation. With the onset of the Korean War, York once again mobilized for war.

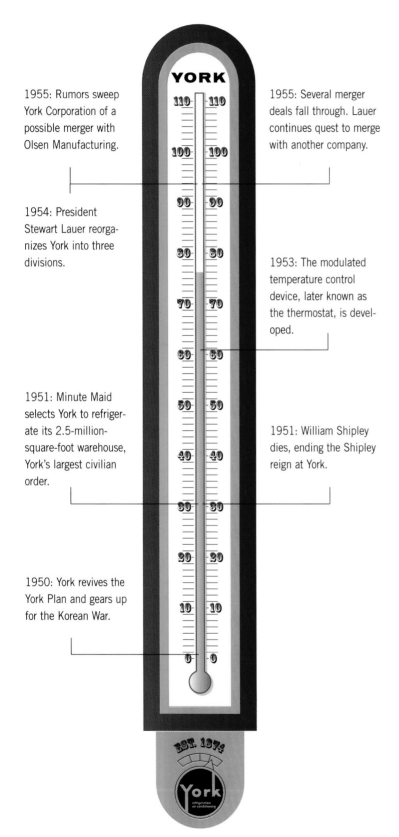

1955: Rumors sweep York Corporation of a possible merger with Olsen Manufacturing.

1954: President Stewart Lauer reorganizes York into three divisions.

1951: Minute Maid selects York to refrigerate its 2.5-million-square-foot warehouse, York's largest civilian order.

1950: York revives the York Plan and gears up for the Korean War.

1955: Several merger deals fall through. Lauer continues quest to merge with another company.

1953: The modulated temperature control device, later known as the thermostat, is developed.

1951: William Shipley dies, ending the Shipley reign at York.

Corporation's legal advisor, Lauer wrote, "If Truman does not die of a heart attack and the bill goes through, the country will be started on the way to socialism and to hell compared to our present way of life."[3]

The Front Line of the Cold War

The Korean War led to a return of wartime controls under the federal Controlled Materials Plan. During the brief mobilization period, York revived its York Plan, devised during World War II to improve productivity through cooperation among industries.[4]

The company devoted substantial time and energy to pursuing government contracts, hiring more than 1,000 new employees to help produce refrigeration and air conditioning for the nation's defense. At the end of 1950, the company completed a million-dollar contract to design and build weather test chambers for research on rockets and guided missiles at the Navy's Ordnance Test Station in Inyokern, California.[5] York also supplied refrigeration for altitude chambers at the Naval Aeronautical Turbine Laboratory in Trenton, New Jersey, to simulate varying weather conditions. The company also won a contract to conduct noise and vibration studies on Navy equipment for use on ultra-quiet submarines. York constructed a unique laboratory for this purpose and was the first and only manufacturer to develop a complete and scientifically advanced sound and vibration facility. Four test chambers, totaling 50,000 square feet, were placed under one roof to fulfill the exacting requirements for submarine applications.[6]

The DER-10 FlakIce Machine returned to combat in a much more critical role than it ever played before. The machine was used in conjunction with anesthesia and helped prevent shock during surgery at Mobile Army Surgical Hospitals, or M.A.S.H. units, that often operated within a few miles of the front lines in Korea.

Peacetime Expansion

Great Britain emerged from World War II damaged, but in much better condition than continental Europe. Repairing and retooling Britain's industries for peacetime production occurred at a rapid pace, and the demand for York's refrigeration and air conditioning soon exceeded supply. York Corporation poured money into its London subsidiary and in 1950 purchased a production plant in Nottingham.

Meanwhile in the United States, York Corporation continued to perfect its automatic ice-making line. York introduced a complete ice service unit that froze and stored ice — called Yorkcubes by the sales force — in a self-contained unit that measured less than seven feet in height and occupied just six square feet of floor space.[7] At the heart of the updated automatic ice maker was York's three-cylinder hermetic compressor. To eliminate moisture buildup, it was factory-sealed, which also prevented the Freon refrigerant and permanent lubrication oil from escaping. The unit was remarkably easy to maintain. At the flip of a switch, the machine's circulating pump sent water from the stainless steel reservoir to the top of 16 brass freezing-tubes encircled by copper refrigerant coils filled with Freon-22. The water froze quickly as it cascaded down the tube, lining the square cylinder with ice. At the end of the process, only a small hole remained in the column of ice. The refrigeration cycle reversed itself to warm the tube until the ice loosened and began to drop. Then, needle-sharp points of stainless steel cut the

Operating on a Cold War footing, York recognized that atomic bomb shelters opened up potential markets for air conditioning.

Altitude test chambers, under construction at York for the military.

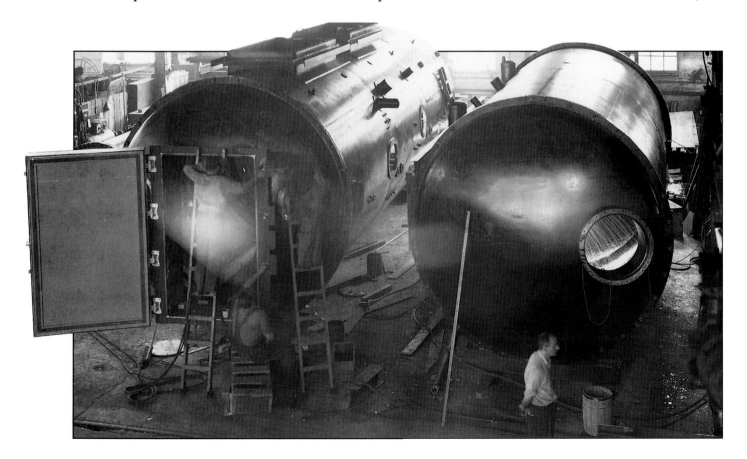

columns of ice into cubes. The machine could make up to 8,000 ice cubes a day.[8]

York also continued to contribute to peacetime research into nuclear energy. Yorkco workers installed a 24,000-horsepower refrigeration plant to help cool hot atomic piles at Hanford, Washington. A similar unit was designed and installed at Argonne Laboratories at the University of Chicago.[9] But even as York Corporation worked for peace, it was also preparing for war.

Air Conditioning the Bomb Shelters

On January 1, 1951, the company adopted the adages "Defense is Our Business" and "Every effort will be made to keep a steady flow of York air conditioning and refrigeration products flowing to you." Profits in 1950 were 31 percent higher than the year before.[10] Yorkco officers elected not to introduce additional products, predicting that demand for existing production lines would grow, particularly in areas of national defense. Sales Director John R. Hertzler stated that air conditioning sales would increase as people, industries and cities prepared for atomic war with the Soviet Union. "The need for civilian defense on a national scale ... brings up potential business of terrific magnitude, such as air conditioning the New York City subway system to make it usable as a civilian bomb shelter in case of an atomic bomb attack," Hertzler told his sales force.[11]

End of a Legacy

As revenue soared in 1951, tragedy struck. Chairman William Shipley, 71, died on January 13, 1951. Shipley had just attended a Washington, D.C., conference about the nationwide enactment of the York Plan. After flying home to Bayport, Long Island, he retired for the night at 10:30 p.m. Around midnight, his daughter, Ruth McNaught, was awakened by a noise. She discovered her father slumped

Resolved that we record, with profound sorrow, the death of our past president and Chairman of the Board, William Stewart Shipley.

His services to our industry and the Corporation were many and varied, including notable contributions to the advancement of the arts of refrigeration and air conditioning and to the consistent growth of the Corporation, in which his chief interests and loyalties were centered.

Because of his gracious nature and humanitarian impulses, he earned and preserved the admiration, love and respect of his associates and of the entire York organization.

His activities were not confined to business matters alone. He gave generously of his time, talents, energies and means to charitable enterprises, to patriotic movements, to national and civic affairs and to community projects.

During World War II, he earned national personal honors and built universal recognition for York as an industrial city, by his genius, leadership and enthusiasm in making the "York Plan" an effective and vital program for increased production through community cooperation.

He was a citizen of any community he visited or in which he resided.

His name, his deeds, his tolerance and personal charm, his wise, simple wholesomeness will long remain as an inspiration to the York organization in carrying on the work which he helped so soundly to establish during his 50 years of continuous service.

Resolved that we extend to his family our heartfelt sympathy in their bereavement, and that a copy of this resolution sent to his family.

over the bathtub, dead from a massive heart attack.[12]

"His evident good health and high spirits [at York the day before] made his sudden passing all the more shocking," Stewart Lauer wrote in a letter to a friend.[13] Shipley had remained active in Yorkco's affairs following his retirement. He once said that the company, passed to him by his brother, Thomas, was his

---

Following the death of William Shipley, York's board of directors officially recognized its chairman's contributions with this resolution.

life. "I must keep in touch. If I didn't, it would be just like lying down in a hole and piling the dirt in on top of my head."[14]

Shipley was remembered as a man who "never lost the common touch which so impressively endeared him to men of all walks of life whether they were workmen, with whom he labored side by side in the ranks of industry, or persons of renown who received inspiration from his contacts," wrote John Padden for the Manufacturers' Association of York.[15] Shipley's death represented the end of the Shipley line at the helm of York Corporation.

In the month following Shipley's passing, President Stewart Lauer initiated a number of organizational changes. To increase efficiency, a number of upper-management positions were eliminated. Although 1951 began with eight vice presidents serving the company, several would step down to fill lower management jobs as a result of the reorganization.

New Milestone

Meanwhile, the company reached yet another milestone in its history. Minute Maid, the successful orange juice company, retained York to refrigerate its 2.5-million-square-foot warehouse in Plymouth, Florida. The refrigeration contract was York's largest civilian order to date. The warehouse was cooled by York's advanced design of an ammonia refrigeration machine, which also met the needs of the dairy, brewery, meat packing and cold storage industries.

The York Turbo Refrigeration System, which used centrifugal compressors and Freon-12, was also popular as orders doubled for the textile, chemical, oil refinery, aircraft and passenger ship indus-tries. The Turbo compressors used the automatic Prerotation Vane Control, capable of holding the chilled water cooling medium within a range of one-half of one degree. The system was used in buildings such as the U.S. Naval Aeronautical Turbine Laboratory and the National Institute of Health.

The Naval laboratory used the three sets of Turbo compressors to assist in the development of jet engines. The Turbo compressors had a combined horsepower rating of 7,200 and could bring the temperature down to a frigid 67 degrees below zero. The Turbo systems used at the National Institute of Health assisted in vital research into heart disease and cancer.

We have always recognized that the wide acceptance accorded to York-built air conditioning and refrigerating equipment can be maintained and increased only by designing the very best quality and performance into our products. In doing so, our Development Engineers have long found PRODUCT ENGINEERING a very valuable source of new ideas and diversified design-engineering know-how.

Rodney F. Lauer
Vice President,
Engineering and Research
York Corporation

THE MEN WHO DESIGN

Center: By 1951, air conditioning sales comprised the highest percentage of new business as more efficient units were developed.

Right: Rodney Lauer, President Stewart Lauer's brother, helped keep York in the forefront of research and development.

Above: York Mayor Felix Bentzel (center) and his wife inspect the London-based York-Shipley, Ltd., plant on their 1951 goodwill trip to England.

Right: Bentzel was accompanied by Trevor Evans, Mayor of Willesden (right).

As York's big-ticket items gained popularity, the company also improved existing designs for one- and two-horsepower models that provided inexpensive air conditioning for small offices, suites and retail stores. This smaller Yorkaire system also provided affordable residential cooling.

Within a few months, the highest percentage of new business would come from air conditioning sales, ranging from one-half horsepower single-room air conditioners to central systems as large as 5,000 horsepower. Sales of refrigeration products and systems, accessory equipment, supplies, repair parts and maintenance contracts also increased. However, development of new products was delayed in anticipation of an increase in war-related production. The Training and Education Department of York's Industrial Relations Division expanded operations within the York Institute of Refrigeration and Air Conditioning building. The facility, established at the Grantley Plant after World War II, was

enlarged to include a special course developed around Air Force requirements.

Despite civilian control over strategic materials, net sales for 1951 showed a 17 percent increase compared to 1950, to more than $57,536,00. A tax increase took a large bite out of York's earnings, while the cost of expansion further cut profits. Operational expenses continued to weaken profits in 1952, despite successful efforts of Yorkco salesmen to expand business. The sale of York's packaged air conditioners and automatic ice makers to consumers reached a new high in 1952, with a 3 percent increase over 1951. However, net earnings after taxes decreased 4 percent. Lauer attributed the higher overhead costs to wage, salary and fringe benefit increases, mandated by the Federal Wage and Salary Stabilization Board.[16]

Worry over York's financial position grew in 1952, even after the company installed eight 220-ton turbo compressors aboard the 990-foot SS *United States*, hailed as the world's fastest peacetime ship. The Turbo system installed by York provided air conditioning to cool, filter, dehumidify and uniformly circulate air to prevent seasickness. York refrigeration also provided for 50,000 cubic feet of refrigerated cargo space using four six-cylinder compressors with the air circulated by eight air units.[17]

In the second half of 1952, sales estimates continued to fall. The economy was sound and continuing to expand, a time when York Corporation should have reflected significant growth. The company's inability to compete with Carrier Corporation's success with multiple-room air conditioning systems irritated President Stewart Lauer, who did not want to relinquish York's lead in air conditioning sales or earnings.[18] Lauer blamed the company's slowdown on a lack of coordination between its sales force and engineers. He told York's board of directors that if both departments worked together to get contracts with the government, the company would turn its declining fortunes around.

In 1953, York Corporation returned to developing new features for its products. Determined

Above: York achieved completely automatic indoor climate control with its compound compression heat pump.

Left: The new Heironimus Department Store, in Virginia, was the first building to be heated and cooled by the heat pump.

to set itself apart from rival Carrier, Lauer announced that York Corporation would adapt its units to both heat and cool residential homes. This would make York air conditioners useful from early spring to late fall and, Lauer hoped, triple York's earnings.[19]

That year Yorkco engineers also worked on improvements to a modulated temperature control device, commonly known as the thermostat. The engineers experimented with methods to connect air conditioning and heat pump components with individual room thermostat controls to allow people to set different temperatures in different rooms of a building. To assist in the research effort, York Corporation constructed a 36,000-square-foot engineering research and development facility. The new offices, drafting rooms and studios were devoted to the research of packaged products sold through York's expanding distributor organization, and included certain types of units for integration with large air conditioning systems. The facility also contained a shop for manufacturing test models of products before full-scale production began. Several test homes were also built for year-round air conditioning research. Each was equipped with a different air conditioning system to compare operating

Above and below: About $2.5 million was spent expanding and retooling the Grantley plant in 1954, although York suffered from a decline in sales.

costs, air distribution, degree of quietness, convenience and flexibility from the homeowner's perspective.[20]

By the end of 1953, profits had increased 8 percent over the previous year, and 6,830 employees were on the company payroll.

Year-Round Air Conditioning

The intense research paid off in 1954 when York Corporation introduced its revolutionary year-round air conditioning window units and induction units to the market. The induction products, built into the structure of a building for central air conditioning and heat, stimulated sales commercially for homes and multi-level buildings. The company had 21 operating or contracted induction air conditioning units on its books by the middle of January.[21]

The new year-round window unit, developed on the heels of the larger central system, was predicted to be just as successful, attracting the Philco Corporation, which suggested York could manufacture the units under the Philco name. During the Great Depression, the two companies had sold room air conditioners under the Philco-York name. Prior to World War II, the corporations had given each other a hand under various guises in which York designed and manufactured while Philco funded advertising, selling and field training. Immediately following the war, the York-Philco name had been put to rest. However, York had continued to produce room air conditioners to be sold under the Philco name and also manufactured its own York brand of air conditioners with a different exterior. Since both Philco and York interior components were the same, York could mass-produce to lower costs and keep retail prices competitive.

When Philco showed interest in obtaining a similar contract with York to manufacture a Philco self-contained store and residential package, Lauer jumped at the chance. He believed a continued relationship with Philco would increase net profits and lower production costs.[22]

York's move into the induction and central air conditioning field was aimed at undercutting Carrier's lead in the market. However, Cloud Wampler, president of Carrier, launched a counter-attack, claiming that York had infringed upon the Carrier-patented induction system air conditioner called the Weathermaster. "We spent large sums of money in pioneering, developing and perfecting the conduit Weathermaster system and we do not propose to have it appropriated," Wampler said.[23]

York Vice President Keith Louden responded, "We intend to contest [the suit] vigorously and welcome this opportunity to have the matter tested in court." York's attorneys and executives immediately began researching patents in Europe and the United States to find a central or conduit system air conditioning unit registered earlier than Carrier's patent. Meanwhile, York sold its induction units by advertising the differences between York and Carrier units. For example, York's unit had a damper control mechanism that was not built into those sold by Carrier.[24] The suit was dropped by Carrier in 1955. York agreed to pay royalties from past sales and was licensed for future use of Carrier's patented induction units for year-round air conditioning-heating systems.

Continuing Setbacks

By July 1954, the company reported a lower profit margin than usual,

A 1953 York one-horsepower air conditioning unit.

despite several layoffs to cut operational costs. The company could not absorb increased wages and salaries and still turn a profit, while a price increase would cause York to lose its competitive edge.[25] To make matters worse, the sales of room air conditioners were far below what Lauer had promised to stockholders. However, the company continued on its program to expand the physical size of its facilities.

The stockholders had already agreed to increase the corporate common stock from 1,500,000 shares to 2,500,000. Nearly $23,177,500 was raised in proceeds from the public sale. About $10.5 million of this money was designated for improvement and expansion of the West York and Grantley plants over a five-year period.[26] About $2,550,000 was scheduled for the expansion, rearrangement and some retooling of the Grantley plant in 1954. Lauer intended to transform the York Corporation into several divisions that divided domestic industrial products from other types of commercial lines. He also wanted to turn York's overseas business into a separate division.[27]

Lauer was preparing to lay the groundwork for the division plan when poor sales and profit returns for room air conditioners persuaded him to delay. The poor returns were a more immediate concern because company morale began to suffer.

Above: In 1954, intense research paid off with the introduction of the revolutionary year-round air conditioning induction unit, which was an immediate success. The unit was built for York by C.A. Olsen Manufacturing Company.

Sales of the Yorkaire Model 150 (below), Model 200 (right) and other York products dropped when competitors began to crowd the market.

"If we look upon this transition as a 'most terrific' task and try to have all the answers before we start, we will fail, due to resistance. I say this from personal experience," Lauer said. "We must think, too, that only a few months ago we made pretty strong promises to the public through our financing. If we admit now that some of that was sheer guesswork, you know the answer," Lauer wrote.[28]

York Corporation was not the only company in the industry reeling from the effects of weakened room air conditioner sales. On August 5, a meeting of air conditioning company representatives was held at the Links Club in New York City to discuss the problem. Cloud Wampler, president of Carrier Corporation, conducted the meeting, which was centered solely on the "good name of the industry." Wampler believed the sale of room-sized air conditioners had been seriously damaged by several newcomers in the industry whose inferior quality, bad applications, misleading advertising and a wide variety of prices ruined the product's reputation.[29]

Wampler was taking the lead in developing standardization within the industry, much like Tom Shipley of York had done at the turn of the century. Lauer was already aware of the problems with the room air conditioner and had taken steps earlier that summer to report some misleading claims made by other manufacturers in the industry. Lauer resented Wampler's attempt to pretend leadership on a problem that Lauer had already recognized. On the other hand, Wampler believed the only solution to correcting the "mess" was to formulate industry standards in pricing and advertising claims. He accused the national Air Conditioning & Refrigeration Institute (ARI) of being partially to blame for wildly publicizing statistics on the growth of the air conditioning industry, which encouraged "every

Dick, Jane and Harry to jump into the business to make a fortune," Wampler said.[30]

As a result, the industry was flooded with too many room-sized air conditioning units, causing price wars and unsubstantiated claims among the numerous companies selling the products.

Wampler was a thorn in Lauer's side because of his media appeal within the industry and success at diverting industry leadership from York. Wampler's presence became even more bothersome when York started having labor relations problems in the field. Work stoppages began occurring at sites where the company was installing industrial air conditioning because York, with its "company union," paid lower wages than its competitors. It was pointed out that Carrier Corporation, which had AFL union shops, had no labor problems. Leaders of the United Mine Workers Union hinted that they would prefer to work with Carrier Corporation's employees to install air conditioning in multistoried buildings since they, too, were national union members.[31]

The problems kept piling on Lauer's shoulders. By the end of August it was reported that a federal income tax audit of the company for 1950, 1951 and 1952 showed a tax deficiency of $36,407 for those years. The practice of the corporate financial office in preparing tax returns was to "take advantage of deductions where the language of the law is not specific, leaving it to the income tax auditors to challenge any items they may disagree with." For example, the company saved $1,024,593 over the three-year period on tax credits which were not challenged by the audi-

York room air conditioners. The downturn in the air conditioning industry came just as York expanded several plants to boost production.

After much delay, Stewart Lauer (standing) finally implemented his plan to divide the company into three segments.

tors. York Corporation paid its tax deficits and penalties out of a reserve fund.[32]

Dividing the Company

In October 1954, Lauer finally implemented his plan to reorganize the company. The plan divided the company into three divisions: Industrial, Commercial and International. Each division manager would be responsible for the profits of each operation. Lauer, serving as president of the company, would be responsible for the coordination of the three divisions and the combined results of their operations.[33]

The Industrial Division would be headed by Vice President R.K. Serfass; Vice President J.K. Louden would head up the Commercial Division;

and Managing Director C.B. Morrison would head the International Division with offices in New York and London. The president's staff, with which Lauer would collaborate to assist and advise the divisions, included Vice President M.G. Munce, in charge of marketing, and Vice President J.M. Joslin, in charge of industrial relations.[34] The International Division's creation reflected the company's growing global nature.

Following the announcement of the company's new structure, Lauer turned his attention to York Corporation's diminished reputation. On October 5, Lauer wrote a commentary on publicity and public relations for the corporation. He attacked Cloud Wampler of Carrier Corporation for his "urge for publicity per se by an author who, by self-appointment, made himself the spokesman for the industry." In letters to industry investors, Lauer accused Wampler of wildly forecasting a great potential for the sales of air conditioning products, contributing to a flood of the air conditioning market and excessive inventory carry-over.

"It is within the realm of possibility, too, that these statements may have performed a disservice to the public and to the industry if some of the entrepreneurs are producing and installing room air conditioners that do not incorporate the exacting standards of those produced by the originators of the product through their greater knowledge and experience and their constant patient and painstaking technical development."[35]

Instead of backing Lauer in his stance against Wampler, York's directors actually suggested that Lauer make amends. In December, the two corporate presidents met for lunch in New York to discuss their personal differences. The constructive chat resulted in an amiable "agreement to disagree." Wampler later wrote to Lauer, saying "Please know how much I appreciate the attitude you are now taking. Also, let me assure you that I will certainly meet you halfway."[36]

This was not a surprising response by the popular leader of Carrier. Despite Lauer's efforts to gain a lead over the company, Carrier's lead continue to grow. Wampler's sound business decisions included the improvement of its competitive position through intensive cost reduction, vigorous promotion and new product development. Wampler also shelved Carrier's construction program that was to be financed through the 1953 sale of common stock. Instead, Wampler invested the funds in government issue.[37] York Corporation, by contrast, went ahead with its plans for expansion.

The result was devastating to York. In November, the company cut its labor force by 90 people because of a reduced production schedule in the Industrial Division at the West York plant. New business had fallen by 6.2 percent compared to 1953, and the company's backlog orders had decreased about 41 percent.[38]

Lauer began holding confidential discussions with York's board of directors about a possible merger with C.A. Olsen Manufacturing Company. "If it should leak out around the organization that we are giving some thought to this matter of merger, it could eventually be damaging to York or Olsen if nothing would happen," Lauer wrote.[39]

C.A. Olsen, president of C.A. Olsen Manufacturing Company of Ohio, had purchased 10,000 shares of Yorkco stock in April. Olsen's company manufactured a complete line of gas- and oil-fired furnaces and accessories. In December, Olsen had been appointed to the York Corporation's board of directors. This foothold by Olsen led to an agreement from York to manufacture cooling systems used in Olsen equipment. The C.A. Olsen Manufacturing Company had already published its interest in the development of year-round air

Above: An inside view of a 1955 York air conditioner.

Below: York set itself apart from competitors by emphasizing quality at the 1955 A.M.A. convention held in Atlantic City.

An advertisement for the year-round residential air conditioning induction unit.

conditioning units that would provide both winter heat and summer cooling for the home, and rumors of a possible merger circulated in the industry that year.

Lauer believed that the corporation should acquire the assistance of an established manufacturer of heating units, such as Olsen. Then York could obtain greater profits from the sale of year-round heating and cooling merchandise.[40] But as the merger approached, problems developed. It appeared that Olsen would have replaced Lauer as president of York while Lauer remained chairman of the board. York's management feared that a change in leadership would hurt their salaries and job security.

In June 1954, York and Olsen publicly confirmed discussions of a "possible merger," but at a June 15 meeting, York Corporation stockholders refused to allow Lauer to continue with the merger. The company had returned to profitability, with quarterly earnings rising to $1.4 million, and the future appeared even brighter. York had just begun construction of a huge new air conditioning system with a single central power plant to replace its original installation in seven major Washington, D.C., buildings. The $500,000 contract called for four centrifugal refrigeration units using nearly 10,000 horsepower for chilled water for the Capitol, Supreme Court, two House offices, the Senate office, the Library of Congress and its annex.[41]

York Corporation executives were optimistic as the year 1955 unfolded. The company appeared strong with substantial new capital investment, new products and forecasts for renewed hiring. Orders during the first 24 days of January were eight times greater than those of December.[42] By March, net earnings were roughly 69 percent greater than the previous year.[43]

Bad News on the Horizon

The good news would not last. Lauer received a letter from his friend, Ray Rich of Philco Corporation, stating that Philco was sustaining unacceptable losses after purchasing $30 million worth of what proved to be an unpopular air conditioning unit. Philco's contract with York for the manufacture of room air conditioners would end October 31, 1956, and Philco would not renew the contract.[44]

York's statistics for 1955 showed sales were down by 11.3 percent, with net earnings dropping from $2.12 per common share in 1954 to a low of $1.72 per share by the end of 1955. The only good news was a 16 percent increase in sales in the International Division. Competition was stiff, particularly with the Carrier Corporation. Jim Harnish, a York engineer hired in 1951, recalled one battle that York almost lost to Carrier when both vied for a 1955 government contract. The $1 million contract was to supply refrigeration as low as minus 120 degrees at the Wright Field installation to test the strength and efficiency of aircraft propellers under extreme conditions. Harnish said he and his mentor, Neil Hopkins, were given the task of securing the $1 million contract.

"We were $50,000 higher than Carrier. So the government came back to us and said, 'York, you've done a lot of good work for us in the past. You stuck by your designs, and if it didn't work, you'd work at it till you got it going. If you can get your price down to just $10,000 higher than Carrier, we'll give you the order.' The president, Stewart Lauer, told Neil that this was a big risk

for us. We could lose a bundle. Was there any way we could minimize those risks?"[45]

Hopkins and Harnish went to work and discovered that Carrier had made a mistake in the amount of brine needed to reach the required temperatures, and as a result its bid was lower.

"So Neil went back to Lauer and said, 'Let's request that the government have the contractors resubmit bids but have the government pay for the brine. So we did, and York was well within the $10,000 limit and we got the award. But by the time we completed the design, propellers had become obsolete. Now they went to jets. The government had an obligation to pay for the work completed and was required to have us prove that our design would work. So we built the equipment anyways and then tore the whole thing down. I guess that's the way our government operates."[46]

Lauer continued with his quest to merge York Corporation with another manufacturer to help boost profits. He was rebuffed by Philco when he broached the subject and had been blocked by York's stockholders regarding Olsen. Lauer sought the advice of his executive management committee and then pursued the acquisition of a heating appliance manufacturer. To avoid repeating past mistakes, Lauer hired Andrew Freimann to head the acquisition committee. Formerly a member of the management team for General Motors, Freimann was given the title as York's vice president of Marketing. Lauer hinted at Freimann's real job with the company when he said, "We are very pleased to have one of the outstanding figures in home heating and cooling, which we believe has great future possibilities."[47]

The next step was to investigate well-grounded heat appliance manufacturers. Freimann started obtaining information on various companies that fit York's needs and invited them to tour York's facilities. The search for an appropriate corporate partner began in earnest, and would result in York's becoming owned by one of the world's most prestigious holding companies.

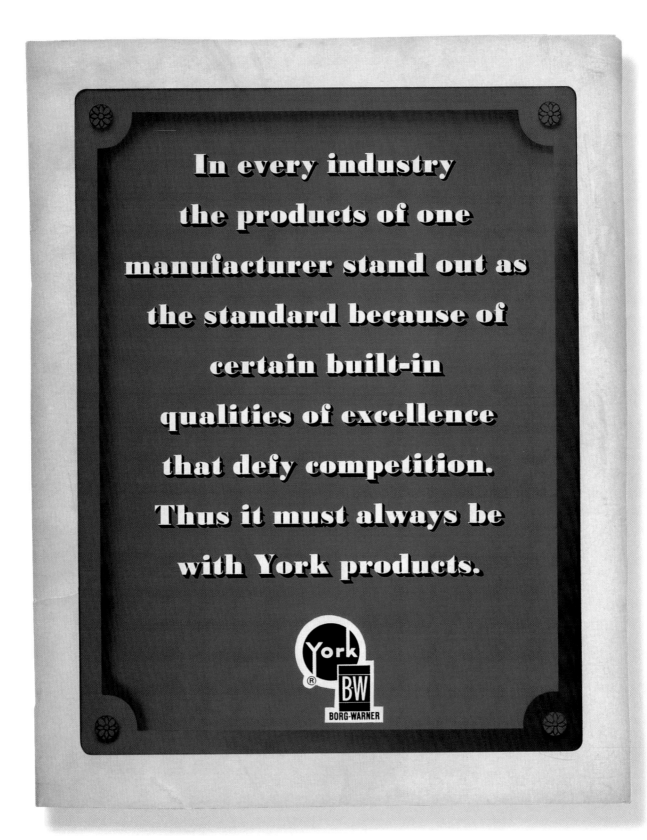

The corporate creed continued by York/Borg-Warner after the takeover in 1956.

CHAPTER TEN

BORG-WARNER

1956-1960

"We tried to be sort of avant-garde in the things we set out to do."

— Jack Schultz, 1996[1]

THROUGHOUT ITS HISTORY, the York Corporation's financial health literally ebbed and flowed with the changing seasons. President Stewart Lauer wanted to merge York with a financially secure company that could compensate for the sluggish fall and winter sales months. This quest would ultimately lead to a tumultuous relationship with international conglomerate Borg-Warner.

On June 9, 1955, Borg-Warner's president, Roy Ingersoll, met with Lauer and York Director Robert Wolcott in New York to discuss a possible acquisition.[2] Borg-Warner was an attractive potential partner because it maintained a reputation as a decentralized corporation. Under Borg-Warner's umbrella, York could retain its unique identity as a leader within the air conditioning and refrigeration industry.

Meanwhile, Lauer and his executive management team were interested in the purchase of the Thor Company, a Williams Heating Division of the Eureka Williams Corporation of Bloomington, Illinois. Pending stockholder approval, Lauer accepted a proposal made January 24, 1956, by C. Russell Feldman, president of Eureka Williams Corporation, to purchase the property, equipment and other assets for $1.8 million by June 30, 1956.[3] Eureka Williams had an impressive history of engineering, production, sales, earnings and growth, but the asking price was high.[4]

Lauer and Ingersoll spoke by telephone on February 27, but when Lauer did not hear from Ingersoll again by March 5, he decided to conclude negotiations with Eureka Williams.[5]

A few days later, Borg-Warner contacted York, offering a two-for-one exchange of shares on the stock market. York's attorney, George Munson, suggested that York solicit an opinion from its bankers. "My own feeling is that on their two-for-one suggestion, we could never get to first base with our stockholders," Munson said.[6]

"I sincerely believe that there is merit in the principle involved in this type of a proposed merger," Lauer replied. The York Corporation was in financial difficulty, with its common stock trading at only $2.05 a share. Borg-Warner represented the company's best chance to expand facilities to meet the year-round heating and cooling market.[7]

In March 1956, Lauer and Ingersoll concluded an initial draft of the agreement, which included a restriction of York's dividends to 30 cents a share until the closing date, originally scheduled for April 2. In addition, York had to change its

The new York/Borg-Warner logo. In 1956, Borg-Warner purchased York for $50 million.

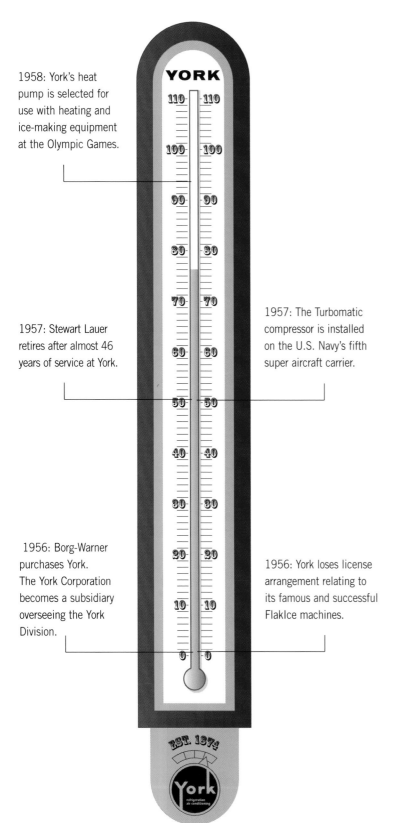

1958: York's heat pump is selected for use with heating and ice-making equipment at the Olympic Games.

1957: Stewart Lauer retires after almost 46 years of service at York.

1957: The Turbomatic compressor is installed on the U.S. Navy's fifth super aircraft carrier.

1956: Borg-Warner purchases York. The York Corporation becomes a subsidiary overseeing the York Division.

1956: York loses license arrangement relating to its famous and successful FlakIce machines.

legal name to the Lauer Corporation, liquidate York Corporation and then distribute $2 per share to York stockholders, along with $100,000 in cash to conclude the liquidation.[8]

Lauer and Ingersoll's agreement also included continuing York's employment contracts, group insurance, pension insurance and a retirement plan. However, York's management incentive plan would be dropped after September 30, 1956. In addition, all salaries and employment were frozen until Borg-Warner was totally in control of York.

Discussion of a merger with Borg-Warner was kept under tight wraps, and the stock remained stable until the boards of both companies gave their approval at a secret meeting held April 4 in York. At noon the following day, the merger was announced to the public. Still subject to approval by stockholders, the plan called for an exchange of a half-share of Borg-Warner stock plus $2 cash for each share of York stock, an arrangement that was appealing to York directors and stockholders.[9]

With all this going on, Lauer elected to terminate York's agreement with Eureka Williams. On June 20, a settlement of $35,000 was reached for any damages against York Corporation in connection with the aborted Eureka-Williams Company negotiations.[10]

A History of Borg-Warner

Borg-Warner was established June 5, 1928, as a holding company for three automotive specialty firms, Borg & Beck Company, Warner Gear and Marvel Carburetor Company. Borg & Beck had developed an inexpensive single-plate clutch, Warner Gear had cut transmission costs, and the Marvel Carburetor Company was the leading carburetor manufacturer at the time. "What we want," said George Borg, the first president of Borg-Warner, "is a corporation which cannot be made or broken by the fortunes of any single division or the market for any one product."

"We have organized so that we can fight better. A manufacturer who might be ruthless toward the producer of a single automobile part will think twice before attacking the maker of many parts. Let us make as many parts as we can — so that if our

competitors press us too hard in one line, and we must sacrifice it, we can still operate on the others."[11]

The new Borg-Warner Corporation acquired nine subsidiaries within a year, including Norge, one of the top five refrigeration manufacturers. Norge had pioneered the development of the self-contained kitchen refrigerator by moving the compressor unit from the basement into the case of the "ice box," and had developed the coin-operated dry cleaning business.

Other acquisitions that year included Galesburg Coulter Disc Company, which made discs for plowing; Long Manufacturing, which made radiators and clutches; and Morse Chains, the leading producer of bicycle chains. Borg-Warner's com-

bined sales in 1929, before the stock market crash, were $54 million.

The company survived the Great Depression under the leadership of Charles Davis, and in 1935, Borg-Warner converted from a holding company to an operating company so it could consolidate sales and earnings records. Individual divisions maintained their autonomy and even found themselves in fierce competition for customers. The company contributed automotive goods and other products during World War II and entered the fifties with record earnings of $29 million.

In 1950, Roy C. Ingersoll became chief executive officer. Ingersoll's father, the late Stephen A. Ingersoll, had founded the Galesburg Coulter Disc Company, which had been acquired by Borg-Warner in 1929. In April 1958, the 73-year-old Roy Ingersoll was succeeded as chief executive officer by his son, Robert S. Ingersoll, 42. Roy Ingersoll remained chairman of the board until 1961.

By 1962, Borg-Warner was operating 55 plants in 13 states, along with plants in 18 foreign countries, for a total workforce of 33,000. Its 35 product lines included appliances, automotive products, aviation equipment, nucleonics, defense equipment, environmental controls, industrial equipment, materials and petroleum.[12]

While the two companies waited for the stockholders' vote, York launched a public relations campaign explaining how valuable the merger would be to York. Both York and Borg-Warner paid for full-page advertisements in the two local papers, explaining the details of the merger if approved by the stockholders. One component of the campaign was York's cooperation with Borg-Warner on the development of a combination heating and cooling unit for residential use.[13]

Who could know more about the cold than an Eskimo? This stuffed fellow appreciates the benefits of York's refrigerants in this DuPont display.

From May 23 through June 25, shareholders mailed York their votes on proxies. In a special meeting of stockholders on June 25, the votes were announced: 79.3 percent of the shareholders had voted in favor of the merger, and 4.9 percent of shareholders voted against it.[14] At noon on June 30, York Corporation passed from an independent manufacturing enterprise to a link in the vast Borg-Warner chain. With more than 6,000 employees on its payroll, the area's largest manufacturer had lost a certain degree of independence.

Life under Borg-Warner

Under Borg-Warner's ownership, the York Corporation was known as the York Division of Borg-Warner. Borg-Warner directors agreed that the York name had attained worldwide recognition and prestige in refrigeration and air conditioning. York maintained relations with contracting companies in China, England and other parts of the world. While the company exported compressors to Europe, the Far East and Latin America, the contract companies built heat exchangers locally.

York was also supposed to retain its policies, management and personnel.[15] York's affiliation with Borg-Warner would lead to expansion, increased production and more employment at York facilities, Lauer remarked in a letter to York stockholders.[16]

"Borg-Warner has the type of diversification and organization we were seeking. Borg-Warner has a unique concept of operating a multi-division industrial enterprise. It is probably the most completely decentralized large company in the country. Each division of Borg-Warner has freedom of action, authority, responsibility and relationship that is normally associated with an independent company. We look forward under this plan to a continuity of York management and policy, quietly strengthened by Borg-Warner organization and experience."[17]

Borg-Warner would prove to be a wealthy but inattentive parent to York. From the beginning, it was clear to York's personnel that Borg-Warner did not understand the refrigeration and air conditioning business. Bill Eastman, product manager for York, was at the company at the time of the acquisition. He recalled how Borg-Warner both helped and hurt York.

"They contributed a great deal to the company's growth in terms of equipment and research, but they provided inadequate guidance from a marketing standpoint. We were simply something they didn't understand. They were parts manufacturers for the automotive industry, and they didn't understand dealing with customers in any way, shape or manner."[18]

Robert Berger, who worked at York from 1946 to 1991 in several areas of the company, noted that the product catalog kept shrinking

Fred Schiding, mayor of York, offered Stewart Lauer his blessing and congratulations on the Borg-Warner merger.

under Borg-Warner. "As Borg-Warner, we started to lose our feel for more products, especially in the engineered machinery line. Borg-Warner had dropped products and let the field purchase them from other companies."[19]

Borg-Warner, for its part, had its problems with its new acquisition, as a 1978 Borg-Warner publication made clear. The publication stated that after spending $50 million for York, Borg-Warner shelled out another $17 million to warranty defective products "even though most of the defective work antedated the acquisition."[20]

The York Division

On July 3, 1956, Roy Ingersoll was elected chairman and Lauer was elected president and chief executive officer of the new organization. Borg-Warner had spent $50 million to get York, taking over its assets as well as debt of $18 million. Much of the physical plant was seriously deteriorated and operations were not efficient.

Within its first month as the York Division, the company introduced its Turbomatic compressor. Available in capacities between 100 and 600 horsepower, the lightweight compressor was adaptable for upper floor installations in multistory

buildings. York's new cooling systems, which employed the Turbomatic compressor, were the closest thing to a hermetically-sealed system of any centrifugal compressor on the market. It was selected for the U.S. Navy's fifth super aircraft carrier still under construction, as well as for escort vessels for the Canadian Navy.[21]

Jack Schultz helped design and test the centrifugal compressors series, which he believes is among the finest product lines developed by York. Schultz, who joined York in 1953 and retired in 1985, is now a consulting engineer and an adjunct instructor of Thermodynamics at Penn State University. He said York led the way to developing the highly efficient, compact and simple single-stage compressor. "It was another industry first for York and was followed by all the other manufacturers. We tried to be sort of avant-garde in the things we set out to do."[22]

York also announced the completion of its role in air conditioning the Empire State Building. The initial installation in 1950 had

---

York introduced its line of Hermetic Condensing Units soon after the merger with Borg-Warner. From left to right are the air-cooled, water-cooled and combination air- and water-cooled units.

York
refrigeration
air conditioning

York Hermetic Condensing Units

FOR EVERY REFRIGERATION NEED

Air Cooled or Water Cooled

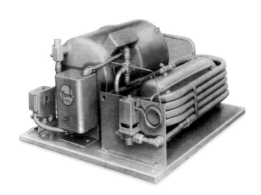

**The YORK Snorkel
...has the thinnest
line of all!**

Just 12¾" front to back

Unlike earlier air conditioners, the York Snorkel air conditioning unit did not take up an entire window or mar the front of a home by jutting outside.

consisted of two turbo water-cooling systems with a total capacity of 1,100 horsepower. In 1952, York installed two additional systems of identical capacity, and in 1956, York received an additional order for two systems of 3,800 horsepower.

Meanwhile, the management structure within the York Division began to change. In September 1956, the supervisory board of directors formed the York Corporation, which served as a subsidiary of Borg-Warner and was respon-

sible for all factory and field sales operations of the York Division. The York Corporation had the same officers and directors as the York Division. A month later, the Borg-Warner officers formed another division that assimilated and coordinated all sales to major home builders. This division handled sales for the York Corporation, Ingersoll-Humphreys, Reflectal and Norge.

More changes were in store, including the cancellation of York's license arrangement with the FlakIce Corporation. Borg-Warner purchased all the domestic and foreign patents pertaining to York's FlakIce machines and cube machines so that the machines would be sold under the Borg-Warner trade name.

Adjusting to a New Role

In January 1957, Stewart Lauer retired from his job as president and CEO of the York Division, ending an active role in York's business that had lasted almost 46 years. He served two more years as chairman of the board of the York Division and York Corporation. Henry Haase, the York Division board chairman who replaced Ingersoll, was elected to succeed him.

One of the bright spots of 1957 was Borg-Warner's purchase of a line of automobile air conditioning compressors made by Lehigh Manufacturing Company, in Pennsylvania. This line of compressors was turned over to York for production, becoming the division's top money-maker for years.[23]

Also during 1957, York moved the manufacture of hermetic compressors to Borg-Warner's Marvel-Schebler Products plant in Decatur, Illinois, and began manufacturing a line of lightweight, high-speed automobile air conditioning compressors there. Additional products were moved from York to Decatur over the next few years. The West York plant buildings were either put up for sale or leased. Most of the York Grantley plant's foundry operations were transferred to the foundry at the Byron Jackson Division of Borg-Warner in Lawrenceburg, Indiana.[24]

In 1958, the York Division's revolutionary heat pump was selected for heating and ice-making equipment for the 1960 Olympic Games ice-skating installations in Squaw Valley, California.

In theaters around the nation, York demonstrated that it was still the leader in the air conditioning industry.

The heat pump would be adapted in a most novel way to both cool the ice and handle the heavy snowfall in northern California.

Also that year, the company introduced its High-I heating and cooling system for induction systems within multistory structures. The unit could heat and cool different rooms in a building at the same time, so it was perfectly suited for apartment buildings, hospitals or multi-office buildings. York also introduced Acoustamatic room air conditioners, a line of residential units that was unusually efficient, quiet and attractive.[25]

In 1959, two gigantic tractor-trailers stocked with the latest York products traveled the United States as the "York Cavalcade of Products." The tour was designed to show that York was still the leader in the air conditioning field.

By the end of 1959, Lauer announced his retirement as chairman of the board of the York Division and York Corporation (the sales subsidiary of Borg-Warner).

The company had survived the acquisition as a financially sound leader of the industry, with 1,800 employees. York would find itself in a position to join the technological race to the moon, as well as continue its contribution to the nation's defense. But it would continue to struggle against rising costs, continuing losses and changes in its organization and relationship within Borg-Warner.

This hyperbaric chamber, designed by Borg-Warner and manufactured by the York Division, was considered valuable in the treatment of many ailments and injuries. It was installed at the Lutheran General Hospital in Park Ridge, Illinois, in 1965. Dr. Jack van Elk, right, the chief investigator of high-pressure oxygen treatments at the hospital, inspects the machine as Andrew P. Boehmer, chief engineer of hyperbaric research for Borg-Warner, looks on.

CHAPTER ELEVEN

YORK GOES HIGH TECH

1960-1969

"We continue to be extremely optimistic about the future. The national economy looks good, our industry looks even more encouraging, and York's position within the industry continues to improve. I see no reason why the growth we have accomplished during the past five years cannot be repeated during the next five years."

— William Roberts, 1967[1]

THE SIXTIES were a period of technological achievement for the United States, and the York Division of Borg-Warner Corporation played an important role in some of the most important projects of the decade. York provided air conditioning to cool atomic reactors and the Vehicle Assembly Building used in the Apollo Moon Program and designed a hyperbaric oxygen chamber to aid physicians in treating their patients.

Making the Silent Service More Silent

Beginning in 1960, York designed a Sound and Vibration Laboratory to develop ways to reduce noise levels generated by electrical and mechanical equipment. Using data collected from ultrasensitive instruments, York engineers experimented with equipment refinements to reduce sound and vibration levels. The company eliminated vibration within casings and employed superior methods to muffle the equipment's overall noise signature.[2] This laboratory, led by Manager W. Scott Bayless, was used to analyze sounds for all of Borg-Warner's subsidiaries. One of its most important tasks was to reduce mechanical noise aboard submarines, a critical mission because sound travels farther through water than through air. In time of war, noise

reduction could mean the difference between stealth and detection, between life and death.

In 1960, the Navy's requirement for ultraquiet refrigeration and ice machinery led to the thermoelectric system, which replaced noisy compressors and moving parts with quiet electronic circuits housed within a copper module.[3] However, the thermoelectric system proved impractical for use on submarines. The system works best to cool small surface areas at very low temperatures. It requires too much energy to cool the interior of a nuclear submarine operating in warm waters.[4]

The Navy needed a powerful, quiet and relatively compact cooling system for both the Polaris submarine, capable of launching intercontinental ballistic missiles from beneath the sea, and the smaller, more maneuverable attack submarines.

York's search for a low-noise solution led to advances in reciprocating compressors, installed in the USS *Thresher* nuclear attack submarine in 1961. The packaged water chilling system used twin motor-driven 16 cylinder compressors designed to minimize vibration, which is transmitted by water over long distances and is easily

A 1968 promotional clock.

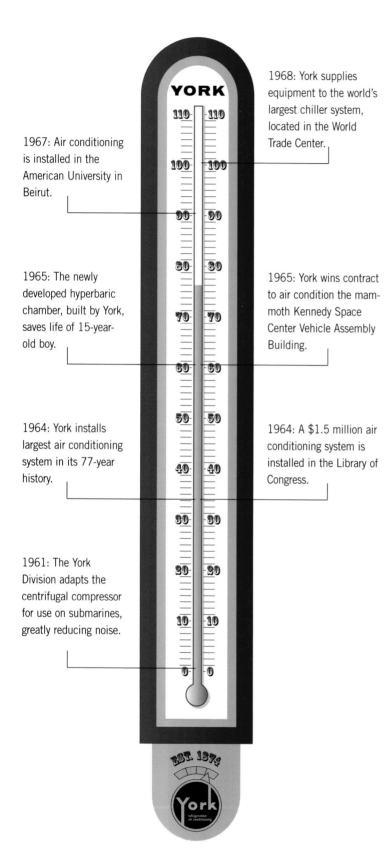

1968: York supplies equipment to the world's largest chiller system, located in the World Trade Center.

1967: Air conditioning is installed in the American University in Beirut.

1965: The newly developed hyperbaric chamber, built by York, saves life of 15-year-old boy.

1965: York wins contract to air condition the mammoth Kennedy Space Center Vehicle Assembly Building.

1964: York installs largest air conditioning system in its 77-year history.

1964: A $1.5 million air conditioning system is installed in the Library of Congress.

1961: The York Division adapts the centrifugal compressor for use on submarines, greatly reducing noise.

detectable. Acoustic noise was muffled by a special valve cage and muffler assemblies.[5] Attack submarines are smaller than the Polaris, designed to hunt surface ships and other subs.

The Polaris submarine, on the other hand, was designed to lie quietly at station, as undetected as a hole in the ocean. The first such submarine, the USS *George Washington,* was built by the Electric Boat Company, a division of General Dynamics. Launched in November 1960, it carried 16 nuclear-tipped missiles, designed to be fired from underneath the sea. Nicknamed "boomers," these subs stayed on duty for months.[6]

The reciprocating compressor was installed on the USS *Ethan Allen* as well as the USS *Lafayette.* But York achieved a breakthrough in 1961 with the centrifugal compressor design. This system greatly cut gear, motor and other mechanical noises, used less energy and took up less space than any other compressor design. Dr. Kenneth Hickman, vice president of Engineering in the Applied Systems Division, noted that the basic centrifigal compressor principle is still used in the latest submarines built by Electric Boat.

The impractical thermoelectric unit, on the other hand, found a useful life as part of infrared missile targeting systems and night vision goggles. Infrared waves are generated by any body above the temperature of absolute zero. The thermoelectric unit cools a small surface area of a sensor, creating enough of a contrast to make it easier to detect the heat signature. A new division, Borg-Warner Thermoelectrics, Inc., was created to develop these units for the military.

Development of the Heat Pump

Although the thermoelectric unit was one innovation that did not have the impact initially envisioned, it was around this time that York's engineers pioneered the industrial and commercial heat pump. The goal was to develop a unit that could operate as a source of both heat and air conditioning, which would make it attractive year-round. The difficulties in developing a cost-effective unit intimidated most other manufacturers, recalled Jim Harnish, a retired York engineer. Harnish helped develop the air-source industrial

York led the industry in developing the heat pump. These six heat pump outdoor sections served double-duty in winter and summer.

"If the architects had to build a roof over that arena to withstand 11 feet of snow, which had fallen over three days in 1959 — it would have been a monster. They came up with the idea of heating the roof, and we just figured out the way to do it."[8]

The Total Quality Concept

heat pump in the late fifties. "It was a new field, and there wasn't much known about it. You couldn't go into textbooks and find out the answer to a problem."[7]

Harnish said he and other engineers devised an unusual and untried scheme: one compressor pumping into another one to make it more efficient, using a centrifugal compressor and a reciprocating compressor operating in parallel. In the summer, gas flowed through both. In winter, the compressors operated in a series, the centrifugal pumping into the reciprocating compressor. "I'm sure that was the first time it was ever done," Harnish added.

York's heat pump led to several firsts during the 1960 Winter Olympics, held in Squaw Valley, California. It was the first time artificial refrigeration was used for cooling the ice for an Olympic event. And as the ice was cooled, the heat pump kept the underside of the arena roof warm, melting the massive amount of snow that traditionally fell in northern California.

Borg-Warner's 1963 Annual Report describes a massive conglomerate with 47 divisions, subsidiaries and affiliates providing more than 2,000 products and services. The company had 33,000 employees, working in 55 plants in 13 states, plus additional plants in 18 foreign countries. Borg-Warner stock was listed on both the New York and Midwestern stock exchanges and had paid a dividend annually since it was founded in 1928.

During this period, York installed air conditioning equipment at the Chicago Civic Center; the United Nations Apartment and Office Building in New York; the Equitable Building in Chicago; the Maritime Terminal Building in New Bedford, Massachusetts; Century City in Los Angeles; and the Cadillac Division of General Motors Corporation.

As part of an aggressive new strategy to reduce costs, York created the Value Engineering

Committee in 1963. Representatives from the Purchasing, Industrial Engineering and Design Engineering departments found ways to cut costs without sacrificing quality. Based on the committee's recommendations, York substituted materials, developed new manufacturing methods, combined manufacturing functions and standardized parts and materials across product lines. To help achieve these goals, a Materials Section was established within the Engineering Department.[9]

Finding ways to cut costs was the responsibility of every employee. "Cost continues to be one of our major problems, and we would like to remind you that COST IS EVERYBODY'S PROBLEM and EVERYBODY'S JOB. Your suggestions on cost reductions and means of reducing expense are always welcome."[10]

In 1964, York introduced "Total Quality Control," a concept that would remain important to progressive American manufacturing companies through the 1980s. As Manager P.K. Miller explained, "Quality is designed and built into a product. The secret of accomplishing this economically is to do it right the first time! Emphasis must be placed on error prevention, not error correction! This is the Total Quality Control concept."[11]

Cooling the Capitol

In 1964, Borg-Warner was America's largest independent manufacturer of automobile components, selling products to all of the major U.S. auto manufacturers. Its broad range of automotive products included transmissions, overdrives, clutches, universal joints, differentials, torque converters and timing chains. It also provided components to most of the major truck and farm machinery manufacturers, both at home and abroad. York was the leading source of automotive air conditioning compressors for Ford Motor Company, and supplied components to other customers such as American Motors.

Under Borg-Warner, York continued to set the pace within the air conditioning industry. In 1964, Johns Hopkins University in Baltimore, among the world's leading medical schools, asked York to install two units that would provide air conditioning to all buildings on the 2,000-acre campus. At the time, central heating and air conditioning was rare on college and university campuses. By the end of the decade, however, universities and public schools across the nation adopted York central air conditioning.[12]

The same year, York landed a $1.5 million contract to install a comprehensive air conditioning system in the Library of Congress in Washington, D.C. Proper atmospheric control is vital to maintaining the integrity of archival records and rare books because humidity is extremely destructive to paper and glue. The pipes and ducts of the modern heating and cooling system were tastefully hidden within masonry flues, originally designed to use the building's vintage 1897 coal-fired warm air heating system.

York also installed heating and cooling systems for the Capitol Building, Supreme Court, the two Senate Office Buildings and the three House Office Buildings.[13]

Late in 1964, the company completed the largest installation in its 77-year history at the National Bureau of Standards. Originally spread out among many buildings in the Washington, D.C., area, the Bureau, in charge of regulating all types of weights and measures, consolidated its operations in a new complex on 200 acres near Gaithersburg, Maryland. Four York 3,000-ton turbo systems provided chilled water to all the buildings in the complex.[14] Such high-visibility contracts made York's name synonymous with large, comprehensive climate control systems.

The Peach Bottom Atomic Power Station

Another important York installation completed in 1964 built upon the company's experience working with nuclear power facilities during World War II. Converting its expertise to the peacetime applications of atomic energy, York fabricated a low temperature control refrigeration system for the Peach Bottom Atomic Power Station at Peach Bottom in York County, Pennsylvania.

Operated by the Philadelphia Electric Company, the Peach Bottom plant employed a new breed of atomic reactor recently developed by the General Atomic Division of General Dynamics Corporation. This was the world's first high-temperature, helium-cooled nuclear plant for generating commercial electric power at modern steam pressures and temperatures. York installed an R-12 compound refrigeration system using a series of three compressors: a Single-Wheel Centrifugal Booster Compressor, a Four-Wheel Centrifugal Compressor, and two 12-Cylinder V/W Reciprocating Compressors. These compressors were capable of "flash cooling" the refrigerant to minus 123 degrees.[15]

Thirty years after it was built on the western shore of the Susquehanna River, the Peach Bottom Nuclear Power Station continues to supply power for the Philadelphia Electric Company.

Aiding Medicine

In addition to helping provide power, York technology was credited with saving lives. In 1962, the company entered the field of hyperbaric medicine by helping to build a research chamber at Lutheran General Hospital in Park Ridge, Illinois. Developed by Borg-Warner's Roy C. Ingersoll Research Center and manufactured by the York Division, this invention worked by increasing the oxygen pressure in a patient's lungs.

This woman is holding a Yorkaire Purifier, a filter introduced in 1962 that destroyed odor and bacteria in the air.

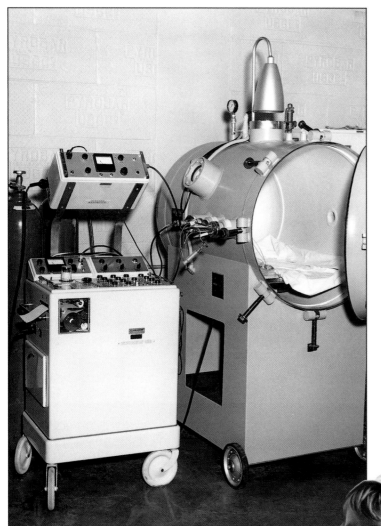

Though still regarded as experimental in the early 1960s, hyperbaric treatment was considered beneficial to patients suffering from strokes, coronary heart disease, strep infections, burns, gangrene, tetanus, shock, heart surgery and plastic surgery. The anecdotal evidence was compelling.

In September 1962, two-month-old James Patrick Angus of Garden City, Long Island, was suffering from a condition known as blue baby. Born with a defective heart, the tiny infant was turning blue because his body was not getting the oxygen it needed. He needed an extremely delicate heart operation, and the risks were tremendous. When the boy's parents heard about the hyperbaric chamber, they had their son flown to Lutheran General Hospital.

At the hospital, James Patrick Angus was placed within a small steel chamber and given pure oxygen under pressure. Doctors said the oxygen helped him gain much-needed strength to withstand the operation, which was a complete success.

Cylindrical in shape, the hyperbaric chamber rested on four swivel casters, measured 28 inches in diameter and seven feet two inches in length, weighed 1,300 pounds and provided oxygen pressures of 30 pounds per square inch. Half of the chamber was made of aluminum and the rest from a clear plastic. Physician and patient were able to talk by means of an electronic communication system, and the patient's couch could be raised and lowered within the chamber.

A year later, the hospital dedicated the John A. Hartford Hyperbaric Oxygen Research Center, which had three room-sized chambers: one that was 41 feet six inches long, to accommodate six bed-patients; one that was 34 feet seven inches long, enough to permit two simultaneous operations in the case of organ transplants; and one that was 23 feet and four inches, for recompression and research. The chambers were interconnected so that decompression would not be necessary in moving from one unit to another.

The $1 million research unit, designed and built by Borg-Warner, was the largest of its kind in the world. To celebrate the dedication, James Patrick Angus' parents, Mr. and Mrs. John Angus, sent a wire in the name of their healthy and happy son.

One of the first patients to benefit from the treatment center was Chicago resident Robert Pfeifer, who was in danger of losing his left leg following a 1965 car crash. Inside the chamber, his body received oxygen at

Above: A portable hyperbaric chamber, developed in the late sixties.
Inset: James Patrick Angus at 18 months. The hyperbaric chamber gave him strength to withstand a risky heart operation when he was two months old.

high pressure while doctors reattached the leg. His lungs, fortified by the oxygen supply, forced increased concentrations of oxygen through the vital organs and tissues of his body, giving him added strength during the surgery and recuperation period.[16]

A week after Pfeifer's leg was saved, the York hyperbaric chamber was used to treat a scuba diver suffering from the bends. By October 1966, glowing letters were arriving at York Corporation headquarters from patients and family members who had benefited from the York hyperbaric oxygen chamber. C.P. Parsons wrote that his son might have died without the chamber.

"Recently, my 15-year-old son had what appeared to be a minor accident while riding a horse. Having been through the usual knocks, cuts, bruises and fractures that most boys seem to be prone to, we weren't too concerned about his cut shin. After this boy of ours spent a few sleepless nights and didn't show any sign of improving, he

A 1968 rendering of an Apollo series air conditioner, a compact machine with high capacity and quiet operation.

was put to bed in our local hospital. Gangrene had set in. After surgery to open his wound and exposure to oxygen (on the lower part of his leg), they thought they had the problem solved. This wasn't the case. It had already gone above his knee, and he was moved to a larger hospital that was supposed to be able to cope with the problem. We were informed that amputation was necessary and that even that might be too late. Our only alternative was the Borg-Warner-engineered Hyperbaric Oxygen Chamber at Lutheran General Hospital in Park Ridge, Illinois. He was rushed to this facility by ambulance and within hours was within the chamber for his first 'run.' After two more sessions in the chamber, his gangrene was gone."[17]

Following up on this success, York developed a portable hyperbaric chamber.[18]

The Space Program

In 1965, York contributed to the space program, winning the contract to air condition the mammoth $100 million NASA Kennedy Space Center Vehicle Assembly Building on Merritt Island, Florida. The 1.2-million-square-foot building was the largest in the world and required one of the world's largest air conditioning system. The four York Turbomaster water chilling systems were capable of delivering 2,500 tons of refrigeration.[19] The 526-foot-tall building was as high as the Washington Monument and could house four of the massive Saturn V rockets used in the Apollo program. York's system was critical to protect delicate circuits from damage from temperature extremes, which often occurred. A legend circulated among workers that before York installed its system, clouds would form at the ceiling of the immense building and rain would fall.[20] Bill Eastman, project manager for Large Tonnage Systems, commented that designing the system posed a challenge to York's engineers.

"You've got a 40-story open space to cool. You have to almost handle it in zones because the hot air is going to rise and the cold air is going to fall. You have to provide cooling at all levels to maintain the humidity control to prevent condensation and corrosion."[21]

Cool Man...Cool   YORK
Air Conditioning

A 1968 billboard, with room for the name of the individual dealer, features the cartoon polar bear that appears in several advertisements from this time period.

York was so proud of its contribution to the manned space program that it named a line of room air conditioners the Apollo series.

York's products were often chosen because of their reliability under harsh conditions. Four of York's 300-horsepower chillers were installed on the aircraft carrier USS *John F. Kennedy*, under construction at the Newport News Shipbuilding and Drydock Company in Virginia, after passing a shock test. To simulate combat conditions, the air conditioning unit was placed on a floating platform at the Norfolk Naval Shipyard in Portsmouth, Virginia. Explosive charges were detonated underwater as close as 20 feet from the platform. The unit kept on working.[22]

At the 1966 annual Borg-Warner Stockholders Meeting in Chicago, Borg-Warner President L.G. Porter predicted a glowing future for the York Division.

"Another growth area is air conditioning and refrigeration equipment, and in the detailed story on York Division in the Annual Report, we say they are predicting a growth rate of 10 to 15 percent annually for each of the next five years. ... York is well along in its $12 million expansion program at its main plant, and some of the benefits in lower costs and improved manufacturing

efficiency should begin to apply to its operations in the latter part of 1966."[23]

Urban Renewal

In 1966 York was part of an exciting building project in Pittsburgh, developed by a partnership between Aluminum Corporation of America, Oliver Tyrone Corporation and Lewis Kitchen. A 79-acre tract in Allegheny County, occupied by decaying rooming houses and shoddy retail stores, was replaced by the Allegheny Center, a complex of upscale retail stores and residential homes. The Allegheny Center was the first large building project of its kind to be heated and cooled from a central gas energy system. Designed and constructed by the Equitable Gas Energy Company, the system involved 4.5 miles of pipeline to provide year-round climate control to 1,350 apartments, 220 townhouses, 750,000 square feet of commercial retail space and an eight-story office building. York installed three Centrifugal Water Chillers capable of providing 6,000 tons of refrigeration. At the time, York engineers calculated that this capacity would have been sufficient to serve the daily water requirements of a city the size of Savannah, Georgia.[24]

Jubilation over projects of this scale was overshadowed by evidence that consumer demand was falling. In 1967, the *Wall Street Journal* reported that the York Division had been overly optimistic.

"Borg-Warner Corporation's York Division expects the value of installed air conditioners to rise 10 percent this year to $3.3 billion. But such an estimate is based on manufacturers' shipments to dealers, and dealers in some big markets say their sales to consumers are sluggish. 'Sales? What sales?' quips Duke Doyle, a Dallas appliance retailer. He says his air conditioner business is running 50 percent under a year ago. ... Smaller air conditioners are moving especially slowly, some retailers say. Window unit 'specials' at less than $100 are offered in several cities."[25]

In spite of evidence that demand was slowing, the York Division plowed ahead with plans for expansion. At a company gathering in October 1967, York President and General Manager William H. Roberts predicted that sales would grow 20 percent by the end of 1967, and announced that the $12 million expansion at the Grantley Avenue plant would include a new machine shop, expansion of the engineering department and a new 100,000-square-foot addition.[26]

Despite the optimistic tone of the address, it was apparent that the comparatively high cost of some of York's product lines continued to hurt sales. As a remedy, prices on the new CM line of residential air conditioning units were set at lower levels than the Flex-O-Matic or Champion models they were designed to replace. To lower prices, York needed to lower production costs by investing in new equipment and continually rethinking its designs. In closing his remarks to York's employees, Roberts concluded:

"We continue to be extremely optimistic about the future. The national economy looks good, our industry looks even more encouraging, and York's position within the industry continues to improve. I see no reason why the growth we have accomplished during the

past five years cannot be repeated during the next five years."[27]

Though consumer demand softened, York's commercial lines of refrigeration products continued to grow.

Soaring International Growth

International business was also thriving during this period. One of York's largest overseas projects was providing air conditioning to the American University of Beirut, Lebanon. Chartered by the State University of New York in 1863, the American University was the oldest university in Lebanon. Classes in the schools of Arts and Sciences, Medicine, Pharmacy, Nursing, Public Health, Engineering and Agriculture were taught in both English and Arabic. In 1967, it was gradu-

These models are holding mock-ups of York's thermoelectric products. The woman on the left is holding a mock-up of a York thermoelectric air conditioner, while the one on the right is holding a mock-up of a thermoelectric water cooler.

ating 2,500 students a year from 52 nations and 24 religions.

York was also enjoying rapid international expansion through licensing and acquisitions. John Walsh, hired as a manager of Licensing and Acquisitions in 1960, oversaw this expansion, much of which took place in Asia. In 1963, he became director of International Operations. "I was in charge of licensing the York know-how in countries in which we could not export readily," he commented. Walsh said companies were licensed to import and install York products in such countries as India and Japan. Other contract companies were acquired, such as York France, which started out as a joint venture with a local business.[28]

In 1967, York air-conditioned the Medical Center at the University of Beirut with three 600-horsepower centrifugal compressors, each capable of producing 650 tons of refrigeration. The system included coolers, intercoolers, 454 fan coil units and several air handlers.[29]

Beginning in 1967, the York Division literally took to the skies with the creation of the York Flight Department and purchase of a twin-engine, four-passenger Model G18-S Beechcraft. Pilot Richard Beckner and copilot Kenneth St. Clair conducted the maiden flight from the York Airport to Newark Airport in New Jersey in one hour and 45 minutes on January 5, 1967. The following day the two pilots flew two executives to a meeting in Chicago and brought them home the same evening. In its first year, the Blue Max, as the Beechcraft was affectionately known, logged 623,000 miles carrying 589 York personnel and customers to 96 airports in 24 states and Canada.[30]

During 1967, York moved boldly to increase its market share in the emerging market to supply air conditioning and refrigeration systems for schools, introduced a new line of refrigeration units for railroad cars and "piggyback" trucks, and expanded its offerings for large commercial installations.[31] The end of fiscal 1967 marked the climax of a five-year $226-million-dollar capital improvement campaign for Borg-Warner Corporation. Corporate sales surged to $951 million, up from $913 million in 1966.[32] Performance in the builder and consumer sales markets, including York air conditioning and refrigeration lines, was particularly strong.

In 1968, York supplied the major components for the world's largest chilled water air conditioning system in the World Trade Center in lower Manhattan. The system was designed to cool four low-rise buildings and two 110-story towers, each occupied by 50,000 people a day. When complete, York's $2.65 million, 49,000-ton system had enough capacity to cool 25,000 homes. The system included seven massive 7,000-ton multistage centrifugal compressors, installed in a one-acre room that was on the guided tour through the famous building. Two hundred and fourteen miles of copper tubing moved chilled water through the air conditioning circuits of the vast building complex.[33]

The units installed were so massive that many of the components withstood the 1994 World Trade Center bombing, leading industry experts to call York's machinery the only proven "terrorist-proof chillers." Victor McCloskey, vice president of Corporate Development, said the devastating blast took place directly above York's engine room in the building.

"When the bomb went off, the parking lot literally fell into our engine room. When you went into the place a few days later, you found burned-out cars and humongous chunks of concrete alongside our centrifugal chillers. We had the task of helping [the New York] Port Authority rebuild that air conditioning facility. Not only did we provide some new equipment in record time, but the old equipment literally withstood this blast. Control panels were ripped off and destroyed, but these huge heat exchangers, compressors and motors are all still there today, in operation. We received an award from Governor Mario Cuomo for the response to the disaster."[34]

About a dozen of York's employees were in the building at the time of the explosion, noted York employee Robert Dolheimer.

"They were in a room being trained on, I think, variable air volume, and there was a plate glass window in the room where they were studying, and fortunately most of the people were faced away from the glass. The people facing the glass did get some cuts on their faces. If you were watching TV at the time, you would have seen several

York service guys being helped out of the building after the bomb went off."[35]

The Computer Age

In 1968, York began using computer programs written in FORTRAN to help design and select components for major installations. The computer helped to calculate the heating and cooling requirements of specific buildings. The computer-generated simulations, developed at the Borg-Warner Roy C. Ingersoll Research Center, were the most sophisticated programs of their type in existence. By avoiding the installation of oversized heating and air conditioning systems on large projects, both York and its customers enjoyed substantial savings.[36]

In 1968, the headquarters for the York International Division was moved from Chicago to York, where new headquarters were constructed on the east side of Richland Avenue south of Codorus Creek. Erected by R.S. Noonan, Inc. of York for $2.5 million, the five-story, 97,000-square-foot office building housed executive offices, Marketing, Financial, Data Processing, Purchasing, and Printing departments. The adjoining two-story 19,000-square-foot York Institute of Air Conditioning and Refrigeration included a 200-seat auditorium with public address and film projection systems.[37]

The new buildings were a monument to York's great success during the 1960s. By 1969, York air conditioning was at work in the New York Hilton at Rockefeller Center and the new J.C. Penney Building in New York City,[38] the $5 million Federal Office Building in St. Petersburg, Florida,[39] and Kent State University in Ohio.[40]

As the company looked forward to the 1970s, York's employees and managers spoke with pride of York's contribution to Borg-Warner's overall performance and of the technological achievements that rendered America's homes, offices, apartment buildings, shopping malls, theaters and transportation facilities the most comfortable in the world.

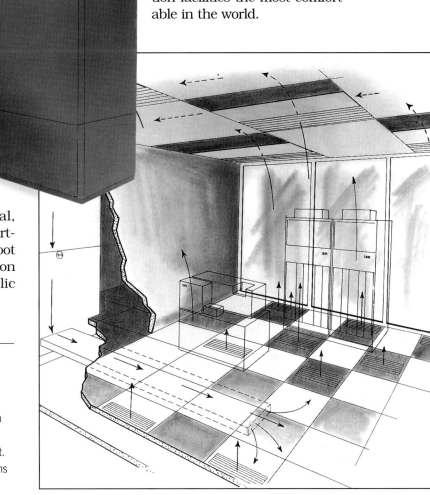

Above: An environmental control system manufactured by York in 1966 for use in one of IBM's computer rooms.

Right: A 1966 rendering of the air flow pattern in a computer room cooled by a York system. In the sixties, large computers powered by thousands of vacuum tubes generated a tremendous amount of heat. To keep the machines from breaking down, they were stored in rooms that were heavily air-conditioned.

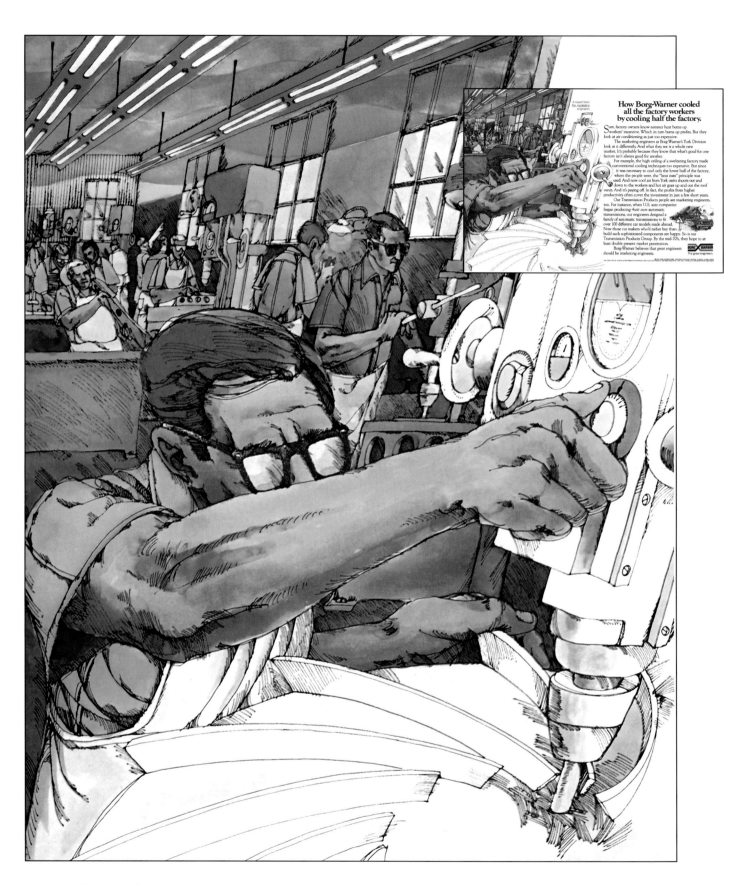

A 1972 advertisement touts the York Division of Borg-Warner for finding innovative ways to tap the office and factory markets.

CHAPTER TWELVE

THINKING GLOBALLY

1970-1979

"In the long run, though, as long as the sun shines and the laws of nature hold, there is no energy shortage. We can make use of solar energy and nuclear fusion for billions of years. ... In this connection, the booklet you now hold is a remarkable public service by the York Division of Borg-Warner Corporation. It goes into the nuts and bolts of energy conservation in the home, describing what you can do to help yourself and others."

— Isaac Asimov, introduction to "Energy and Your Home," 1978[1]

THE SEVENTIES emerged with the expansion of York products in Europe, where the air conditioning market was growing at nearly twice the rate of the American market, especially throughout Italy and France. York also installed air conditioning in Osaka, Japan, for Expo 70, the first such expo approved by the International Bureau of Exhibitions outside Europe or the United States. Between 30 million and 50 million people visited Expo 70 between March 15 and September 13, 1970. The 815-acre center was air conditioned with York's time-proven Turbomaster system, the same type installed in the NASA Kennedy Space Center Vehicle Assembly Building on Merritt Island, Florida.[2]

Military Contracts

During the first few months of 1970, the York Division landed an important Navy contract through Litton Systems, Inc. of Pascagoula, Mississippi. The division would outfit nine new amphibious assault vessels, as well as the refurbished aircraft carrier USS *Midway,* with air conditioning and refrigeration systems. Each of the amphibious vessels, designed to carry troops, tanks, helicopters, landing craft and supplies, received four 300-ton York centrifugal water chilling packages for air conditioning and three Marinepaks to maintain the ship's stores at minus 20 degrees.[3]

Reconstruction of the aircraft carrier at Hunter's Point Naval Shipyard required four years and more than $202 million. York supplied five 300-ton air conditioning systems to meet the needs of the massive ship, which could carry a crew of 4,300.

In 1970, Jack Kennedy was elected president of the York Division, succeeding Gerard V. Patrick, who had served as both president and chairman of the board since 1969. A graduate of Purdue University in Indiana, Kennedy was formerly president of Rudy Manufacturing Company of Dowagiac, Michigan, and La Crosse Cooler Company of La Crosse, Wisconsin.[4] As president of the York Division, Kennedy concentrated on upgrading product lines and experimenting with new technologies.

One new product line was the Turboguard, a compressor-free system that could "telephone" a human operator to warn of a leak in the system. "Smart" systems to alert maintenance crews of pending problems before catastrophic breakdowns became increasingly common as the seventies progressed.

York celebrated its 100th anniversary in 1974.

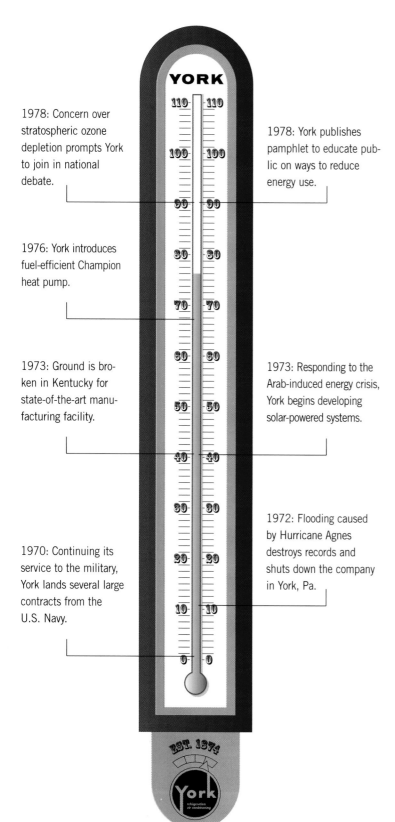

YORK

1978: Concern over stratospheric ozone depletion prompts York to join in national debate.

1978: York publishes pamphlet to educate public on ways to reduce energy use.

1976: York introduces fuel-efficient Champion heat pump.

1973: Ground is broken in Kentucky for state-of-the-art manufacturing facility.

1973: Responding to the Arab-induced energy crisis, York begins developing solar-powered systems.

1970: Continuing its service to the military, York lands several large contracts from the U.S. Navy.

1972: Flooding caused by Hurricane Agnes destroys records and shuts down the company in York, Pa.

EST. 1874

York

Employers were discovering that air-conditioning their facilities was a good investment because comfortable workers were more productive. A 1971 report by the American Society of Heating, Refrigerating and Air Conditioning Engineers took this point a step further, demonstrating that students performed better on exams in climate-controlled schools.[5] As a result of the study, sales of York air conditioning systems to schools and universities grew throughout the decade.

Hurricane Agnes

The summer shower that began on June 21, 1972, turned into Hurricane Agnes, dumping more than 20 inches of rain on York County, forcing hundreds of people from their homes and shutting down industries. After the storm, a bright and eager Scott J. Boxer, just hired by York following his graduation from the University of Rhode Island, arrived for his first day as a York engineer wearing a freshly-pressed shirt and tie. Boxer, former president of York International's Unitary Products Group, recalled his first assignment.

> "'Go home. Put on the worst clothes you have. Codorus Creek overflowed and filled up the basement. You are going to be shoveling mud.' So on my first day, I shoveled mud from the training room."[6]

Thousands of records, forms and printed material were destroyed or damaged in the flood. The York Institute lost hundreds of trans-

Jack W. Kennedy was president of the York Division from 1970 until 1986.

parencies and slides and countless charts, demonstrators and simulators. Its closed- circuit television system was severely damaged. Employees helped with the cleanup, and by June 25, the York plant was operating at 80 percent of its production capacity.[7]

The Middle East

Searching for new market opportunities, York focused on the Middle and Far East. E.P. Carpenter, vice president of International Markets, discussed the vast potential of these regions in a 1974 speech to the sales staff. "In these areas climate conditions and the availability of oil add up to higher incomes and more sophisticated tastes and desires," he said.[8] York had recently increased its visibility in the Middle East when it completed an air conditioning project at the Aryameher Sports Center in Teheran, Iran.

York's growing international presence created some interesting experiences for the sales staff, recalled Sales Order Administrator James Stambaugh, who joined York in 1973 and has handled orders all over the world.

"This was my first exposure to working with different cultures, from the Japanese who were so polite that they would not ask you a question for fear of offending you, to the Middle Eastern kind of culture, which is a little more of a table-pounding, get-your-attention kind of thing. We'd get involved in countries that I thought we would stay away from because of volatile situations. For example, we used to do a lot of business in Beirut, and there was a guy who I dealt with on a regular basis. When things started to go really bad in Lebanon, we had to find creative ways to ship into the country. We'd ship into a different country and the guy would make arrangements to get it from that country into his. It got pretty challenging."[9]

On the domestic front, the division constructed a state-of-the-art manufacturing facility at Madisonville, Kentucky. Groundbreaking was in June 1973, and the facility opened a year later. Terry Bowman, director of purchasing for the Unitary Products Group, said the facility helped the company meet a growing demand for residential air conditioning.

"Air conditioning was just transitioning from a real luxury to a necessity in new homes. The early seventies was an expansion period in our country, and a lot of homes were being built. Air conditioning was starting to become something that people really desired. So we built a brand-new factory with the latest concepts in mind. We had consultants, and they were counseling us on the open management concept, in which everyone is on a first-name basis. There were no private parking places. The plant manager had an open door, meaning that anybody in the factory

How to get an extra 8 hours work per week from this man.

When work conditions become hot and uncomfortable, workers lose interest and productivity is lost. It doesn't make economic sense, does it? Not like York central air-conditioning.

It's a proven fact that people work harder and produce more in cool, comfortable conditions. York conditions.

And increased productivity means increased revenue. So, in no time, York central air-conditioning will pay for itself.

Think about it. York makes economic sense.

We'd like you to know more about York commercial air-conditioning installations, so why not contact us, or one of our carefully selected dealers.

EFFICIENT **YORK** BORG WARNER AIR-CONDITIONING

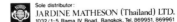

Sole distributor:
JARDINE MATHESON (Thailand) LTD.
1032/1-5 Rama IV Road, Bangkok, Tel. 869951, 869961

YBW 2-75

York capitalized on studies showing that productivity increased in climate-controlled work environments. This advertisement is for a distributor in Thailand.

could walk in and talk to him. A very positive culture was built."[10]

York also introduced the FlatTop evaporator coil, which allowed central air conditioning to be added to heating units in existing home systems. The coil was exceptionally compact and easy to install. York advertised it on CBS-TV, during the *Evening News with Walter Cronkite*, in spots that featured Judy Carne, the "sock-it-to-me" girl from *Laugh-In*.

New Sources of Energy

In 1973, the American public was abruptly confronted with the knowledge that it had grown dangerously dependent on oil from the Middle East. When Arab nations refused to sell oil to countries that supported Israel during the 1973 Yom Kippur War, gas prices ballooned and lines at gas pumps stretched for blocks. Panicked drivers topped off their tanks whenever the needle quivered below full.

Research into alternate fuels became a national imperative. The York Division established itself as a pioneer in the suddenly popular field of solar energy when it helped create the first solar-energized school in the nation. The Timonium Elementary School in Maryland was heated and cooled by a sun-powered absorption system that used water heated by solar collectors. The innovative system saved an estimated 1,200 gallons of oil over a period of seven weeks. The solar equipment, which relied on a York absorption chiller system, worked best in summer and required assistance from an oil-operated system during winter. Designed by AAI Corporation of Baltimore under a contract funded by the National Science Foundation, it used a 5,040-square-foot solar collector and a 15,000-gallon water storage tank.[11]

York consultant Alwin Newton, former director of Research and Advanced Engineering, believed that solar power could become the energy choice of the future.

"The beauty of the arrangement is that the absorption unit used is one York has been pro-

Above: Judy Carne explains the benefits of the FlatTop evaporator coil.

Opposite page: York employees work on the enormous compressor rotor used to cool the Empire State Building. York began air-conditioning the New York landmark in 1950. This picture was taken in the seventies.

ducing for years. No modifications were necessary to incorporate it into the solar system. ... Many believe that solar energy for heating and cooling in the immediate future will be restricted to commercial applications, but I see it coming to private residences very quickly — within the next 10 years. We've had the Space Age and the Atomic Age; the 1980s will see the entrance of the Solar Age."[12]

The drive for fuel efficiency resulted in widespread acceptance of the heat pump, used for both cooling and heating. The pump cooled buildings by pumping heat away from the interior and heated buildings by pumping heat in. The energy-efficient pump used only the amount of energy needed to maintain a certain temperature. In 1976, York

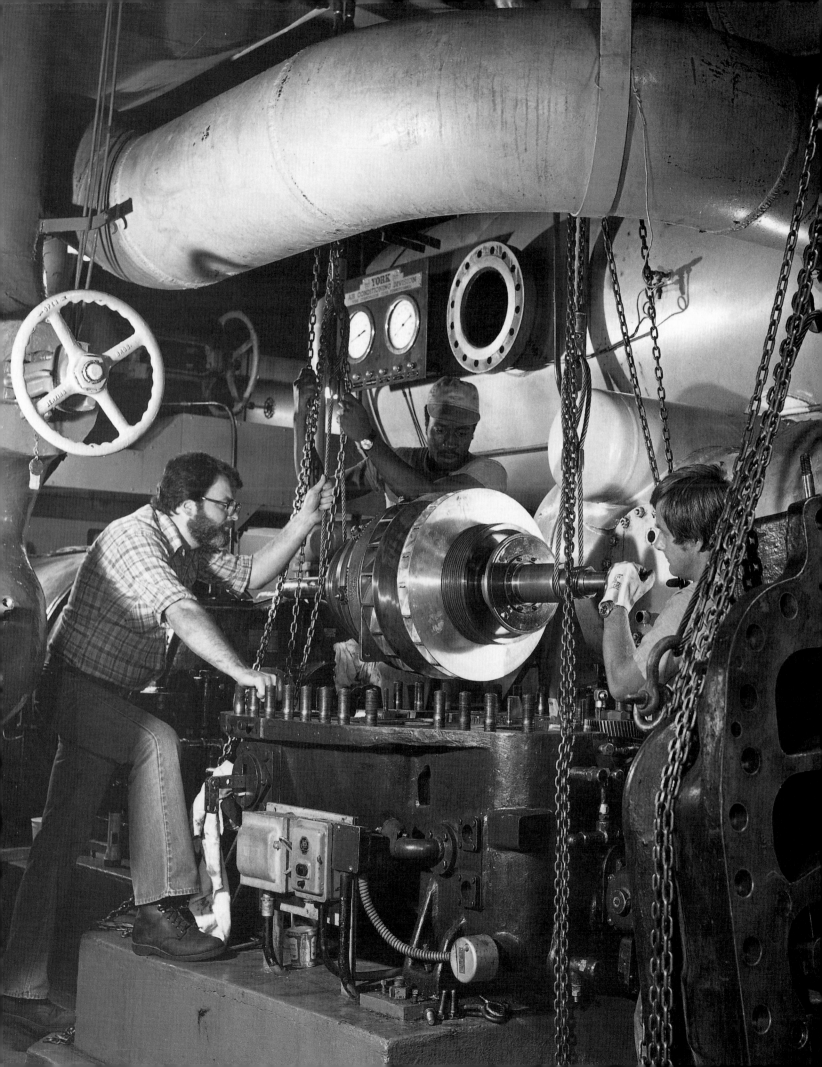

introduced the world's first computer controlled heat pump, called the Champion Split System Heat Pump. The Champion was 16 to 20 percent more efficient than competitive pumps. Heat pump sales in general took off in 1976, according to *Business Week*.

"In the first seven months of this year alone, manufacturers sold 170,000 units, and they now expect sales to approach 300,000 units by year end. Nationwide, heat pumps are going into nearly half the homes built with electric heating. In Cincinnati, they have already captured 75 percent of the new housing market. In Washington, they have 80 percent."[13]

In 1978, York published a booklet called "Energy and Your Home" to educate consumers on ways to reduce the cost of heating and cooling. Renowned science writer Dr. Isaac Asimov wrote the preface.

"There is an energy crisis. We saw it at the end of 1973, when the Middle East imposed an oil boycott and we discovered that the United States could not live on its own oil supply. ... In the long run, though, as long as the sun shines and the laws of nature hold, there is no energy shortage. We can make use of solar energy and nuclear fusion for billions of years. There is a variety of subsidiary sources available too — wind, running water, tides, ocean warmth, Earth's internal heat, even coal and fission. In this connection, the booklet you now hold is a remarkable public service by the York Division of Borg-Warner Corporation. It goes into the nuts and bolts of energy conservation in the home, describing what you can do to help yourself and others. For every person who reads and acts, there will be a small extension of the deadly deadline that faces America and the world. And if enough people act, as a result of reading this booklet or for any other reason, the deadline may be lifted forever."[14]

By July 1978, more than 180,000 copies had been distributed, and favorable reviews flooded in from the *Boston Herald American, New England Progress, New York Daily News, New York Post, New Haven Register, Chicago Tribune, St. Louis Globe Democrat, San Francisco Examiner and Chronicle,* and *Akron Beacon-Journal,* as well as radio stations from New Jersey to Iowa.

Above: York's revolutionary ENMOD (energy modulator) thermostat and heat pump, the first in the world, saves energy by adjusting usage throughout the day.

Left: York's energy conservation book was hailed by such prestigious newspapers as the *New York Daily News,* the *New Haven Register* and the *Chicago Tribune.*

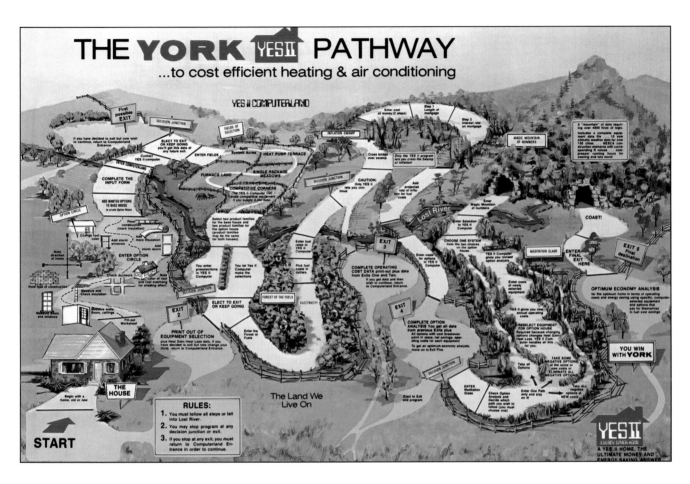

The booklet gave tips and methods for calculating the efficiency of heat pumps and air conditioning systems. These units were rated according to the number of British Thermal Units (BTUs) they removed from a room per amount of energy supplied to them. Under the new system, called the Energy Efficiency Ratio (EER), the cooling capacity calculated in BTUs per hour, was divided by the electrical consumption in watts. For a 12,000 BTU air conditioner using 1,900 watts of electricity, the EER would be 6.3. A 12,000 BTU air conditioner using only 1,400 watts would have an EER of 8.6 and would cost roughly 25 percent less to operate than the first. York considered any unit with an EER ratio above seven to be good, but

units with EER ratios higher than eight were considered better buys.[15]

York also created **YES**, an acronym for York Energy Saver Residential Computer Analysis. A major cause of inefficiency in many home heating and cooling systems was oversized systems, especially in homes with efficient insulation. In February 1979, York introduced a new line of 55,000-BTU Borg-Warner oil-fired furnaces specifically sized for the better insulated homes under construction around the country. During the same period, York's Deluxe Climaster IV gas-fired furnace was redesigned with an energy-saving flue damper to prevent the escape of heat through the chimney. York estimated that the addition of the new flue damper alone would reduce the average household heating bill by 20 percent.[16]

York joined with Honeywell Inc. to develop a solar energy heating and air conditioning system.[17] York supplied two high-efficiency Turbopaks, which were connected to Rankine cycle turbines. The product provided 82 percent

---

This illustrated brochure is modeled after a board game, but it actually helps determine needs and effective solutions with the YES II energy-saving plan.

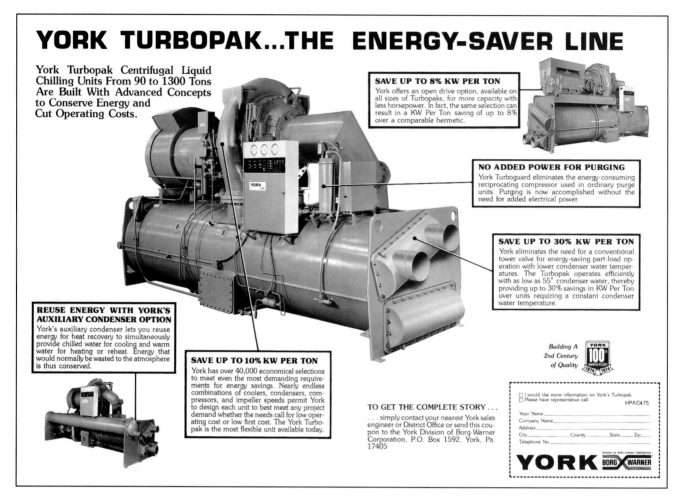

of the annual cooling requirements, 53 percent of the annual heating needs and all of the hot water for an eight-story, 100,000-square foot office building in Minneapolis. The system, designed by Honeywell Energy Resources Center, stored heat to run on cloudy days and could operate in temperatures as low as minus 30 degrees.[18]

Between 1971 and 1976, the York Division worked to comply with changing requirements in the federal Toxic Substances Control Act, which governed the disposal of polychlorinated biphenyls, or PCBs, a toxic chemical with fire-resistant properties.[19]

During this time period, the York Division was selling products to the very OPEC nations responsible for driving up oil prices. York provided air conditioning equipment for 15 train cars on the 400-mile-long Saudi Arabian rail line running from Riyadh to the Persian Gulf. Roof-mounted

This highly efficient 1974 Turbopak centrifugal liquid chilling unit conserves energy, a goal that became increasingly important during the energy crisis of the seventies.

air conditioning units supplied by the York Transportation Equipment Group ensured that the train interiors would remain a comfortable 76 degrees, even when outside temperatures soared to 120 degrees. Other installations included the Mecca Conference Center, Saudi Ministry of Aviation, Jeddah International Airport, Riyadh Airport, Saudi Government Employees Office Building, King Abdul Aziz University, Saudi Planning Organization, Saudi Cement Company, King Faisal Specialist Hospital, ARAMCO, Redec Compound, Bin Zaqr Building, Medina Airport, Taif Airport, Jeddah Broadcasting Studio, Jeddah Library, Saudi Airlines, Lockheed Compound, the

Saudi Public Telephone and Telegraph Exchange buildings and the Saudi Industrial Studies and Development Center.[20]

Acting Locally

In 1979, Borg-Warner directors and executives toured York's $2 million, 30,000-square foot Industrial Refrigeration Building, recently opened at the Grantley Avenue plant. The facility would be used to construct special units weighing up to 100 tons and also to improve the transfer of Borg-Warner products to the sandblast area, paint shop and shipping docks.

Responding to President Jimmy Carter's request to set thermostats no higher than 68 degrees in winter, the York Division improved energy conservation within its own facilities. York Utilities Foreman Dick Knaub explained the importance of oil conservation.

"To operate York Division facilities for 1979-80, oil budget requests alone are estimated at well over $1 million. When I started at York in 1971, home heating oil was selling at 16.9 cents per gallon. That same oil, #2, is used to heat our shops and buildings. Eighty-six percent of this particular oil is required for heating, not production. In January of this year, it sold for 47.3 cents per gallon. Last month, the price had increased to 66.9 cents per gallon for bulk rate, and we estimate we will need 434,500 gallons."[21]

Concern for the Environment

Toward the end of the decade, one of the greatest challenges confronting the air conditioning and refrigeration industry was to find a replacement for Freon-12. In 1978, officers from the York Division, led by Dick Barnett, general manager of Unitary Products, joined the national debate over chlorofluorocarbon-based refrigerants such as Freon-12. Studies showed that fluorocarbons were harmful to the ozone layer that protects the earth and its inhabitants from the most damaging effects of the sun.

Concerned about ozone depletion, the federal Environmental Protection Agency held hearings to decide whether refrigerants should be regulated. This action would have tremendous impact on York, which relied on Freon-11 and Freon-12 for its air conditioners. The use of CFCs in aerosol cans had already been outlawed, and York officials were naturally anxious to see if the ban would be expanded to refrigerants.[22]

As the York Division of Borg-Warner prepared to take on the challenges of a new decade, it was able to point with pride to a number of recent successes. The seventies, however, ended amid continuing worries over high inflation and economic recession, a prolonged energy crisis and increasing concern about the environment.

Ronald Reagan set the tone for the dawning decade by arguing in the 1980 presidential campaign for a downsized government and lower taxes that would spur the growth of business. Big changes were on the horizon for the York Division as Borg-Warner moved to consolidate its markets and refocus its priorities.

York's "can-do" attitude helped it survive depressions and world wars. The company's ability to seek out new opportunities served it well after the energy crisis of the seventies. With the nation more concerned than ever with conservation, York introduced dozens of products and programs to help customers cut down on fuel consumption.

Workers at Borg-Warner's Central Environmental Systems plant in Norman, Oklahoma, assembling single-package commercial air conditioning and heat pump units in 1982.

CHAPTER THIRTEEN

YORK GOES INDEPENDENT

1980-1989

"They never knew what they had. Borg-Warner just sent in one president after another, and none of them knew how to handle the company. It was a continual reorganization that never seemed to go anywhere. I don't think we ever had the proper direction."

— Elwood Spangler, 1996[1]

WHAT BEGAN AS a promising decade for Borg-Warner soon degenerated into deep recession, rising foreign competition, high unemployment and widespread corporate anxiety.

In 1981, Borg-Warner acquired the Westinghouse Air Conditioning Division, bringing the well-known Luxaire brand name to York's line of products.

The division had started in 1939 as the C.A. Olsen Manufacturing Company of Elyria, Ohio. It had been acquired in 1955 by Westinghouse Electric Corporation. This was the same C.A. Olsen that had almost merged with York in 1953. In 1963 Westinghouse organized a subsidiary company under the name Luxaire, which became the Westinghouse Air Conditioning Division in 1979.[2] With these established brands among its offerings, the Borg-Warner Air Conditioning Group expected to substantially increase its market share in the domestic marketplace.

In the early eighties, the Air Conditioning Group of Borg-Warner began placing a heavy emphasis on Computer Aided Design (CAD), Computer Aided Manufacturing (CAM) and Computer Integrated Manufacturing (CIM) technologies. By 1983, more than 50 percent of the drawings for York's new product lines were created by CAD, and roughly 40 percent of York's machine tools were computer controlled.[3]

Computers also helped facilitate some of the more mundane aspects of York's daily operations. In 1983, the company installed a computerized inventory control system capable of tracking 43,000 parts in 20 different storerooms. This task had previously required more than 300 York employees to periodically come in on Saturdays or Sundays to count inventory.[4]

Cost-Cutting Measures

The Air Conditioning Group posted profits of $30.4 million in 1981 and profits of $33.8 million the following year. In mid-1982, team captains of the Engineered Machinery Cost Improvement Program (CIP) presented management with more than $13 million in annual cost savings.[5] York's various departments continued to send four to ten employees to "quality circle meetings" once a week to analyze problems and formulate solutions to further reduce production costs and boost profit. Eventually, seven quality circles emerged, with such creative names as Pareto's People (Materials

---

In 1986, York became an independent company once again. This image is from a newsletter celebrating the spin-off.

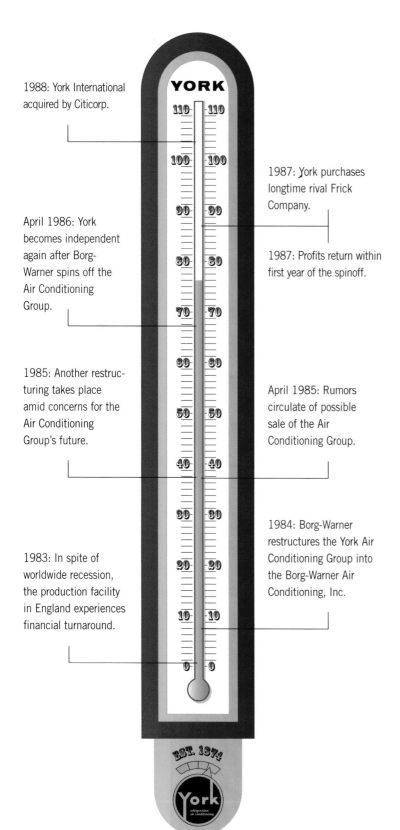

1988: York International acquired by Citicorp.

April 1986: York becomes independent again after Borg-Warner spins off the Air Conditioning Group.

1985: Another restructuring takes place amid concerns for the Air Conditioning Group's future.

1983: In spite of worldwide recession, the production facility in England experiences financial turnaround.

1987: York purchases longtime rival Frick Company.

1987: Profits return within first year of the spinoff.

April 1985: Rumors circulate of possible sale of the Air Conditioning Group.

1984: Borg-Warner restructures the York Air Conditioning Group into the Borg-Warner Air Conditioning, Inc.

A Triton heat pump.

Department), Force Five (Engineering Department), the Compressor Circle (Compressor Assembly Department), Riptide (Final Assembly Department), People in Progress (Testing Laboratory), Women in Progress (Text Processing), and Up with People (Condenser-DX Coolers Department).[6]

A Turnaround in England

In 1983, Scott J. Boxer became managing director of Manufacturing Operations in Basildon, England. The facility, operating at the site since 1973, shipped a variety of packaged air conditioners, chillers and heat pumps across Europe and to Scandinavia, Africa, Australia, Asia and the Middle East. It won the prestigious Queens Award for Export Achievement in 1979.[7] In 1983, however, it posted a loss of $2.2 million.[8] In the previous 10 years, the division had suffered through eight rounds of layoffs. One of Boxer's first steps was to restore morale, noted a 1989 magazine article about the facility's subsequent turnaround.

"He believes part of the problem at York at that time was common to many UK organizations: a lot of Middle East business producing boom projects that loaded the factory to the gunwales, followed by a slump in orders that led to redundancies. Small surprise, then, that management's and the workforce's loyalty had plunged very low. Taking time to introduce himself to every one of the workforce, Boxer recalls the tense atmosphere and comments such as, 'When are you going to lay us off again? Is the company going to close?'"[9]

Boxer worked hard to improve communication, build trust and turn the plant into a world-class manufacturing unit. One of his first initiatives was to establish five multidiscipline teams, each with a design engineer, manufacturing engineer, buyer, foreman, inspector and several volunteers from the shop floor. The groups were asked to identify and remedy problems that had caused warranty costs to skyrocket. Dennis

Kloster, who is now vice president of Marketing, North America, for York's Unitary Products Group, noted that Scott Boxer's management method was among the reasons he joined York.

"Politics is one thing that is flat-out not tolerated, at least in our division. If Boxer senses any of that going on, he puts an immediate end to it. You can stay focused on doing your job and not worry about office politics."[10]

Improved Communication

During these lean times, the division made a concerted effort to improve communication among employees. Regular columns in the employee newsletter, *The York Communicator,* explained the workings of Borg-Warner Corporation, specifically the Air Conditioning Group. A "Your Turn" section was added, in which management answered questions posed by employees. The company printed questions from even the unhappiest employees and made a good-faith effort to explain the reasoning behind the cost-cutting measures.

In a late 1983 letter to employees, Robert J. M. Fisher, president and chief operating officer of Borg-Warner's Air Conditioning Group, acknowledged that the past year had been challenging.

"As we entered 1983, we recognized we were heading into some difficult times. ... Unfortunately,

This image from a 1987 brochure illustrated that York's new reciprocating liquid chillers were easy to maintain. Of course, the real chillers were much larger.

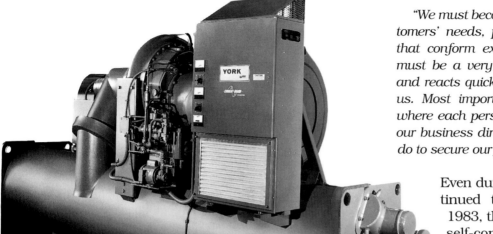

*our results did not come close to
our expectations. The International
scene remained unsettled with weaker
economies and a continued strengthening of the
U.S. dollar in relation to other currencies, combining to reduce our sales. The U.S. market was good
for residential products but non-residential construction did not improve over last year. We saw
fierce competition in all markets and our prices
and profit levels dropped as a result."[11]*

The York Division remained optimistic, and
began referring to itself as "The Can-Do Company."
A 1984 issue of *The York Communicator* quoted
Henry Wadsworth Longfellow's line that "The lowest ebb is the turn of the tide."

A New Way of Doing Business

The Borg-Warner Air Conditioning Group
began to seriously rethink how it did business.
Instead of building products it believed customers wanted, and training its sales teams to
market those products, York began to formally research the marketplace and tailor its
products for specialized markets and established customers. In 1984, Dave McEwan,
vice president and general manager of
Engineered Products, explained the strategy in
The York Communicator.

*"We must become a business driven by our cus-
tomers' needs, producing products and services
that conform exactly to their requirements. We
must be a very lean organization that monitors
and reacts quickly to the changing world around
us. Most importantly, we must be a business
where each person has a clear understanding of
our business direction and the job we must each
do to secure our future."[12]*

Even during the worst of times, York continued to introduce new products. In
1983, these included the York PoolPak, a
self-contained unit that reduced
humidity and energy costs in large
indoor swimming pool installations.
Developed in Great Britain, the
PoolPaks were capable of reducing
overall pool energy costs by a remarkable 40 to 60 percent.[13] In addition to
such new product lines, York also continued
to offer a superior line of 17 models of room air
conditioners ranging in capacity from 4,900 up to

The evolution of a product. The Current-Guard solid state motor
starter (above) ensured smooth, reliable starting of centrifugal water
chillers. The York Turbo-Modulator motor speed controller (below),
introduced in 1979, eliminated the need for a starter altogether, leading to energy savings as high as 30 percent.

30,700 BTU. The smaller units employed the new rotary compressor design while larger models utilized the time-tested re-ciprocating compressors.

Corporate Restructuring

On January 1, 1984, Borg-Warner Corporation announced that York's Air Conditioning Group would be known as Borg-Warner Air Conditioning, Inc., a wholly-owned subsidiary of Borg-Warner Corporation, and that Borg-Warner Central Environmental Systems would become a wholly-owned subsidiary of Borg-Warner Air Conditioning, Inc.[14]

That day, Borg-Warner Chairman James F. Beré announced that Jerry Dempsey would be replaced by C.E. "Red" Johnson as president and chief operating officer of Borg-Warner Corporation.[15] Dempsey left to become vice president of Waste Management, Inc., the nation's largest waste disposal company. His departure caused quite a stir at York. According to an article in *Business Week*, Dempsey had clashed with Beré over management styles, particularly after annual earnings dropped 3 percent. While Dempsey had spent much of his career immersed in Borg-Warner's core businesses, such as air conditioning and automotive parts, Beré's new corporate strategy was heavily focused on services. Dempsey's hands-on leadership style conflicted with Beré's inclination to let subordinates make their own decisions. Perhaps the issue that hastened Dempsey's departure was his push to acquire Westinghouse Electric Company's home air conditioner business in 1981. Though this acquisition greatly helped the York Division, York remained one of Borg-Warner's weakest performers following the acquisition. Some business analysts predicted that the loss of Dempsey would hurt Borg-Warner because he was widely regarded as the one individual who kept the various departments within their budgets.[16]

In November 1984, 80 salaried Borg-Warner employees were laid off as a result of a prolonged United Auto Worker labor strike in which nearly 1,200 York employees had walked off the job.[17] To settle the strike, Borg-Warner offered an average wage of $23,000 plus cost-of-living increases over three years, lump-sum increases of 1.3 and 2 percent in 1986 and 1987 respectively, a return-to-work bonus of $400, as well as a generous list of health care, life insurance and vacation concessions.[18]

With the end of the strike, an ambitious plant restructuring was implemented by Borg-Warner

With the help of a savings analyzer, a York dealer quickly compared operating costs and energy savings for furnaces, heat pumps and air conditioners.

management. In April 1985, Borg-Warner Air Conditioning, Inc., was reorganized into three business units: Central Environmental Systems, Industrial Systems and Applied Systems.

The restructuring took place amid ominous rumblings about the future of York and the entire Air Conditioning Group under Borg-Warner. While Central Environmental Systems was still headed by R.C. Barnett and Industrial Systems by Jack R. Walsh, the formation of the new Applied Systems unit out of the Engineered Machinery and the International divisions required an entirely new corporate structure. Applied Systems came under the direct control of Borg-Warner Executive Vice President R.J. Doyle, who was responsible for human resources, group finance, financial analysis and the MIS functions formerly handled by Headquarters and Engineered Machinery Division. The new vice president of marketing and strategy, D.L. McEwan, was put in charge of various segments of Applied Systems. Walsh became president of York Europe; Ken E. Hickman, vice president of Engineering; and R.C. Thomas, vice president of Manufacturing.[19]

Throughout 1985, rumors circulated about the possible sale by Borg-Warner of its Air Conditioning Group. In a bulletin to employees dated April 25, 1985, Borg-Warner Air Conditioning Group President and Chief Operating Officer Robert J.M. Fisher tried to reassure York employees.

"It is very important for everyone to understand that Borg-Warner is not negotiating the sale of our air conditioning business; that our policy has not changed from that I mentioned in January. The main emphasis is for all of us to improve our company's performance."[20]

This statement was prompted by an April 24, 1985, *Wall Street Journal* article suggesting Borg-Warner was considering a possible sale, merger or joint venture for its troubled Air Conditioning Group. The article appeared after Borg-Warner's profits plummeted by 11 percent during the preceding quarter, not including large loan losses experienced by Borg-Warner's Acceptance Unit.

On April 29, 1985, Borg-Warner President C.E. Johnson rushed to quell rumors of a possible imminent sale of the Air Conditioning Group, the result of statements made by Borg-Warner Chairman James Beré that the air conditioning industry required "restructuring."

"Mr. Beré said the industry is in need of restructuring, that there's an overcapacity right now — production capacity — in the industry. And if we felt the industry was trying to restructure, we would consider the possible sale, merger, or joint venture for the Air Conditioning Group as an option to contribute positively toward the restructuring within the entire industry. But it was not that we are on the brink of selling York."[21]

Independent Again

Nevertheless, a spin-off of the Air Conditioning Group was precisely what Borg-Warner had in mind. "They shopped the company in the early 1980s and seriously shopped it from 1982 to 1985, when the company really began to go downhill," said Robert Pokelwaldt, who would become chairman and CEO of York International. "I mean, it was getting a little threadbare." Pokelwaldt said Borg-Warner hampered York's ability to make money.

"Borg-Warner really hadn't spent a lot of time and effort nurturing the refrigeration and large component business. The Borg-Warner people let those traditional areas drift a bit because they were into transmissions, drives, that sort of thing."[22]

Elwood Spangler, who joined York in 1954 from the engineering training program, agreed that Borg-Warner did not manage the company properly.

"They never knew what they had. Borg-Warner just sent in one president after another, and none of them knew how to handle the company. It was a continual reorganization that never seemed to go anywhere. I don't think we ever had the proper direction."[23]

In July 1985, Borg-Warner announced it would launch an independent air conditioning company by distributing all of the shares of its air conditioning subsidiary on a tax-free basis to holders of its common stock. The plan called for the independent company to have a capital investment of $230 million, a debt of $60 million, and an equity base of approximately $170 million. According to the announcement, air conditioning sales were down to just 16 percent of Borg-Warner's business and accounted for just 2 percent of its profits.[24] The new company was expected to be owned by Borg-Warner's 43,000 shareholders.[25]

Robert Fisher, president of the Borg-Warner Air Conditioning Group, attempted to quiet the growing anxiety of York employees, who were nervous about facing stiff competition in a weakened market without Borg-Warner's financial support.

"While at first the possibility of being separated from Borg-Warner may seem a little frightening, it's important to look at how it could be a positive move. We would be a very large public company with a strong financial base. In fact, not taking our Australian or joint venture operations into consideration, we would rank among the Fortune 500 industrial companies."[26]

York supplied the steam-powered air conditioning system for the 2.2-million-square-foot Hartsfield Atlanta International Airport, which opened in 1980.

In September 1985, Borg-Warner's board of directors approved a plan to distribute the shares of the air conditioning subsidiary and announced that Stanley Hiller, Jr., a veteran of such corporate turn-arounds as G.W. Murphy Company and Bekins Company, would succeed Robert J.M. Fisher at the helm, as well as become chairman of York.[27]

A senior partner in the Hiller Investment Company of Menlo Park, California, Stanley Hiller, Jr. had founded Hiller Aircraft during the 1940s. The company merged with Fairchild Industries in 1960 to form Fairchild Hiller Company. By the time Hiller resigned as president in 1965, he had helped create one of the largest helicopter manufacturers in the world.

Hiller's interest in York was accidental. In a 1986 interview, he explained that he only became aware of the possibility of a York spin-off while pursuing other business matters with Borg-Warner.

"The value of a spin-off intrigued us, the added value versus the more common straight purchase approach. There are many messes with takeovers. One company acquires another, then infiltrates that company with its own people. We're totally differ-ent. We don't have a huge organization, and the spin-off concept fit that nicely."[28]

The constraints imposed by Borg-Warner's ownership were suddenly cast off in 1986. On April 9, the Air Conditioning Group of Borg-Warner Corporation ceased to exist, and York International became a publicly held corporation listed on the New York Stock Exchange. The Borg-Warner Corporation distributed one share of York International Corporation common stock for each 10 shares of Borg-Warner common stock.[29] York officials began looking for a new name for its international segment, which was also known as York International.

York's new president and chief operating offi-cer, Thomas J. Vincent, immediately set out to return York to the independent powerhouse it had once been. A specialist with 25 years of expe-rience in engineering corporate turnarounds, Vincent had served for 10 years as president and COO of four separate companies under the Baker International Corporation: Pacific Concrete and

Rock Company of Honolulu, Hawaii; Ramsey Engineering Company of St. Paul, Minnesota; Kobe, Inc., of Los Angeles, California; and Milchem, Inc., of Houston, Texas.[30]

Hiller also brought aboard Hiller Group asso-ciates James T. Dresher as chief financial officer and William J. McSherry as director of Planning and Programs. In other management changes, Richard C. Barnett of York was promoted to vice president and general manager of Central Environmental Systems, while Jack Walsh of York was promoted to vice president and general manager of Applied and Industrial Systems.

Following the spin-off, Vincent reported that York's first-year earnings were just 50 cents per share in 1986. By 1987, York's earnings had increased to $2.82 per share.[31] As lower interest rates spurred residential construction in the United States and the falling value of the dollar abroad revitalized foreign markets, York devoted a significant amount of attention to the interna-tional marketplace. International sales comprised roughly 87 percent of the increase in York's prof-its by early 1987.

The transition to independence was challeng-ing for many of York's managers and employees. "It was a period of the unknown," said Dennis Kloster. "From a kind of fat, dumb, happy and stable — to whatever degree things are stable — to something that was totally unknown. It left you with kind of an uneasy feeling."[32]

Hiller assured employees that "there is great opportunity for industries in change. ... Those who don't change in how they respond are in seri-ous trouble. That, to us, is opportunity."[33]

In the aftermath of the spin-off, Borg-Warner faced problems of its own as Minneapolis-based investor Irwin Jacobs, among the most cunning of corporate raiders, threatened a hostile takeover of Borg-Warner after acquiring 6.1 percent of its stock. According to industry analysts, the York spin-off was part of a larger Borg-Warner corporate restructuring effort aimed at recovering from a 13.4 percent decline in profits the previous year. The spin-off of York allowed Borg-Warner to finance a stock buyback program designed to fend off unwelcome takeover attempts, such as that by Jacobs.[34] In February 1987, Borg-Warner laid off more than a fifth of its corporate staff and reduced its research and development budget by a third in a desperate effort to foil Jacob's takeover attempt. By that date, Jacobs and his allies already held 12.4 percent of Borg-Warner's stock, while New Jersey-based GAF Corporation had acquired another 9.6 percent stake of Borg-Warner stock in an independent takeover attempt.[35]

New Products

With the shackles of a conglomerate thrown off, York began to turn out and market its products faster than its competitors. Bob Schmitt, marketing manager for the Applied Systems division, remembered the painstakingly slow product development process while under Borg-Warner.

"You'd wait maybe eight or nine months for a product to be approved by Borg-Warner, and then it would take three or four years of development before the product got to market. Nothing was in a hurry. Within a year of the spinoff, we could get a major product development approved in three to four weeks, maximum. With our headquarters here, we had everybody who could make a decision in one place."[36]

During this period, about 60 percent of York's sales were in the commercial sector, with the remaining 40 percent in the unitary products sector. York continued to market its products under the York, Luxaire and Fraser-Johnston brand names. The international segment of the company became known as York Air Conditioning and Refrigeration, Inc.[37] In 1986, York International introduced several new products, including an expanded line of Stellar 2000 9 SEER (Seasonal Energy Efficiency Ratio) air conditioning systems in the 3- to 5-ton capacity range. These were designed for new single family homes and light commercial applications. The introduction of the new line coincided with the introduction of a 10 SEER line of H1CF models intended to help homebuilders qualify for utility rebates.[38] York also introduced a line of Stellar 2000 high efficiency heat pumps with capacities ranging from 1.5 to five tons and SEERs of nine or higher. Equipped with the Yorkguard Control Module, an integrated control and diagnostic center, these units offered automatic defrosting, low voltage protection, a five-minute turn-on delay, a five-minute anti-recycle timer, system sensing and lockout protection, and a staged control for the supplemental heater to prevent operation of the blower when the heating element was not operating.[39]

York's new product lines were topped off during this period with the introduction of super-high efficiency upflow gas-fired furnaces. Available in capacities ranging from 57,000 to 115,000 BTU, these furnaces were equipped with a glass-coated primary heat exchanger, a secondary heat exchanger, and a forced-draft fan and motor to deliver maximum efficiency.[40] By the spring of 1987, these new product lines were followed by similar new lines of Luxaire and Fraser-Johnston heating and cooling systems offering 10 SEER efficiency.[41]

Back to Basics

By the conclusion of the 1986 fiscal year, Hiller's "back to basics" approach of concentrating on capital equipment, computers and

The patented Yorkguard Module regulated frost build-up by automatically causing the heat pump to defrost only as needed.

research paid off when York generated $8.2 million in profits, a considerable turnaround from 1985's loss of $1.2 million.[42] In the summer of 1987, York implemented an Employee Stock Purchase plan. The price of York stock was set by subtracting 15 percent from the $26.25 closing price of York International stock on July 31, 1987.[43]

A renewed focus on quality and efficiency became the new corporate mantra. February 24, 1987, marked the company's first "zero defects" day, held at the Madisonville, Kentucky, manufacturing plant. The zero-defects goal would soon catch on throughout the organization. "ZD Day is

the last phase of our new beginning in the pursuit of quality excellence," Materials Manager Terry Bowman commented in an employee newsletter. "ZD Day itself will be the day we go as a plant and announce to all who will listen that we intend to make quality number one. It is up to each one of us to build a chain of quality products that reaches all the way to our customers."[44]

In mid-1987, the only operation not showing a profit was Applied Systems, which dealt primarily with centrifugal and reciprocating chillers, as well as the compressors required for them. F.R. LePage, vice president of Manufacturing, announced that York would eliminate duplicated efforts by returning to a single-plant concept of management. Certain lines, including compressors and chillers, would no longer be regarded as separate operations. The reorganization allowed York to eliminate 39 salaried and 24 hourly jobs through a combination of layoffs and attrition.[45]

York International had 1,500 workers in York County. The company was the largest independent manufacturer of air conditioners in the United States, and one of the three largest manufacturers of heating, air conditioning, ventilating and refrigeration equipment. Its nine manufacturing plants around the world employed more than 7,500 workers.[46]

International and Domestic Expansion

York's independence from Borg-Warner Corporation led to an era of tremendous growth in international production and sales. While roughly 20 percent of York's business was composed of overseas sales in 1986, by the middle of the 1990s nearly 50 percent of York's business was in international sales. In 1987, York International expanded its presence in England by acquiring Industrial Cooling Equipment, Ltd., of Manchester, England, a company that had been designing and installing large refrigeration systems throughout northwest England since 1935 and had been a distributor for Borg-Warner

Quality is a top priority at all York facilities. Here, Valerie Fitzhugh carefully installs fan grills on central air conditioning units.

Air Conditioning since 1938. With annual sales of roughly $7 million, this firm was the fourth acquisition by York in the months immediately following its break from Borg-Warner.

York also acquired longtime rival Frick Company and Frick/Frigid Coil of nearby Waynesboro, Pennsylvania. Frick, founded in 1853, manufactures industrial refrigeration systems for the food and beverage industries, and cooling systems for the chemical and petrochemical industries. One of the company's recent innovations was a state-of-the-art screw compressor with microprocessor control, which maximized energy efficiency.

Milton Ward Garland, who was born in 1895 and had started working for Frick in 1920, joined York as part of the acquisition. The former chief engineer had earned dozens of patents for items related to refrigeration, including a completely automatic unit that made fragmented ice used by the poultry industry. Though Garland officially retired in 1967, he continued work as a consultant and trainer. At 101 years of age, as of this writing, Garland still works every morning and continues to win patents for his contributions to the science of refrigeration. "I just put one in the mail the other day," he said during a 1995 interview.[47]

Other important acquisitions included Bristol Compressors, a manufacturer of small compressors in Bristol, Virginia, and Lillard Corporation, a distributor of heating and air conditioning equipment having plants in California, Nevada and Oregon.[48] With annual sales of $100 million, Bristol Compressors employed approximately 800 people in the manufacture of air conditioning and refrigeration compressors.[49] Each of these acquisitions strengthened and consolidated York International's hold on the domestic and foreign air conditioning markets. Following up on this highly successful strategy, in November 1987, York International announced it would acquire full ownership of its joint ventures in Mexico. York purchased the joint interest

Above: Milton Ward Garland, now 101 years old, still goes to work every day and continues to submit patents for new refrigeration ideas.

Below: Bristol Compressors, acquired by York in 1987, won the U.S. Senate Productivity Award that year for being the most outstanding manufacturing company in the state of Virginia.

of the Ibursa, a private investment group, in York Aire of Monterrey, Mexico, and Recold, located near Durango, Mexico.[50]

The emphasis on international sales paid off in 1987 with an 87 percent increase in operating profits from markets located outside of North America.[51] By balancing domestic and foreign manufacturing capabilities, York maximized profits on all fronts. The new policy was first implemented when the Central Environmental Systems Group began producing mini-split air conditioning units for both the domestic and the foreign market. The acquisition of Bristol Compressors dramatically boosted foreign compressor sales. An agreement between Le Froid Industriel York, based in France, and Brown-Boveri York in Germany led to the purchase of a large number of screw compressors from York's new Frick subsidiary. Largely as a result of these initiatives, gross profits in 1987 soared to $213.8 million.[52]

But even with burgeoning sales, the company did not give marketing a high priority, recalled Chuck Russ, hired in 1987 as manager of Marketing Communications. "Not a lot of money was spent in that area," he said. "It was not considered a highly necessary area. ... My first impression was that it would be an uphill battle."[53]

Citicorp

In 1988, York International was acquired by Citicorp Venture Capital in a leveraged buyout that cost approximately $750 million.[54] A leveraged buyout is essentially a debt-financed acquisition in which the assets of the company being acquired are used as security for borrowed money. Such buyouts are often used by management to take over its own company by acquiring the outstanding stock.

CEO Robert Pokelwaldt noted that the stockholders "didn't fare too badly" as a result of the leveraged buyout.

"It was a classic example of taking equity out of a company that has built up over the years and giving it to the shareholders, letting the company take itself public again. There wasn't much to complain about in this particular case."[55]

Pokelwaldt came to York in 1988 to run the worldwide Applied Systems Division. He became CEO in 1991. In the aftermath of the leveraged buyout, York International and its holding company faced cash interest payments of $80 million per year and annual principal payments scheduled to escalate from $30 million in the first year to higher amounts in following years. The immediate and deferred debt payments totaled $790 million. As a consequence of the buyout, Stanley Hiller, Jr., ceased to be chairman of the board and was no longer associated with the company. He was succeeded by Michael R. Young. However, the net result of the dramatic transaction was to increase

York's market value from $115 million in 1986 to $750 million in 1988.[56]

Pokelwaldt bought back the airside business that had been made into an independent company a few years earlier. In 1988, York also acquired Tempmaster Industries of Kansas City, Missouri, said Joe Smith, vice president and general manager of the Air Products Group. Smith, who had been an engineer at General Motors and a factory manager for Harley Davidson, was hired by Pokelwaldt in 1993 as vice president in charge of special projects. He said the Tempmaster acquisition "was the start of the growth of the Airside Products business."[57]

In 1988, York posted sales of $1.2 billion, and by 1989 York's net sales had climbed to $1.4 billion.[57] The growth was partly due to a growing

market for replacement parts and service to the large number of residential and commercial air conditioning systems sold by the Applied Systems Division in previous years.

York introduced several new products during this period, including Sunline 2000 light commercial air conditioners employing Frick screw compressors, the only compressors available in these sizes in the U.S. market. The year 1989 also witnessed York's acquisition of RECO International, Inc., of San Antonio, Texas, for $21 million. RECO employed about 250 workers in the manufacture of industrial refrigeration systems used in the food and petrochemicals industries.[58]

In 1989, York began to reduce the massive debt incurred by becoming an independent company. In April, James T. Dresher took the reins as York International's new chairman, president, and COO, replacing Michael R. Young, who resigned after York made the transition from a publicly held to a private company.[59]

To help knock down its debt, York aggressively sought large foreign contracts. In September 1989, York announced a $17 million contract to build and design an air conditioning system for the Prophet's Mosque in Medina, Saudi Arabia. The oldest mosque in the world, the building can serve 250,000 worshipers at a time.

The $16 billion renovation project was the most expensive mosque renovation ever. When it was complete, the Prophet's Mosque had 59 gates, 10 minarets and 27 domes.[60] The air conditioning contract called for six multistage York centrifugal chillers, 24 direct air-cooled heat exchangers, and six refrigerant transfer units designed to generate a total of 20,500 tons of refrigeration capacity.[61]

Mark Bodell, principal engineer for York, remembered the project. He said the cooling plant is located about five or six miles from the mosque. "So they had some very large piping, maybe 48 to 60 inches in diameter, running tens of thousands of gallons of water that we cooled down to the mosque itself, through the fan cooling units to blow cold air down on the central area where all the Muslims would go to worship."[62]

To help land other large contracts, York held product exhibitions in Minsk, U.S.S.R., and Beijing in 1989. On the domestic front, York Snow, Inc., a division of Le Froid Industriel-York in France, was awarded contracts for snow-making systems at the Hunter Mountain Ski Bowl in New York and the Squaw Valley Ski Area in California. A lean and energized York International had found its footing.

As York International Corporation prepared to enter the last decade of the 20th century, its highest priorities were to further reduce its debt and free itself of its relationship with Citicorp Financial through a public stock offering. With unprecedented success overseas and a resurgent American economy, the goal was well within reach.

York air conditioning keeps 250,000 worshipers cool at the Prophet's Mosque in Medina, Saudi Arabia.

Products such as this 90 percent fuel-efficient Diamond-90 residential furnace keep York at the forefront of tomorrow's energy requirements.

CHAPTER FOURTEEN

PREPARING FOR THE 21ST CENTURY

1990-1997

"Build on the York International tradition of innovative technology to become the worldwide leader of environmentally responsive heating, ventilation, air conditioning and refrigeration systems designed to improve the quality of life."

— The York Mission, established in 1994[1]

SALT LAKE 2002

TM

TM © 1997 SLOC

THROUGHOUT THE 1990s, York International maintained its position as the largest corporation devoted solely to the manufacture of air conditioning, refrigeration, heating and ventilating equipment in the United States. By 1996, it had capped 10 years of double-digit growth, surging to a record $3.2 billion in sales. Selected for such prestigious commercial installations as the Kremlin, the British Houses of Parliament, the United States Capitol Complex and the World Trade Center, York had established the industry standard for reliability and quality engineering. York is a world leader, with manufacturing plants in the United Kingdom, France, Germany, Mexico and Australia, and joint ventures in Saudi Arabia, Egypt, Malaysia and Taiwan, as well as licensees and branch offices in more than 100 other countries.

The company closed its Madisonville, Kentucky, facility and moved its operations to a larger manufacturing site in Elyria, Ohio. The company's corporate restructuring was completed in 1991 with an initial public offering in October of 12.1 million shares. Another 5 million shares were offered in March 1992. Just before the company went public, Robert N. Pokelwaldt was promoted from chief operating officer to chief executive officer. Pokelwaldt had joined York in 1988, when he was put in charge of the Worldwide Applied Systems Division, and had become chief operating officer in 1990. Pokelwaldt had been chairman and CEO of the Frick Company from 1983 to 1988. He would become chairman of the board in 1992, following the retirement of Chairman James Dresher. Under Pokelwaldt's leadership, which includes an unwavering commitment to research and development, York has grown steadily throughout the world. This growth was in part fueled by a number of key acquisitions, which added new plants, trained personnel and expanded sales channels. York's strategy was to obtain specific assets which would ensure the company's growth.

Phasing out Pollutants

York opened the new decade with net sales of $1.45 billion and a net income of $12.8 million. In 1992, despite a soft economy, York posted sales of $1.94 billion and a net income of $50.9 million. The sales increase was fueled in part by growing worldwide concern over the depletion of the ozone layer. Millions of old refrigeration systems were fitted with new environmentally friend-

---

The provider of choice for the 2002 Winter Olympics in Salt Lake City, Utah, York has been a long supporter of the Olympics.

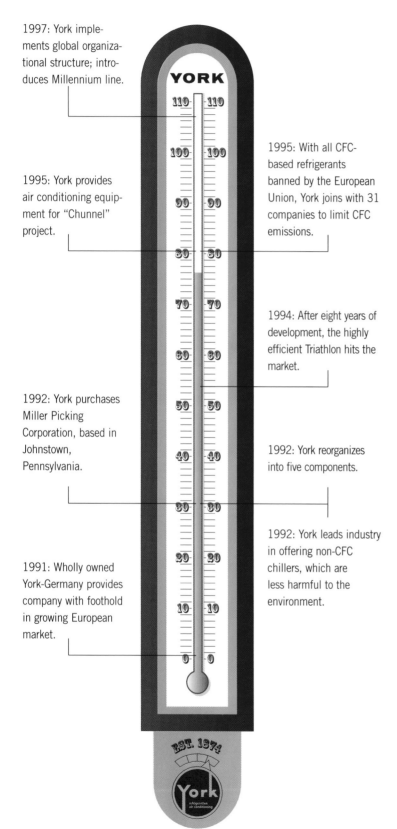

1997: York implements global organizational structure; introduces Millennium line.

1995: York provides air conditioning equipment for "Chunnel" project.

1992: York purchases Miller Picking Corporation, based in Johnstown, Pennsylvania.

1991: Wholly owned York-Germany provides company with foothold in growing European market.

1995: With all CFC-based refrigerants banned by the European Union, York joins with 31 companies to limit CFC emissions.

1994: After eight years of development, the highly efficient Triathlon hits the market.

1992: York reorganizes into five components.

1992: York leads industry in offering non-CFC chillers, which are less harmful to the environment.

ly refrigerants and components. Nestlé Foods Company was one of the first companies to transition away from chlorofluorocarbon-based refrigerants. With 440 factories and 360 industrial refrigeration systems worldwide, Nestlé vowed to replace CFC refrigerants in 70 percent of its plants by 1996. The Swiss-based company turned to York in 1992 to begin the process.[2]

York was able to switch to non-CFC refrigerants with few difficulties, said Bill Stewart, a systems analyst who has been with York since 1977.

"We have had a lot of experience in this field, and we know what has to be reviewed and what you have to deal with in using these different refrigerants. Because York didn't standardize as rigidly, we were able to make the necessary changes with ease. For example, we were familiar with one of the interim replacements, R-22, since the mid-1970s because it was more cost-effective. Changing to the newest non-CFC refrigerant posed some problems, but we still could make the changes easily."[3]

In 1992, York International offered the widest range of CFC-free chillers in the industry. HCFC-22 refrigerant was used in large Turbomaster centrifugal chillers, smaller CodePak centrifugal chillers, CodePak screw chillers, and RecipPak reciprocating chillers. Some of the Turbomasters were also using HFC-134a refrigerant. York's ParaFlow absorption systems utilized ordinary water as the refrigerant.[4]

By the end of 1994, all CFC-based refrigerants were officially banned by member countries of the European Union.[5] At the close of 1995, York International joined with 31 other companies worldwide in a cooperative effort to limit CFC emissions by adding high efficiency purge units to chillers that used older CFC refrigerants. These units were installed as the first part of a three-phase program aimed at reducing refrigerant emissions. Later phases of the program called for retrofitting and converting chillers to alternative types of refrigerants and replacing all older chillers in service. All of this activity was geared toward meeting the January 1, 1996 deadline for the phaseout of all CFC refrigerant production.[6]

Worldwide Growth through Acquisitions

In 1992, York acquired Miller Picking Corporation of Johnstown, Pennsylvania, a manufacturer of custom air handling equipment, as well as France-based Airchal Industries. Both companies designed customized systems specifically for customers' needs. To strengthen York's international business, the company acquired Email, Ltd., of Australia and New Zealand as an addition to its recent acquisition of Tempmaster-AustralAsia. This acquisition was followed in June by the purchase of Imeco, Inc., a subsidiary of Continental Materials Corporation. During 1993, York-Uruguay commenced production of commercial and industrial air conditioning equipment for sale in Argentina, Brazil, Paraguay, Uruguay, Chile and Bolivia.[7] Pokelwaldt said York chooses its acquisitions carefully.

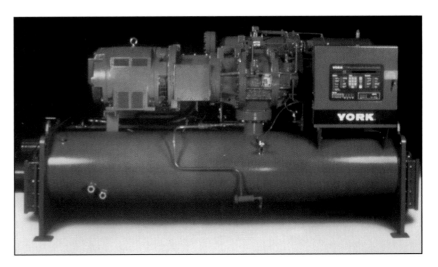

York adapted its Rotary Screw CodePak to use environmentally-friendly refrigerants, free of CFCs, in response to worldwide concern about ozone layer depletion.

"We take a slower approach than perhaps some other companies when it comes to squeezing the synergies out of an acquisition. The companies that we try to acquire are good companies with good management. We're not bottom-fishing for good companies. We want to buy them at a good price, but we want a good company. We don't tout ourselves as turnarounds. ... A good acquisition has to have not only a product synergy but other synergies as well. You might look at a company and say it fits York to a tee, but maybe there is no way to merge the two marketing forces without losing a great deal of distribution and user access. When that's the case, you might be better off passing it up and not spending money to lose market share. You really have to look at every market and every geography as an independent stand-alone company."[8]

For example, in 1997, York purchased assets of Pace Company, a Portland, Oregon-based manufacturer of air handling units, as well as its subsidiary, Pace-Gamewell, Inc., in Salisbury, North Carolina.

The additions provide York with 330,000 more feet of manufacturing space, a testing facility, as well as a strong presence with manufacturers of integrated circuits and a bigger foothold in the automotive industry.

"This acquisition is a good fit for York International," noted Airside Products Group President Joe Smith. "It provides new channels for the sale of both Pace and York products. In addition, we immediately benefit from added capacity, with a trained workforce."[9]

Pokelwaldt's ability to determine what company to buy based on the quality of its products has been one of the keys to York's continuing success overseas, noted Helen Marsteller, vice president of Investor Relations and Communications.

"A lot of the acquisitions you've seen us make from 1986 forward have been filling in the product line. You look around the world and the most complex and highly visible jobs belong to York. We expect our international presence to grow, and therefore we set a target for ourselves to achieve 50 percent of our revenue from abroad."[10]

Major domestic sales contracts in 1993 included an agreement from Apple Computer to purchase York systems for its new 32-acre research and development campus in Cupertino, California.

Valued at roughly $1.3 million to York, this contract included CodePak screw chillers ranging from 200 to 300 tons of capacity, as well as central air handlers and air volume diffusers. More interesting to Apple executives, however, was that York was the only company to offer an Apple Macintosh interface for its digital Facility Manager system, which controlled all the heating, cooling and lighting systems in Apple's new 856,000-square-foot complex.[11]

Increased Efficiency

In the nineties, York International took several important steps to increase competitiveness and responsiveness. In 1993, York reorganized itself into five components: Applied Systems Group, devoted to commercial air and environmental con-

trol systems; Unitary Products Group, which builds small air conditioning units; Refrigeration Group, comprising Frick and York Food Systems; Marine Refrigeration, for ships; and the Bristol Compressors Manufacturing Division.

The reorganization also meant a change in the company's basic Unitary Products Group manufacturing philosophy. York became a leader in adopting the Japanese concept of "Just in Time" manufacturing. Instead of building up a large inventory through an assembly line process, departments were set up to produce individual units from start to finish. This allowed York to react faster, keep lower inventories and build more frequently. The practice was more efficient because it allowed to company to produce only what it needed and created a more flexible atmosphere so setup time and waste were greatly reduced.[12]

During 1994, the product names of York, Miller Picking and Tempmaster were folded into York's Airside Products Group, which also introduced several products to address Indoor Air Quality (IAQ) and Indoor Environmental Quality (IEQ). These products were particularly popular with pharmaceutical and computer chip manufacturers, who required exceptional air quality.

One of the company's long-standing goals was to engineer air conditioners that improved indoor air quality. In addition, York's new Millennium line of commercial centrifugal chillers provided unprecedented levels of energy efficiency.[13]

Product Development

Under Pokelwaldt's leadership, York aggressively developed products for new markets. "Our product development efforts respond to and anticipate market needs," he said in a 1994 interview.

"All our people are looking for these kinds of opportunities. We make sure they are aware that the company has a management that is receptive

Combining technology from York and Apple Computer in 1992, Apple executive Glenn Barber (left) and York senior engineer Art Osaki created a cutting-edge R&D complex in Cupertino, California.

York's cooling technology is vital to products as diverse as delicate circuitry and frozen chickens.

to these kinds of opportunities, that it has a good strong balance sheet, and that it can fund programs, projects and acquisitions. ... In fact, ever since our company was spun off in 1986, we have increased our spending on capital programs and research and development. I think that indicates a strong dedication to products that are state-of-the-art in terms of efficiency, performance and quality."[14]

One result of this philosophy is the Triathlon, introduced in 1994 after eight years of development. The innovative heating and cooling system is powered by natural gas, which is considered more environmentally friendly and efficient than electricity. Instead of having a compressor inside of a heat pump that runs by electricity, as in a standard unit, the Triathlon unit has a gas-fired engine that drives the compressor.[15]

Developed in cooperation with the Gas Research Institute, Battelle Memorial Laboratories, Briggs & Stratton, Johnson Controls and other manufacturers, the highly efficient Triathlon rates an equivalent of 126 percent Annual Fuel Utilization Efficiency (AFUE), compared to around 90 percent AFUE for the most efficient gas furnaces. It can cut residential heating and cooling bills in half.

The product's high start-up costs prompted York to join forces with the natural gas industry to create the York Triathlon Consortium, brought together under the auspices of the American Gas Cooling Center, which is working to make the new product a success. York is cooperating with gas utility companies to market and distribute the Triathlon.

The Triathlon's introduction generated considerable publicity. "The company is committing sig-

Triathlon™

nificant resources to make the innovative product a success," *Appliance* magazine commented.

> *"This is a high-profile introduction, with considerable interest in the HVAC industry, the natural gas industry and even among the consumer press. A successful product introduction will not only open a new market for York, but will help build its image as a technological leader."[16]*

York executives agree that the carefully orchestrated introduction has paid off. "It's working out great," National Service Manager Bob Napp said in 1995. "It has given us a new niche with the gas utilities."[17]

Dennis Kloster, vice president of marketing for the Unitary Products Group, said the Triathlon "offered us an opportunity to do a number of things we could never have done without it."

> *"The promotional value was great in a number of ways. It helped affiliate us with the gas industry, both on a national and on a local basis, and those relationships can be tremendously helpful in the long run. Secondly, it gave us a promotional push. We could go out in the consumer marketplace as well as the dealer marketplace and say we have something new, something that nobody else has, and here are the benefits of that."[18]*

In 1995, York International was recognized by the U.S. Environmental Protection Agency as a Charter Partner in the agency's Energy Star Program. At a national conference held in April, the EPA lauded York as the only major manufacturer offering high-efficiency air conditioning and refrigeration equipment.[19]

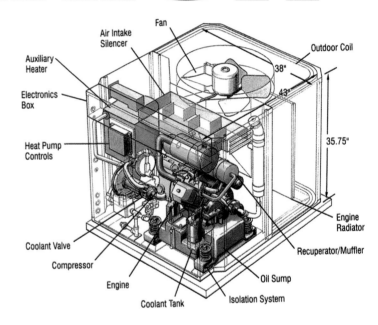

The result of a joint effort with Briggs & Stratton and other companies, York's Triathlon can cut residential heating and cooling bills in half.

A Strategy of Strength

With the Borg-Warner merger and subsequent spinoff still fresh in memory, York management took several steps to protect the company from future takeover attempts. The issue of preferred stock was limited to one vote per share, and York sought the protection of a Delaware corporation law that removed voting privileges from any potential purchasers for three years unless they took 85 percent of the shares in a single purchase. This measure was the result of York's experience in 1990, when 70 percent of the company was owned by Citicorp Investments, Inc., and 30 percent by the Prudential Insurance Company of America.[20]

York International also began acquiring smaller firms as part of an aggressive strategy to consolidate its hold on the heating and air conditioning market at home and abroad. In February 1995, the company announced that it would purchase Evcon Industries of Wichita, Kansas, for $133 million. The acquisition increased York's share of the residential market by 50 percent and dramatically increased its share of the burgeoning manufactured housing market. Employing more than 900 workers, Evcon manufactured air conditioning and heat pump systems, residential furnaces and air handlers under the brand names Coleman Evcon, Airpro and Red T.[21]

Around the same time, York acquired a 50 percent interest in Clima Roca, the residential and commercial air conditioning division of Compania Roca Radiadores of Sabadell, Spain. York also acquired 100 percent of Seveso, an air conditioning manufacturer in Italy.

In May 1995, Virginia-based York subsidiary Bristol Compressor formed a joint venture called Scroll Technologies with Connecticut-based Carrier Corporation. Scroll Technologies operated Carrier's 500-person Carlyle Division, a 342,000-square-foot compressor plant located in Arkadelphia, Arkansas. By combining Bristol's expertise in manufacturing compressors with Carlyle's expertise in manufacturing scroll-type compressors for both home and commercial air conditioning, York increased the volume and reduced the unit cost of manufacturing compressors.[22]

That June, York's Frick Division announced the purchase of two divisions of Gram A/S: Gram Refrigeration and Gram Contractors, which manufacture and install refrigeration systems in Denmark. In July, York acquired a 67 percent interest in the Aeromaster International Division of Aeromaster Industries Company, Ltd., an air conditioning manufacturer in Bangkok, Thailand.[23]

York strengthened its position in the domestic market when its Frick Division purchased Rite Coil, manufacturer of high-quality stainless steel and galvanized steel evaporators and cooling coils.[24] Washington-based subsidiary York Food Systems purchased Northfield Freezing Systems,

a manufacturer of spiral conveyor coolers, freezers, proofers, and dehydrators.[25]

The company reorganized several of these subsidiaries into a single business unit in 1997, placing Gram Refrigeration, Imeco, Frick Refrigeration and Northfield Freezing Systems under the Refrigeration Products Group, with William G. Cowles, Jr. as worldwide president.

In addition to these acquisitions, York constructed a $6 million performance testing facility at its Grantley manufacturing site. The 21,200-square-foot facility will test chillers for energy efficiency and noise reduction. Approved by the Air Conditioning and Refrigeration Institute, it is the most advanced testing facility for large-tonnage chillers the industry.

Saving the Seawolf

When the Navy's Seawolf submarine program, for which York supplied refrigeration and air conditioning systems, was threatened by Congressional budget cutters in 1995, York Vice President and General Manager James A. Bledsoe and Local 1872 UAW President Marlo A. Palmieri worked together to defend the program. In one letter to a York, Pennsylvania, newspaper, Bledsoe stressed the importance of the submarines.

"With more than 158 suppliers that bring in more than $133,667,000 in business to the state's economy, there is a high stake at risk. The stakes are also high for our country. The Seawolf submarine will allow the United States to regain the undersea tactical advantage over the Russians and their quieter Akula class submarine. This is about national security, economic stability, and providing American taxpayers with the most technologically advanced submarine in the world. If the Seawolf does not reach fruition, the public will have paid more than $1 billion in return for absolutely nothing. That just does not make sound business sense."[26]

A letter from Palmieri appeared on the same page.

"Some claim that killing the third Seawolf will save money. The federal government already has

Travelers using the recently-completed English Channel Tunnel, linking Great Britain and France by way of underground railroad (above), are cooled by York air conditioning systems (left).

spent $900 million and can complete the world's most technologically advanced submarine for the same price it will cost to shut the project down. ... The issue is not political pork. It is, however, about maintaining our nation's vital defense industrial base. In the state of Pennsylvania, more than 215 companies and unions contribute to the nation's nuclear submarine industry, generating $133.6 million in revenue for the state. Killing the third Seawolf will force workers with unique submarine construction skills to find other employment."[27]

Recognized internationally for its marine legacy, York currently supplies air conditioning units for the British and French submarine fleets as well. York also air conditions 75 percent of the U.S. Navy's surface fleet.

York enjoyed generally good relations between management and its union. Union membership shrank significantly between 1980 and 1995, partly because of corporate cutbacks and a decline in the number of manufacturing jobs. In 1980, the company employed 2,200 UAW members and 1,800 salaried workers. In 1995, the union membership had shrunk 63 percent to 800 members, and the salaried workforce had dropped 55.5 percent to 800.

York has always been considered a good place to work. "What I generally tell people is that York has been a great place for me over the last 22 years," said Terry Bowman, director of purchasing for the Unitary Products Group. "I've always been able to prosper, and my attitude has always been that I'm going to do my best job and give the company all the loyalty I can give them."[28]

John McDonald, who had been with York since 1968, grew up with the company since both his parents worked at York. McDonald occupied what he described as a high-stress position as a trouble-shooter, responsible for finding solutions to service-related problems with customers.

"There are times I'm just totally drained and frustrated and ask why I'm doing this to myself, but I'm still here. I love it. It's a continuous challenge. And people are recognized. Years ago, I was just a number down in the factory."[29]

Engineers and other employees agree that York's commitment to providing superior customer service makes their jobs more gratifying. Chuck O'Neal, a sales engineer who joined York in 1968 after graduating from New Mexico State University, said maintaining York International's reputation for doing the right thing is one of the most enjoyable aspects of his job.

"I've been involved in a number of projects in which, many years after the product's warranty was over, somebody determined that York was, in some way, responsible for a failure. Every time, York has stepped up to the plate and made it right. I remember one time in the late seventies, in Dallas, when York spent between $400,000 and $500,000 to correct a mistake. Several years after a unit had been installed, it was discovered that a wrong component had been used. York removed the old component, manufactured a new one, and installed it. York paid for all of that to make it right for the customer."[30]

In 1995, York International sales reached a record $2.93 billion, representing a 21 percent increase over 1994. This increase pushed profits up 23.7 percent, to $629.4 million. All three product groups posted sales gains, with residential units up 20 percent, refrigeration up 35 percent and commercial products up 16 percent. Dennis Kloster, vice president of Marketing, North America, for the Unitary Products Group, noted that residential units are rarely customized. "It's more like, you spit them out like popcorn, and you just sell standard products."[31]

The Refrigeration Group's strong performance was largely due to industry-wide capacity expansion as well as the sale of redesigned non-CFC refrigerant chillers for retrofitting Navy ships and submarines. International sales of commercial equipment were up 21 percent, while domestic commercial sales increased 12 percent.

By the end of 1995, York neared its long-sought goal of certification for all facilities under the tough quality control requirements established by the International Standards Organization (ISO).[32] York's reputation for engineering excellence helped it win a lucrative contract to provide air conditioning for the English Channel Tunnel, often referred to as the "Chunnel."

Air-Conditioning the World

York enjoyed its position as the largest independent air-conditioning company in the world. While the company faced stiff competition for residential sales from Trane and Carrier, the two companies with comparable product lines, York remained a leader in commercial markets. It provided HVAC systems for the world's tallest buildings, including the Empire State Building, the World Trade Center, the Sears Tower and the new Kuala Lumpur City Centre in Malaysia, which was not only the tallest twin tower building in the world but also the largest office and retail complex in all of Asia. Air-conditioning this enormous building required six 5,000-ton Turbomaster centrifugal chillers with a combined capacity of 30,000 tons of refrigeration.[33]

Bob Pokelwaldt noted that York's growing international presence called for a new way of thinking about the world.

Six huge Turbomaster chillers were required to air-condition the new Kuala Lumpur City Centre, the tallest building in the world.

"There's been a real deliberate move towards looking at the global aspects of the business, even to the point that we recently announced we will have global product managers rather than there being separate little companies of York all over the world."[34]

With this system, products were produced to the needs of the particular market, regardless of geographic destination. For example, the United States is a 60-hertz market but since most of the world operates on 50 hertz, the product design must be global. At the same time, products must be built to the code specifications maintained by individual nations.

Peter Spellar, president of Applied Systems Worldwide, believes that adding environmental conservation is an important global concern.

"We need to listen to the rest of the world about what the product needs are, what the key is to the future of energy conservation and the future and direction of refrigerants. There is a whole world out there that has the same view as we do but with different product needs and requirements. To get the results, because of energy requirements and environmental requirements, they have a different appearance and have a different cost structure. People need to understand that, because there will be a time when more than 50 percent of our business for York International Corporation will be outside of North America."[35]

As the company grew, new environmentally friendly products continued to emerge. In 1996, York's Unitary Products Group announced plans to market new residential and Sunline rooftop air conditioners with new R-410A refrigerant to replace the R-22. In addition to being non-ozone-depleting, the R-410A promises to increase operating efficiencies 10 percent over R-407c and R-134a, two refrigerants with which York has experimented.[36]

"One of the company's most popular air conditioners is the standard 10-SEER condensing unit," Kloster said. It is also one of the most inexpensive systems on the market.

"The federal government has legislated minimum efficiency levels, and 10 SEER is as low

as you can go. We try to make it easier to install and service. A high percentage of the time, the brand is going to be determined by the servicing dealer at the site. He's going to say, 'Well, your air conditioner died, and it's not worth fixing.' The homeowner is going to say, 'I trust you. What do you recommend?' If we make our units easier to install, easier to troubleshoot and easier to service, he's going to lean toward York over another brand."[37]

A Pivotal Year

In the annual letter to stockholders, Pokelwaldt noted that 1996 "was a pivotal year for York International" in terms of successes and challenges. York launched an initiative to increase its return to stockholders after the company grew from $690 million in business in 1986 to $3.2 billion in 1996. "This initiative, which we call Total Stockholder Return, builds on the strength we have achieved through this last decade of growth," Pokelwaldt explained.[38]

Growth on a global basis, with the exception of Germany and France, continued. To streamline costs, improvements on engineered systems began in 1996. By April 1997, York was able to consolidate chiller production in the Grantley Plant, allowing it to close its facility in Houston, Texas.

Olympic Caliber

When the world's attention turned to the 1996 Olympic Games in Atlanta, newscasters broadcasted stories about the Georgia city's wilting, humid heat. Temperatures in the weeks between July 19 and August 4 climbed into the 90s on some days, with humidity spiraling up into the high 80th percentiles. Water became an expensive commodity for the sweating crowds.

But when those crowds entered a games venue, the AT&T Global Olympic Village or the Centennial Olympic Stadium, a refreshing blast of chilled York air greeted them. York International, the preferred HVAC&R provider, poured a tremendous amount of resources into the 1996 Olympics. More than 44,000 tons of cooling were provided — more than what the Pentagon uses, and enough to cool 22,000 homes in the Atlanta metropolitan area.[39]

Mike Ricci, director of Olympic and Sports Marketing, remembered the incredible effort York put into the Atlanta Summer Olympics.

"Most people would likely assume this was a pretty straightforward challenge. Air conditioning is a science that is all too often taken for granted. There is the perception that unless it's a technology related field, it must not be too difficult. This couldn't be further from the truth. During the course of the Games, York and its partners deployed thousands of pieces of equipment throughout all of the Olympic venues. We also installed our equipment at the many of the technical nerve centers of the Games, including the International Broadcast Center. Our job was to keep things cool so competitions were staged without incident and the television feed was transmitted to the world without interruption. We had one of the most technically daunting challenges that faced any supplier associated with these Games. And unlike some of the technology suppliers who were crucified in the media for failures, we operated flawlessly and without incident."[40]

Many of the air distribution systems developed for the Olympics were custom-made for the event by the Airside Products Division. "Virtually each and every one of them is designed specifically for an application," noted Joseph Smith, vice president and general manager of the Airside Products Division.[41]

By the time the Atlanta Games took place, York had 35 years of Olympic experience. The company's first exposure to the international event was the 1960 Olympics at the Squaw Valley Winter Games, where York provided cooling all the skating venues.

With each subsequent Olympics, York's involvement grew: at the 1968 Mexico City Summer Games, York provided air conditioning for indoor venues; at the 1992 Albertville, France Winter Olympics, York was responsible for making all the artificial snow and refrigeration for the skating venues; in the 1992 Summer Olympics in Barcelona, Spain, York provided air conditioning equipment for every indoor venue; and the company installed refrigeration systems for the luge and bobsled runs, as well as all the ice

skating rinks at the 1994 Winter Games in Lillehammer, Norway. In each of these instances, York equipment was selected and purchased by the Olympic organizing committee.

York's involvement in the Olympics makes good business sense, but it also comes with an deep belief in the spirit of the games. York has established a history of Olympic sponsorship by backing teams from around the world, including teams from Puerto Rico, Australia, Canada and Britain. The company has also sponsored athletes including Bonnie Blair, winner of five gold medals and named in 1994 as *Sport's Illustrated* Sportswoman of the Year.

One particularly interesting story relates to the U.S. Luge Team. "We got involved with the U.S. Luge Team back in the late 1980s," Ricci remembered.

"In the case of the U.S. Luge Association, they came to us back in the late 1980s and, at the time, they believed strongly that the only thing separating them from becoming one of the world powers in this sport was a dedicated training

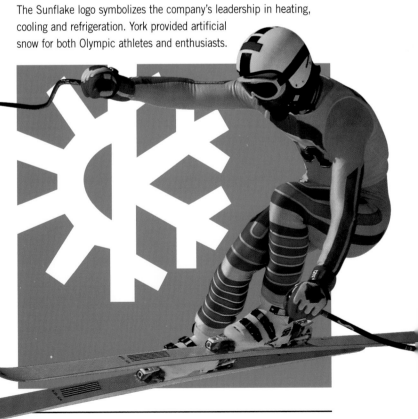

The Sunflake logo symbolizes the company's leadership in heating, cooling and refrigeration. York provided artificial snow for both Olympic athletes and enthusiasts.

United States   Canada   Australia   Puerto Rico   Great Britain

facility. Given our track record in building bob and luge tracks, they asked us whether we would consider applying our technology and expertise to this exciting athlete development project. If we are going to become involved, we generally wish to find an opportunity where our equipment and technical expertise can make an important difference to given federation's athlete development programs. Now, the U.S. Luge Team is recognized as one of the preeminent world powers in the sport of the luge and our athletes are routinely medaling in World Cup competition and positioned to finally bring home Olympic medals for the first time. This wouldn't have been possible had it not been for the involvement of many talented people in the York/Frick organization."[42]

Through its sponsorships and its unblemished record of success, York has turned the Olympics into a profitable business tool. The company has already been chosen as the provider of choice for the 2002 Winter Olympics and will also provide cooling for the 2000 Summer Olympics in Sydney, Australia. York will not fail, Ricci said.

"Within the Olympic world, it's fairly well established that failure isn't an option. Each organizing committee has but one opportunity to stage these Games and they can't afford to fall on their face on such a large and visible stage. With this in mind, our unblemished track record of helping to build venues and stage events for the past 35 years is something that makes us an extremely attractive partner for any potential Games organizer. That's one of the many reasons we have been so successful in making this an important business focus for the York organization. York has chosen to become involved because it's a significant area of

business opportunity and it's also an arena that we have clearly established ourselves as the undisputed leaders in."[43]

The company's exposure to Olympic-sized challenges, aside from being profitable in itself, has led to York's involvement with a number of the nation's largest sporting venues, including the United Center in Chicago, Turner Field in Atlanta, Georgia, and the BancOne Ballpark in Phoenix, Arizona. For all of its effort and success, the company was recognized in 1996 as the world's leading "business to business" sports marketing organizations by *Sports Marketing Letter*, a business periodical.[44]

The acquisition of Snomax Technologies in 1997 enhanced York's ability to help Olympians prepare for the winter games. Based in Rochester, New York, Snomax was owned by Genencor International, Inc. The Snomax subsidiary improves snowmaking performance by reducing production costs, lowering energy consumption and improving the quality of machine-made snow.

Looking to the Future

As the turn of the century approaches, York International recognizes that the world is getting smaller every day. The distinction between domestic and international business continues to blur, as about 46 percent of York's sales and projects occur in other nations. By 2000, more than 50 percent of York's business is expected to take place outside the United States, noted Peter Spellar.

"People are saying that by the year 2005, China will be the world's third-largest air con-

ditioning market, after the United States and Japan. Whether it's 2005 or 2010, it will become a huge market, and we will have to be inside the market."[45]

In March 1997, York launched several joint ventures in China to produce a wide range of HVAC&R equipment. Under the agreements, York is manufacturing fan coils, air-handling units and water-cooled, reciprocating packaged units in a Guangzhou plant. York has also taken an 80 percent interest in a joint-venture agreement with Tailian Refrigeration Equipment Installation & Maintenance Co. Tailian is the original manufacturer of York's current line of fan-cooled units.

Meanwhile, a York plant in Wuxi, near Shanghai, will produce large centrifugal and absorption chillers. Most of the products will be sold within China.

As York International continues to grow in far-flung places around the world, the future is bright, Pokelwaldt predicts.

"When I look at the opportunities, combined with our dedication to this industry, the fact is that we are a financially strong company and have a global presence. I think we are very well poised for future growth."[46]

Even as it becomes increasingly global, the company remains intimately intertwined with the city and county of York, Pennsylvania, continuing to set standards for the industry. The York creed, established during the last century, remains true for the next: "In every industry the products of one manufacturer stand out as the standard because of certain built-in qualities of excellence that defy competition. Thus it must always be with York products."

NOTES TO SOURCES

Chapter One

1. York Manufacturing Company 1884 Products Catalog, p. 46.
2. George R. Sheets, "Made in York," *A Survey of the Agricultural & Industrial Heritage of York County, Pennsylvania,* (Agricultural & Industrial Museum of York County: York, Pennsylvania, 1991) pp. 12-13.
3. John Gibson, *History of York County, Pennsylvania,* 1886, p. 46.
4. General John B. Gordon, *Reminiscences of the Civil War,* (Charles Scribner and Sons: New York, NY, 1903).
5. *Ibid.*
6. "Made In York," pp. 91-93.
7. George R. Prowell, *History of York County Pennsylvania Vol. II,* (Chicago: H.H. Beers & Co., 1907) pp. 759-760.
8. Richard Edwards, *Industries of Pennsylvania,* (1881).
9. Beauchamp E. Smith, "S. Morgan Smith and the Hydro-Electric Industry," *Newcomen Bulletin For North America,* Vol. 30, No. 7, (April 1952) p. 13.
10. F. O. Metz, an officer of York Manufacturing Company hired in 1898. His written comments on the company's history were recorded in 1934 on a document filed in the archives of York International Corporation, Inc.
11. *Ibid.,* p. 9.
12. John Gibson, *History of York County Pennsylvania,* (1886) pp. 8-9.
13. Richard Edwards, *Industries of Pennsylvania,* (1881) pp. 104 - 105.
14. F.O. Metz, information written in 1934 on a brief history of the York Manufacturing Company.
15. *Ibid.,* p. 9.
16. *Ibid.,* p. 15.
17. Richard Edwards, *Industries of Pennsylvania,* (1881) pp. 104-105.
18. Beach Nichols, *Atlas of York County, Pennsylvania, Illustrated* (Pomeroy, Whitman & Company, Philadelphia, PA, 1876).
19. York Manufacturing Company account ledger, 1873-1879, handwritten by Stephen Morgan Smith and archived in the York County Historical Society Library.
20. *Ibid.,* May, 1873 to June 1880.
21. *Ibid.,* 1871 to 1878, filed in the archive library of the York Historical Society.
22. Beauchamp E. Smith, *S. Morgan Smith and the Hydro-Electric Industry:* pp. 13-16.
23. John A. Garraty, *The American Nation since 1865,* (Harper & Row Publishers, New York, 1965) p. 132.
24. Illustrated Catalog of machinery produced by the York Manufacturing Company, 1884.
25. John Gibson, *The History of York County, Pennsylvania* (1886), p. 120.
26. Notes from an interview with George Motter, dated 1934, York International Corporation Archives.
27. SC Frey, *The York Legal Record,* (Vol. III, York, PA, 1883) pp. 37-46.
28. *The Industrial Record:* 1909 (printed material of the York Historical Society).
29. Bernard D. Oldham, *The History of Refrigeration* and *The Journal of Refrigeration,* (January 1966, England) p. 22.
30. York Manufacturing Company 1884 Product Catalogue pp. 9-15.
31. *Ibid.,* pp. 36, 19.
32. *Ibid.,* pp. 36, 20-23.
33. Walter Spahr Ehrenfeld, *York's Factory Whistles,* (1940) pp. 7-8.
34. Willis R. Woolrich, "The History of Refrigeration; 220 Years of Mechanical and Chemical Cold," *ASHRAE Journal,* (July, 1969), p. 34.
35. *Ibid.,* pp. 41, 36.
36. "The Early Days of Refrigeration," written by the staff of an English weekly journal, *Air Conditioning, Heating & Refrigeration News* (Sept. 20, 1976).
37. *Ibid.,* p. 43.
38. York Manufacturing Company 1884 Product Catalogue, "The Jarman" Ice and Refrigerating Machinery.
39. *Ibid.,* p. 46.
40. *Ibid.*
41. *Ibid.*
42. York Manufacturing Company Record of Refrigerating Machines and Air Compressors, (1885) York International Corporation Archives, York, Pa.

Chapter Two

1. York Manufacturing Company, 1892 Product Catalogue, pp. 5-7.
2. Sanborn Map & Publishing Company, Ltd. *Insurance Map of York Pennsylvania* (New York: 1887) p. 22.
3. John Gibson, *History of York County Pennsylvania* (1886) p. 31.
4. York Manufacturing Company, Record of sales from 1885 to 1917, published in the company's *Weekly Record* (Vol. 8, No. 34, 1917) p. 195.
5. York Manufacturing Company, Ltd., Product Catalogue, estimated date of 1886, pp. 6-7.
6. George R. Prowell, *History of York County, Pa,* (Vol. II, J.H. Beers & Co., Chicago: 1907) p. 646.
7. Frick Company booklet, *Celebrating a Century of Engineering Service,* (1952) p. 15.
8. Cash Book for the York Manufacturing Company, 1889-1892, filed in the archives of the PH Glatfelter Company, Spring Grove, Pa.
9. George R. Prowell, *History of York County, Pennsylvania* (Vol.III, J.H. Beers & Co; Chicago: 1907).
10. Armand Glatfelter, *The Flowering of the Codorus Palatinate,* (North Codorus Township Sesquicentennial Commission) p. 282.
11. George R. Prowell, *History of York County, Pennsylvania* (Vol.

III, J.H. Beers & Co.,Chicago: 1907) pp. 219-220.

12. J. Bradley Markward, D.D., board president of the American Missions of the United Lutheran Church in America. His speech given at the funeral of William L. Glatfelter, April 23, 1930. Archives of the P.H. Glatfelter Company, Spring Grove, Pa.

13. *Ibid.*, pp. 7, 282.

14. F.O. Metz, notes from an interview conducted in 1944, filed in the York International Corporation Archives.

15. *Ibid.*, p. 13.

16. York Manufacturing Company, Ltd., 1892 Product Catalogue, pp. 5-7.

17. *Ibid.*, p. 20.

18. *Ibid.*, pp. 10, 21.

19. *Ibid.*

20. *Ibid.*, p. 95.

21. Cash Book, York Manufacturing Company, (1891-92). Filed in the archives of the PH Glatfelter Company, Spring Grove, Pa.

22. Fredrick B. Roe, *Atlas of the City of York*, from railway and recent surveys by the author (1903).

23. S.C. Frey, York Legal Record, Vol. XI, No. 12 (1897).

24. *Ibid.*, Vol. VIII (1895).

25. York Manufacturing Company, 1895 Product Catalogue. Filed in the York International Company. Archives, York, Pa.

26. Thomas Shipley, "Twenty Years Ago," a speech delivered to the American Society of Refrigerating Engineers in New York, 1924. Filed in the York International Corporation Archives.

Chapter Three

1. Louis Morse, notes on his memories of working for Thomas Shipley as a student engineer. Filed in the York International Corporation archives.

2. George Prowell, *History of York County Pennsylvania* (Vol. II, J.H. Beers & Company, Chicago: 1907) pp. 911- 912.

3. The York Manufacturing Company Accounting Records for 1896. Filed in the archives of York International Corporation, York, Pa.

4. Ledger of Accounts for 1897. Filed in the Archives of York International Corporation, Inc.

5. Thomas Shipley, "Twenty Years Ago," a speech given before the American Society of Refrigerating Engineers at their 20th anniversary meeting, Dec. 2, 1924, at the Hotel Astor in New York. The printed speech is filed in the archives of the York International Corporation, York, Pa.

6. *Ibid.*, pp. 3, 8.

7. The York Manufacturing Company Catalogue of Products, 1901. Filed in the archives at York International Corporation, York, Pa.

8. *Ibid.*

9. *Ibid.*, p. 13.

10. Louis Morse, notes written on the history of the York Manufacturing Company, 1934. Unpublished. Filed in the archives of the York International Corporation, York, Pa.

11. Louis Morse, notes written on the history of the York Manufacturing Company, 1934. The unpublished material is filed in the archives of the York International Corporation, York, Pa.

12. The York Manufacturing Company Catalogue of Products, 1917.

13. The York Manufacturing Company Records of sales and shipment, 1874-1900. Filed in the York International Corporation archives.

14. The York Manufacturing Company Record of Accounts, 1897-1900.

15. The York Legal Record, (August 1, 1901, Vol. 15) pp. 33-35.

16. Court of Common Pleas of York County, Pa. records, "Sitting in Equity between the York Manufacturing Company and Charles Oberdick, et. al." (August 1901) pp. 3-11.

17. York Legal Record, (July 1901, Vol. 15, No. 8) p. 30.

18. *Ibid.*, pp. 32, 36.

19. *Ibid.*, pp. 31, 32.

20. Court of Common Pleas of York County, Pennsylvania. "Sitting in Equity between the York Manufacturing Company and Charles Oberdick, et. al." (August 1901) pp. 3-11.

21. York Legal Record, (Vol. 15, No. 39. Feb. 27, 1902) p. 153.

22. Barry Donaldson and Bern Nagengast, "The Growth of Mechanical Heating and Cooling," *ASHRAE Journal*, September 1994.

23. Thomas Shipley, Unpublished notes taken on the meeting. Filed in the archives at York International Corporation, York, Pa.

24. *Ibid.* p. 36

25. Barry Donaldson and Bern Nagengast, "The Growth of Mechanical Heating and Cooling," *ASHRAE Journal*, September 1994.

26. The York Manufacturing Company, Vertical Single-acting Ice and Refrigerating Machines, 1905 company pamphlet.

Chapter Four

1. 1907 Stockholders' Resolution.

2. York Manufacturing Company, Apprentice Book. Unpublished record of men enrolled as apprentices in the company from 1902-1913, York International Corporation archives, York, Pa.

3. York Manufacturing Company Bulletin No. 28, 1906.

4. York Manufacturing Company Record of Sales, 1906.

5. York Manufacturing Company, Ammonia Fittings & Supplies, Fitting Catalogue, second edition, 1906.

6. Tom Shipley, notes on speech given on mechanical refrigeration, undated.

7. H.C. Stuckenbruck, "How Ice Is Made," *Cipsco News*, August 1923.

8. York Manufacturing Company pamphlet, *A Comparison of Ammonia Compressors*, (Bartlet & Company, Orr Press, New York: 1906).

9. York Manufacturing Company, unpublished booklet of reference letters, 1904-1911, York International Corporation archives, York, Pa.

10. George R. Prowell, *History of York County, Pennsylvania*, Volume II, (HH Beers & Company, Chicago: 1907) pp. 912-913.
11. *Ibid.*, p. 9.
12. Edgar A. Altland, *Three Generations of the Glatfelter Family As I Knew Them*, Privately printed, 1948, pp. 2-4.
13. Armand Glatfelter, *The Flowering of the Codorus Palatinate*, privately published, York, Pa.
14. *Ibid.*, p. 12
15. *The York Dispatch*, staff writers, York, Pa., 1918.
16. W.S. Stair, *The York Corporation*, unpublished history booklet.
17. *Ibid.*, p. 16.
18. York Manufacturing Company Bulletin No. 27, sales material published by the company, October 1907.
19. De La Vergne Refrigerating and Ice Making Machinery, 1908 product catalog of the De La Vergne Machine Company, New York.
20. Bernard C. Oldham, "The History of Refrigeration," *Journal of Refrigeration,* (London: 1966) p. 266.
21. W.S. Stair, *The York Organization,* published by York Corporation, 1942.
22. Charles E. Lucke, "Competitive Test," *Ice and Refrigeration Journal*, July 1908.
23. Willis R. Woolrich, "The History of Refrigeration: 220 Years of Mechanical and Chemical Cold," *ASHRAE Journal*, July 1969.
24. York Manufacturing Company Bulletin No, 43, March 1910.
25. G. Drouve, "Machine and Boiler Shops of Improved Construction," *The Iron Age* (Bridgeport, Connecticut, January 19, 1911.)
26. Thomas Shipley, York Manufacturing Company Bulletin No. 27, May 1911.
27. Ron Rose, unpublished historic notes on the Canadian Ice machine Company, 1911-1969, Ontario, Canada.
28. Earl W. Gardner, unpublished Publicity Department minutes, 1897-1922.

29. George A. Goodling, Congressional Record Vol. 120, No. 31, House of Representatives, Washington D.C., March 11, 1974.

Chapter Five

1. "Will the New Year Be A Good One?" York Semi-Monthly Letter 15 (January 1, 1927), pp. 149-150. Filed in York International Corporation archives.
2. York Manufacturing Company, Bulletin No. 27, January 1913. Filed in York International Corporation archives.
3. York Manufacturing Company, unpublished notes on the company's history written, 1954. Author unknown. Filed in York International Corporation archives.
4. York Manufacturing Company, Weekly Letter, August 14, 1915. Filed in York International Corporation archives.
5. York Manufacturing Company, Weekly Letter, Vol. 5, No. 22, July 28, 1917. Filed in York International Corporation archives.
6. York Manufacturing Company, "Weekly Letter, Vol. 6, No. 1, March, 1918, York, Pa. Filed in York International Corporation archives.
7. York Manufacturing Company, "Weekly Letter," Vol. 5, No. 26, August 25, 1917, York, Pa. Filed in York International Corporation archives.
8. Thomas Shipley, "A Bit of History Relating to the York Organization," company advertisement, November 1, 1917. Filed in York International Corporation archives.
9. Bernard C. Oldham, "The History of Refrigeration," *The Journal of Refrigeration*, April, 1967.
10. "A Modern Confectionery Shop," *Between Ourselves* newsletter, (Brooklyn, New York, April 1922), p. 3.
11. *Ibid.*, pp. 2-3.
12. "2500 Machines Sold During 25th Year," York Semi-Monthly Letter 11 (October 1, 1922), p. 56.

13. *Ibid.*, p. 60. Filed in York International Corporation archives.
14. York Manufacturing Company Weekly Letter, Vol. 2, No. 2, January 1, 1919. Filed in York International Corporation archives.
15. "Application of Mechanical Refrigeration Opens New Markets," York Semi-Monthly Letter 12 (September 1, 1923), 64. Filed in York International Corporation archives.
16. "Refrigeration on the Largest Naval Craft in the World," York Semi-Monthly Letter 14 (February 1, 1926), p. 249. Filed in York International Corporation archives.
17. "Frigidaire Machine Replacements," York Semi-Monthly Letter 15 (July 15, 1926), pp. 13-14. Filed in York International Corporation archives.
18 J.T. Bowen, "The Dairy," York Semi-Monthly Letter 13 (May 15, 1925), 390-416. Filed in York International Corporation archives.
19 "The Correct Lubricating Oils for Ice Making and Refrigerating Machinery," Bulletin No. 104, (York Oil and Chemical Company, 1926,) pp. 1-20.
20. *Ibid.*, p. 16.
21. C.O. Fehl, "Plant Expansion," York Semi-Monthly Letter 15 (December 1, 1926), p. 124.
22. *Ibid.*, (January 1, 1927), pp. 187-189.
23. C.W. Vogel, "New Gray Iron Foundry," York Semi-Monthly Letter 16 (February 15, 1928), p. 281.
24. Thomas Shipley, "Plant Improvements and Reasons for Them," York Semi-Monthly Letter 15 (April 15, 1927), p. 394.
25. "Largest Refrigerating Plant," York Semi-Monthly Letter 15 (August 1, 1926), p. 22.
26. "Refrigeration on the Largest Naval Craft in the World," York Semi-Monthly Letter, p. 250.
27. "Theatre Air Cooling Installation," York Semi-Monthly Letter 15 (July 1, 1926), p. 2.

28. "A Modern Theater for the Nation's Capital," York Semi-Monthly Letter 15 (December 1, 1926), pp. 120-121.

29. "Will the New Year Be A Good One?" York Semi-Monthly Letter 15 (January 1, 1927), pp. 149-150.

30. "Arctic-Pownall Stationary Can, Raw-Water System," Fittings and Supplies for Ice Making and Refrigerating Plants Catalog 14 (The Arctic Ice Machinery Company, Canton, Ohio, January 1925), p. 56.

31. "Bad Water Tests with Arctic-Pownall System,'" York Semi-Monthly Letter 18 (January 1, 1930), pp. 275-276.

32. "Henry D. Pownall," York Semi-Monthly Letter 20 (January 15, 1931), unnumbered insert next to page 90.

33. Thomas Shipley, "The Plan and Intent of the York Ice Machinery Corporation," (Address delivered as First Number of 1927-1928 Lecture Course on November 7, 1927), York Semi-Monthly Letter 16 (November 15, 1927), pp. 118-130.

34. Ibid., p. 120.

35. "York Ice Machinery Corporation," York Semi-Monthly Letter 16 (November 15, 1927), pp. 122.

36. Ibid., p. 140.

37. J. L. Rosenmiller, "Accessory Equipment and Supplies, Announcing York Smoke or Ammonia Mask," York Semi-Monthly Letter 16, (June 1, 1928) pp. 407-410.

38. J.L. Rosenmiller, "Accessory Equipment and Supplies, Comparative Data and a Few Hints on Yorkco Cold Storage Doors," York Semi-Monthly Letter 16 (June 15, 1928), pp. 424-434.

39. York Bulletins for 1928, describing each of these products, are contained at the end of a loose bound volume entitled "York Ice Machinery Corporation Bulletins," Archive York International.

40. "Building Experts Consider Iceless Refrigeration Code," New York World, June 24, 1928, p. 1.

41. "Household Refrigerating Machines," York Semi-Monthly Letter 17 (August 1, 1928), pp. 19-26.

42. York Ice Machinery Corporation 1928 Annual Report, p. 3.

Chapter Six

1. Herbert Hoover, 1928 campaign speech.

2. York 1930 Annual Report, December 30, 1930, p. 5.

3. "In Memorium," (Insert to Volume 15, this constituted York Semi-Monthly Letter for February 1, 1930).

4. "Personnel Changes," York Semi-Monthly Letter 18 (February 15, 1930), p. 178.

5. F.A. Weisenbach, "Competitive Machinery and Equipment, Also Sales Methods of Competitive Manufacturers," York Semi-Monthly Letter 18 (April 15, 1930), pp. 230-252.

6. Ibid., p. 234.

7. Ibid., p. 236.

8. "York Refrigeration and Human Comfort," York Semi-Monthly Letter," 19 (August 1, 1930), p. 22.

9. Letter to York Ice Machinery Corporation from T.E. Lapres (October 2, 1930) appearing in York Semi-Monthly Letter 19 (October 15, 1930), p. 74.

10. Ibid.

11. "An Airing for Air Conditioning, The York Coil Type Air Conditioner," York Semi-Monthly Letter 19 (March 15, 1932), pp. 242-244.

12. L.J. Dubois, "York Coil Type Air Conditioners for Fur Storage," York Semi-Monthly Letter 19 (April 15, 1931), pp. 269-271.

13. "A Great Scientific Achievement, " pamphlet published by Frigidaire Corporation, Dayton, Ohio, 1933, pp. 1-15.

14. Milton Ward Garland, interviewed by the author, October 10, 1995. Transcript, p. 10.

15. "Demonstrating Freon," York Monthly Letter (April 1933), p. 369.

16. Section 210-E of York Ice Machinery Corporation Data Sheet, "Freon-12 (Dichloro-Diflouro-Methane) Refrigerant" (October 31, 1938), p. 1.

17. 1932 Annual Report.

18. York Annual Letter, December 21, 1932, p. 3.

19. Ibid.

20. "Fifth 'Yorkco Family Nights To Be Greater Than Ever," The Cooler (April 1927), p. 1.

21. W.S. Shipley, "A Message," The Cooler (June 1937), p. 1.

22. James Stambaugh, interviewed by the author, January 29, 1996. Transcript, p. 21.

23. J. Duane Johnson, interviewed by the author, Jan. 29, 1996.

24. "A Red-ink Department for Aging Workers," The Cooler (June 1935), p. 2.

25. G.E. Buchanan, interviewed by the author, April 23, 1995. Transcript, p. 8.

26. "Relation of Government Debt to National Wealth," The Cooler (January 1936), p. 1.

27. "Financial Statement of Your Company," The Cooler (July 1937), p. 1.

28. "The York Portable Air Conditioner," The Cooler, (May 1935), p. 1.

29. "Abraham and Strauss," The Cooler, (August 1935), p. 1.

30. "Some of the Largest Air Conditioning Jobs in the World Have Been Done by York," The Cooler (May 1935), p. 1.

31. 1939 Annual Report, pp.5-6.

32. "Rigid Tests and Development Made Portable Yorkaire," York News (January 1938), p. 4.

33. Ibid.

34. 1938 York Ice Machinery Corporation Annual Report, p. 7.

35. Stewart E. Lauer, "Americanism in Industry," The Cooler (Picnic Edition, 1940), p. 1.

Chapter Seven

1. "The York Priority Business Plan," (York Ice Machinery Corporation, October 13, 1941), pp. 21-22.

2. Ibid.

3. "York Navy-School," Cold Magic, (Winter 1942) p. 26.

4. Raymond Lecates, interviewed by the author, April 29, 1996. Transcript, p. 2.

5. Austin Diehl, interviewed by the author, January 29, 1996. Transcript, pp. 11-12.
6. W.E. Landmesser, "FlakIce Machines With The Marines," *Sales News* (January 20, 1946), p. 7.
7. York Ice Machinery Corporation 1941 Annual Report, p. 6.
8. 35th Annual Meeting of the Manufacturers Association, February 10, 1941. Published October 1, 1950.
9. James Rudisill, *York Since 1941*, (York Graphic Services, Inc.: 1991) p. 100.
10. York Corporation 1942 Annual Report, p. 4.
11. "Editorial Note," *Cold Magic* (Winter 1942), p. 1.
12. "Stewart E. Lauer, "Our Battle of Production," *Cold Magic* (Winter 1942), pp. 3-4.
13. Internal memo, "Notice to All Branch Managers RE: Synthetic Rubber and Aviation Gasoline Refrigeration Program," (May 29), p. 2. York International Corporation archive.
14. Internal memo, "Presentations and Memoranda on Synthetic Rubber and Aviation Gasoline Refrigeration School," York Ice Machinery Corporation (May 29, 1942), p. 5. York International Corporation Archive.
15. "Synthetic Rubber" memo (June 15, 1942),York International Corporation archive.
16. "Cold Magic Helps Tame Unruly Metals," *Cold Magic* (York Corporation, September 1943), p. 13.
17. "York High-Test Finned Coils," York Sales Brochure, (c. 1942).
18. "Steel Staggered Tube Finned Coils," Circular Letter No. S-1798 (January 7, 1943), p. 1.
19. "Steel Staggered Tube Finned Coils," Circular Letter No. S-1773 Revised (March 30, 1943), p. 4.
20. War Production Board M-28, List A, January 29, 1945, p. 1.
21. "What is L-41?" How? (October 30, 1944), p. 1.
22. S.E. Lauer, "The President's Letter," *Shop News* (January 1943), p. 1

23. *Ibid.*, p. 3-4.
24. "Army-Navy Award Conferred Upon Yorkco Employees," *Shop News* (January 1944), p. 1
25. "Landing Craft Heads Priority Orders as Invasion Approaches," *Shop News* (January 1944), p. 10.
26. R.E. Miller, "Twelve Minutes From Heaven," *Cold Magic* (York Corporation, 1944), p. 28.
27. Neil A. Hopkins, "The Hurricane is Too Slow," *Cold Magic* (York Corporation, undated, c. 1942), pp. 33-34.
28. B.E. James, "Packaged Refrigeration and Air Conditioning," *Cold Magic* (York Corporation, September 1943), pp. 46-48.
29. "Historical Record Production and Services World War II," (York Corporation, 1950), pp. 4-5.
30. "Yorkco Unanimously Selected to Receive Atomic Bomb Award," *Shop News* (March-April 1946), p. 1.
31. "Bulletin #16," York Sales Newsletter (August 6, 1945).
32. "Volume of York Production," in Historical Record Production and Services World War II (York Corporation, 1950), p. 1.
33. York Corporation 1945 Annual Report, p. 1.
34. "York Opens First School of its Kind in Refrigeration and Air Conditioning to Train Field and Factory Employees," *Shop News* (March-April 1946), p. 1.

Chapter Eight

1. "Did You Ever See An Air conditioned Church?" *Sales News* (June 1948), pp. 2-3.
2. "J.J. Murphy, Baltimore, FlakIce Champion — Up To Now!" *Sales News* (December 20, 1945), p. 2.
3. "Nine Plus One (9+1) = A Market For FlakIce Machines Broader Than A Bostonian's Broad A's," *Sales News* (May 20, 1946), p. 3.
4. "World Famous Publisher Uses Yorks," *Sales News* (May 20, 1946), p. 6.
5. "Old Bookbinder's Restaurant Provides An Adventure In Good Eating," *Sales News* (August 20, 1946), p. 2.

6. "Sinai Hospital Operates Three FlakIce Machines," *Sales News* (January 20, 1946), p. 1.
7. *Ibid.*, p. 7.
8. W.E. Landmesser, "What is Happening?" *Sales News* (February 20, 1946), p. 5.
9. *Ibid.*, p. 8.
10. "Yorkco Starts Building Plans to Cost Million," *The York Dispatch* (July 24, 1946), p. 1.
11. *Ibid.*
12. D.C. Seitz, "Key Men Need Training," *Sales News* (February 1947), p. 6.
13. *Ibid.*, p. 7.
14. *Ibid.*
15. George Tindall and David Shi, *America*, (W.W. Norton & Company) pp. 792-793.
16. S.E. Lauer, "Labor Turmoil Among Suppliers Threatens Welfare (of) York Workers," *Sales News* (June 1947) p. 3.
17. "Labor Looks At Communism," *Sales News* (December 1947) pp. 5-6.
18. *Ibid.*
19. Victor Cox, "Taming Neutrons With A Model 350," *Sales News* (December 1947) pp. 1-2.
20. "Did You Ever See An Air conditioned Church?" *Sales News* (June 1948) pp. 2-3.
21. A.F. Avera, "Churches Need Air conditioning," *Sales News* (September 1948) pp. 4-5.
22. *Sales News* (July 1948) p. 1.
23. *Ibid.*, p. 6.
24. ". . . the clearest, purest ice cubes I've ever seen," *Sales News* (March 1949) p. 1.
25. *Ibid.*, p. 2.
26. T.E. Lapres, "Ice the York Way For Chalfont-Haddon Hall Hotels," *Sales News* (May 1949) p. 2.
27. *Ibid.*
28. "World's Largest One-Floor Restaurant Uses York 'Flaker' and 'Cuber,'" *Sales News* (May 1949) p. 3.
29. York Corporation 1948 Annual Report.
30. "Eight Two-Day Field Meetings Launch 'Geared To Go' Program," *Sales News* (March 1949), p. 4.
31. "Suburban Shopping Areas Growing In Popularity," *Sales News* (May 1949) p. 4.

32. Douglas A. Sterner, "Seagoing Yorkaire Conditioners," 40 *Sales News* (September 1949) pp. 1-2.

33. "York Takes Lead In Marine Field," Bulletin #41 York Sales NewsLetter (October 12, 1949), pp. 1-2, and "Queen of the Seas," #43 *Sales News* (February 1950), p. 4.

34. Refrigeration and Air Conditioning (York Corporation, 1951), pp. 35-36.

Chapter Nine

1. John Hertzler, personal letter to his district sales managers, "York Sales News Letter," August 1950.

2. Stewart Lauer, "Letter to the Editor," *Gazette and Daily*, York, Pa.: January 6, 1950.

3. Stewart E. Lauer, note to York Corporation lawyer M.F. Dick on the Economic Control Bill, August 1950.

4. York Corporation, *Shop News*, Vol. IX, No. 3, York, Pa.: December 1950.

5. *Newsweek* magazine, November 1950, as reprinted by York Corporation in *Shop News*, December 1950.

6. J.L. Chandler, "A History of Marine Refrigeration," unpublished article written in 1979 for York Division, Borg-Warner.

7. Crosby Field, "The Manufacture of Small Ice." Paper presented by the president of Flakice Corporation at the American Society of Mechanical Engineers, October 31, 1949.

8. York Corporation, Form 50952-1-10-1 Advertisement Pamphlet, York Model 450A Automatic Ice Maker, 1950.

9. York Corporation, York Sales News Letter, Volume XI, No. 13, December 1950.

10. York Corporation, "York Products and Policies For 1952." Company manual written in October 1951.

11. John Hertzler, personal letter to district sales managers, York Sales News Letter, August 1950.

12. Stewart Lauer, personal correspondence to Norris Benedict of

Waynesboro, Pa. dated February 5, 1951.

13. *Ibid.* p. 21.

14. William C. Moore, *Sales News*, (York Corporation, York, Pa.: Jan.uary 1951) p. 6.

15. John Padden, Memorial Resolution to W.S. Shipley from the Manufacturers' Association of York dated January 13, 1951.

16. Stewart Lauer, Letter to stockholders in the 1952 Annual Report, York Corporation, York, Pa.

17. *New York Herald Tribune*, European Edition, May 15, 1952, p. 1.

18. S.E. Lauer, personal letter to J.R. Hertzler, September 9, 1951.

19. S.E. Lauer, Letter to H.L. Luedicke, executive editor of The Journal of Commerce, New York, January 5, 1953.

20. S.E. Lauer, Speech given to the York Lions Club, "York Corporation and the Air Conditioning Business," October 20, 1953.

21. York Sales News Letter, York Corporation, January 11, 1954.

22. Walter E. Landmesser, York Commercial Department Letter regarding Philco and York Manufactured "Store Coolers," February 5, 1954.

23. "Patent Suit is Filed in Air Conditioning," *The New York Times*, February 11, 1954.

24. York Sales News Letter, Bulletin Edition, No. 53, York Corporation February 12, 1954.

25. *York Gazette and Daily*, York, Pa., June 25, 1954.

26. S.E. Lauer, report to the York Corporation stockholders, July 26, 1954.

27. S.E. Lauer, press release, "Yorkco Moves Ahead on Expansion Program," July 27, 1954.

28. S.E. Lauer, personal letter written to Keith Louden, August 8, 1954.

29. J.K. Louden, report to S.E. Lauer on the Industry Meeting on August 5 at the Links Club, New York, August 12, 1954.

30. *Ibid.*, p. 24.

31. Jack Joslin, York Corporation Personnel Director, letter to SE Lauer, Aug. 4, 1954.

32. D.M. Magor, Personal Report to S.E. Lauer on York Corporation's Federal Income and Excess Profits Tax, August 26, 1954.

33. S.E. Lauer, speech at meeting on the divisionalization of York Corporation, Yorktowne Hotel, York, Pa., October 1, 1954.

34. York Corporation, "Headquarters Staff Organization Chart No. 2," October 1, 1954.

35. S.E. Lauer, "An Observation on Publicity and Public Relations," unpublished essay distributed to York Corporation investors, October 5, 1954.

36. Cloud Wampler, personal letter to Stewart Lauer of York Corporation, December 10, 1954.

37. "Carrier Corporation Head Warns of Rough Year Ahead," *The Wall Street Journal*, November 12, 1954.

38. S. E. Lauer, president of York Corporation, 1954 Annual Report, York, Pa., December 22, 1954.

39. S.E. Lauer, letter to J.K Louden regarding the C.A. Olsen Manufacturing Company, November 29, 1954.

40. S.E. Lauer, letter to York Corporation's Board of Directors regarding the C.A. Olsen Manufacturing Company, December 9, 1954.

41. *Air Conditioning and Refrigeration News*, brief, June 20, 1955.

42. "York Corp. Orders up Sharply," *The Wall Street Journal*, New York, January 31, 1955.

43. C.A. Olsen Manufacturing Company, unpublished news releases to announce merger with York Corporation, April 22, 1955.

44. Ray A. Rich, vice president and general manager of Philco Corporation, letter to S.E. Lauer, president of York Corporation, September 22, 1955.

45. Jim Harnish, interviewed by Alex Lieber, April 29, 1996. Transcript, p. 12.

46. *Ibid.*

47. Gene Walsh, York Corporation press release announcing employment of Andrew Freimann, October 1, 1955.

Chapter Ten

1. John Schultz, interviewed by the author, April 23, 1996. Transcript, pp. 13-14.
2. S.E. Lauer, confidential letter to Roy Ingersoll, June 13, 1955. York International Corporation archives.
3. York Corporation data sheet of proposed purchase of Williams Heating Division of the Eureka Williams Corporation, February 29, 1956.
4. S.E. Lauer, "Unalterable Facts Regarding the Acquisition of Eureka Williams," report presented to York's Executive Management Committee, March 1956.
5. S.E. Lauer, telegram to C.W. Fenninger, March. 5.
6. George S. Munson, letter to S.E. Lauer of York Corporation as its attorney with the Townsend, Elliot & Munson practice in Philadelphia, Pa., March 8, 1956.
7. S.E. Lauer, letter to George Munson, March 7, 1956.
8. S.E. Lauer, "Summary of Sales Agreement- York and Borg," (first draft), York, Pa., April 27, 1956.
9. *York Gazette & Daily*, York, Pa., April 9, 1956.
10. R.C. Ingersoll, letter to Stewart Lauer on settlement with Eureka-Williams, June 20, 1956.
11. H. Lee Davis, "Borg-Warner: The First 50 Years," (Borg-Warner Corporation, Chicago, Illinois, 1978).
12. *Ibid.*
13. S.E. Lauer, memo to J.K. Louden, May 16, 1956.
14. Carl W. Fenninger, York Corporation Proxy Report No. 23, June 25, 1956.
15. Borg-Warner to add York Corp., *The New York Times*, New York, April 6, 1956.
16. "Yorkco Growth Foreseen Under New Affiliation," *York Dispatch*, York, Pa., April 6, 1956.
17. S.E. Lauer, "Letter to York's Stockholders," April 2, 1956.
18. Bill Eastman, interviewed by the author, April 29, 1996. Transcript, p. 10.
19. Robert Berger, interviewed by the author, January 30, 1996. Transcript, p. 6.
20. Borg-Warner Corporation, 1956 Annual Report, Chicago, Illinois.
21. Gene Welsh, York Corporation public relations officer, York, Pa., July 12, 1956.
22. John Schultz, interviewed by the author, April 23, 1996. Transcript, pp. 13-14.
23. Borg-Warner Corporation, 1957 Annual Report.
24. *Ibid.*, p. 35.
25. Borg Warner Corporation, 1958 Annual Report.

Chapter Eleven

1. William Roberts, "Largest Attendance at 25-Year Club Reunion: Roberts Reports on '67 and Future Expansion," *The Weathervane* (York International Corporation, October 1967), p. 7.
2. "York Sound and Vibration Studies Aid Consumers," *The Weathervane* (York International Corporation, July 1966), pp. 5-6.
3. "Thermoelectric Developments By Borg-Warner," Report on Submarine Air Conditioning (York Division, 1961) p. 3.
4. "Final Report Phase I, Thermoelectric Air Conditioner for Submarines," Defense Electronics Products, Radio Corporation of America (Camden, N.J., 1960), p. 1-2. York International archive.
5. Dr. Kenneth Hickman, interviewed by Alex Lieber, September 11, 1996.
6. Jeff Rodengen, *The Legend of Electric Boat*, Write Stuff Enterprises, pp. 116-117.
7. Jim Harnish, interviewed by Alex Lieber. Transcript, p. 7.
8. *Ibid.*
9. "From The Desk of W.C. Moore," *The Weathervane* (York International Corporation, October 1965), p. 1.
10. "Sales Reporting," *The Weathervane* (York International Corporation, December 1963), p. 3.
11. "From the Desk of P.K. Miller," *The Weathervane* (York International Corporation, January 1964), p. 1.
12. "York Absorption and Turbomatic Systems Keep Johns Hopkins University Cool," *The Weathervane* (York International Corporation, March 1964), p. 5.
13. "Valuable Rare Books Need York 'Climate'" *York Sales News* (January 1964), p. 5.
14. "Biggest Job In York's History," *York Sales News* (January 1964), p. 7.
15. "Refrigeration For Atomic Power Station," *York Sales News* (January 1964), p. 6.
16. "New Mobile Hyperbaric Chamber Displayed At First Annual San Francisco Cancer Symposium," *The Weathervane* (York International Corporation, January 1966), p. 6.
17. "York Built Hyperbaric Chamber Speeds 15 Year Old Boy's Recovery," *The Weathervane* (York International Corporation, October 1966), p. 6.
18. "From The Desk of A. Smiley," *The Weathervane* (York International Corporation, July 1966), p. 1.
19. "Environment Control Required In World's Largest Building For Assembly of Moon Rocket," *The Weathervane* (York International Corporation, September 1965), p. 3.
20. Richard Lewis, *Appointment on the Moon*, (Viking Press, New York, 1969), pp. 414-415.
21. Bill Eastman interview, transcript p. 6.
22. "York Units For New USS *John F. Kennedy* Pass Tough Navy Shock Tests on First Try," *The Weathervane* (York International Corporation, February 1966), p. 5.
23. "Excerpts From 'Report of the President' at Borg-Warner Annual Stockholder's Meeting," *The Weathervane* (York International Corporation, May 1966), p. 1.
24. "Pittsburgh Dedicates New Plant To Serve Unique Community Project," *The Weathervane* (York International Corporation, February 1967), p. 6.

25. "Business Bulletin: Air Conditioner Makers Talk of Banner Year, But Retailers Moan," *The Wall Street Journal* (June 15, 1967), p. 1.

26. "Largest Attendance at 25-Year Club Reunion: Roberts Reports on '67 and Future Expansion," *The Weathervane* (York International Corporation, October 1967), pp. 1-2.

27. *Ibid.*, p. 7.

28. Jim Walsh, interviewed by Karen Nitkin, October 31, 1996. Transcript, pp. 6-7.

29. "New Medical Center at University of Beirut is Completely York Air Conditioned," *The Weathervane* (York International Corporation, August 1967), p. 5.

30. "York Employs Wings in Operations," *York Shop News* (July 1968), pp. 1-2.

31. Borg-Warner Corporation 1967 Annual Report, p. 14.

32. Borg-Warner Corporation 1967 Annual Report, pp. 1-3.

33. "Seven 7,000-Ton Centrifugal Compressors to Air Condition New World Trade Center," *York Sales News* (April 1968), p. 1.

34. Victor McCloskey, interviewed by the author, January 29, 1996. Transcript, pp. 8-9.

35. Robert Dolheimer, interviewed by the author, January 30, 1996. Transcript, pp. 12-13.

36. M.R. Schroer," "Cooling and Heating Load Calculations and Optimum Air Conditioning System Selection By Digital Computer," (Roy C, Ingersoll Research Center, Des Plaines, Illinois, September 3, 1968), pp. 1-11. York International archive.

37. "Construction Starts on Office and School Buildings at York HQ," *York Sales News* (April 1968), p. 1.

38. "Look Ma! No Compressors," *York Sales News* (November 1969), pp. 6-8.

39. "York Goes To St. Petersburg," *York Sales News* (November 1969), p. 16.

40. "Kent State Integrates Air Conditioning," *York Sales News* (November 1969), p. 12.

Chapter Twelve

1. Isaac Asimov, "Energy and Your Home," (York Division, Borg-Warner Corporation, 1978), p. 1.

2 "Mitsubishi-York Equipment Air Conditions 'Expo 70'," *York Sales News* (March-April 1970) p. 4.

3. "York Equipment Specified for New Navy Amphibious Assault Vessels," *York Sales News* (January-February 1970), p. 16.

4. "Jack Kennedy Is President!" *York Sales News* (July-August 1970), p. 1.

5. R.D. Pepler, "Variations In Students' Test Performances And In Classroom Temperatures In Climate Controlled And Non-Climate Controlled Schools," Research Report 2193 RP-91, ASHRAE Transactions, 1.1.6.

6. Scott Boxer, interviewed by the author, January 30, 1996. Transcript, p. 3.

7. "York Plant Surrounded By Flood Waters," *York Sales News* (July-August 1972), pp. 1-2.

8. "View From the Top by E.P. Carpenter," *York Sales News* (January-February 1974), p. 15.

9. James Stambaugh, interviewed by the author, January, 29, 1996. Transcript, pp. 3-4.

10. Terry Bowman, interviewed by the author, May 3, 1996. Transcript, p. 11.

11. "Solar Energy Heats and Cools at Timonium, Maryland," *York Sales News* (September-October 1974), p. 3.

12. "Solar Energy Heats and Cools at Timonium, Maryland," *York Sales News* (No. 125), p. 3.

13. "York Heat Pump Hits Headlines," *York Sales News* (No. 129), p. 4.

14. Isaac Asimov, "Energy and Your Home," pamphlet (York Division, Borg-Warner Corporation, 1978), p. 1.

15. *Ibid.*, p. 17.

16. "Half Of U.S. Furnaces Are Too Big For Home," *York Sales News* (No. 132), p. 6.

17. "Solar Energy For Heating And Cooling of Buildings," A York Division Research Report, August 1979, York International archive.

18. "York's Role In Honeywell's Solar-Energy HVAC System," *York Sales News* (No. 133), pp. 2-3.

19. Legislative History of the Toxic Substances Control Act," (Washington, D.C. 1976), pp. 407-513. York International archive.

20. "Did You Know?" *York Communicator* (October 1979), p. 4.

21. "Heating Budget Over $1,000,000," *York Communicator* (September 1979), p. 9.

22. "EPA. Investigates Fluorocarbons," *York Sales News* (No.132), p. 4

Chapter Thirteen

1. Elwood Spangler, interviewed by the author, January 30, 1996. Transcript, pp. 9-10.

2. C. David Kramer, "Luxaire History," (Godfrey Advertising FAX, March 21, 1996). York International archive.

3. Dr.Richard A. Erth, Vice President of Engineering, "From My Point of View," *The York Communicator* (Autumn 1983), p. 6.

4. Tony Michaels, "No More Storeroom Physical Inventories," *The York Communicator* (Autumn 1983), p. 9.

5. "We Are Saving Money For York," *The York Communicator* (Autumn 1982), p. 4.

6. "Quality Circles at York," internal plant memo, July 7, 1984. York International Archive.

7. York Europe Manufacturing Division, Basildon, (1983 insert). York International archive.

8. *Ibid.*

9. Roy Holder, "Anatomy of a Corporate Resuscitation," Works Management, February 1989, p. 20.

10. Dennis Kloster interview, transcript, p. 3.

11. Robert J.M. Fisher, "From My Point of View," *The York Communicator* (Winter 1983/84), p. 1.

12. Dave McEwan, "Where's Our Business Really Going?" *The York Communicator* (Summer 1984), p. 4.

13. "PoolPaks Targeted at Indoor Swining Pool Market," *The York Communicator* (Summer 1984), p. 10.

14. "Borg-Warner Personnel Bulletin #1997," January 5, 1984.

15. "Borg-Warner Personnel Bulletin #1998," January 5, 1984.

16. "Turnover At The Top, Why Executives Are Losing Their Jobs So Quickly," *Business Week* (December 19, 1983), pp. 104-109.

17. "Borg-Warner Lays Off 80, Company Expects More Personnel Reductions If Strike Continues," *The York Dispatch* (November 26, 1984), p. 48.

18. Advertisement, David. L. McEwan "We Are Very Disappointed," *The York Dispatch* (December 6, 1984), p. 35.

19. Borg-Warner Internal Bulletin, "Borg-Warner Air Conditioning, Inc. Organizational Changes," April 18, 1985. York International Archive.

20. Robert Fisher, "In The News," Bulletin posted April 27, 1985. York International archive.

21. "Borg-Warner Has No Plans To Sell York, Firm Says," *Air Conditioning, Heating, & Refrigeration News* (April 29, 1985), p. 1.

22. Robert Pokelwaldt, interviewed by the author, January 30, 1996. Transcript, pp. 6-7.

23. Elwood Spangler, interviewed by the author, January 30, 1996. Transcript, pp. 9-10.

24. "Borg-Warner Eyes Spinoff, Air Conditioning Plant May Go Independent," *The York Dispatch*, p. 44, and "1985 Second Quarter Report," p. 4 (July 26, 1985).

25. Tim Reeves, "Borg-Warner Wants Spinoff of York Plant," *The York Daily Record* (July 27, 1985), p. 1A and "Borg-Warner," *The Wall Street Journal* (July 29, 1985), p. 6.

26. "Independence Would Bring Opportunities," Borg-Warner Interchange (July 26, 1985), p. 2.

27. Press Release: "Borg-Warner Board Approves Air Conditioning Stock distribution," (September 25, 1985), York International archive.

28. Mike Miller, "York International: Reborn of a Changing Industry," *Air Conditioning, Heating & Refrigeration News* (January 20, 1986), p. 23.

29. "York International Corporation Offering Circular," (August 5, 1987), F-8. York International Archive.

30. "Vincent Appointed President and Chief Operating Officer," *The York Communicator* (January 1986), p. 7.

31. York International 1987 Annual Report, p. 1.

32. Dennis Kloster, interviewed by the author, January 29, 1996. Transcript, p. 1.

33. Mike Miller, "York International: Reborn of a Changing Industry," *Air Conditioning & Refrigeration News* (January 20, 1986), p. 23.

34. "6.1 Percent Stake Acquired, Investor Eyes Borg Warner," *The York Dispatch* (October 31, 1986), p. 28.

35. Matt O'Connor, "Bog-Warner Cuts Corporate, R&D Staffs," *Chicago Tribune* (February 17, 1987),6B.

36. "New Stellar 2000 A.C. Units Are Introduced," York Marketing Messenger (February 1986), p. 4.

37. Bob Schmitt, interviewed by Alex Lieber, July 29, 1996. Transcript, p. 3.

38. Stanley Hiller, Jr. and Thomas J. Vincent, Letter to York Employees, March 5, 1986. York International archive.

39. "Heat Pumps Designed For Every Market Segment," York Marketing Messenger (February 1986), p. 5.

40. "90+ Furnaces Introduced," York Marketing Messenger (February 1986), p. 3.

41. "New High Efficiency Luxaire and Fraser-Johnston Units Are Introduced," Focus, A Publication of Central Environmental Systems (Spring 1987), p. 1.

42. Idris Michael Diaz, "York International Thrives on Back-To-Basics, Chairman Succeeding at Largest Challenge," *York Daily Record* (Sunday, November 8, 1987), p. 1D.

43. York International Employee Bulletin, "Employee Stock Purchase Plan Set," August 5, 1987. York International archive.

44. Terry Bowman, "Target — (ZD) Zero Defects," *The Conveyor*, (York International, February 1987).

45. F.R. LePage, York Internal Bulletin, August 11, 1987. York International archive.

46. York International press release, "News From York," August 3, 1987. York International archive.

47. Milton Ward Garland, interviewed by the author, October 10, 1995. Transcript, p. 11.

48. "York International Purchases British Firm," *York Daily Record* (November 12, 1987), p. 1A.

49. York International Press Release, "York Agrees To Acquire Bristol," September 25, 1986. York International archive.

50. Press Release, "York International to Acquire Full Ownership of Joint Ventures in Mexico," November 23, 1987. York International archive.

51. York International 1987 Annual Report, p. 2.

52. York International 1987 Annual Report, p. 3.

53. Chuck Russ, interviewed by the author, April 25, 1996. Transcript, p. 3.

54. Todd Myers,"James Dresser New CEO," *The York Dispatch* (April 25, 1989), p. D1.

55. Robert Pokelwaldt, interviewed by the author, January 30, 1996. Transcript, pp. 6-7.

56. Bill Patalon, "York International: A Buyout That Worked," *York Daily Record* (December 24, 1989), p. 2F.

57. Joe Smith, interviewed by Karen Nitkin, April 29, 1996. Transcript, p. 5.

58. York International Corporation 1991 Annual Report, p. 1.

59. Mark Pearson, "York International, RECO Merge," *The York Dispatch* (July 8, 1989), p. A4.

60. York International Press Release, "News From York," April 13, 1989. York International archive.

61. Constance Walker, "County Firm Lands $17 Million Deal With Saudis," *York Daily Record* (September 26, 1989), p. 1A.
62. Mark Bodell, interviewed by Alex Lieber, August 1, 1996. Transcript, pp. 4-5.

Chapter Fourteen

1. York mission, established in 1994 by York International.
2. "Nestlé Turns to York for CFC Solutions," York International Corporation 1992 Annual Report, p 16.
3. Bill Stewart, interviewed by the author, January 29, 1996. Transcript, pp. 18-19.
4. "York Offers Industry's Widest Range of CFC-Free Chillers," *York Insight*, (1992) p. 13.
5. "Refrigeration and Freezing: Out in the Cold," Food Engineering International (February 1995), p. 49.
6. "GM Using Purge Units To Conserve CFCs," *York Insight* (Winter 1995), p. 13.
7. York International 1993 Annual Report, pp. 4-5.
8. Robert Pokelwaldt, interviewed by the author, January 30, 1996. Transcript, pp. 25-27.
9. "York Acquisition Adds Manufacturing Plants, Sales Channels," York press release, May 7 1997.
10. Helen Marsteller, interviewed by Karen Nitkin, October 25, 1996. Transcript, pp. 6-7.
11. "New Apple Computer R&D Campus Features York Equipment, Controls," York International 1992 Annual Report, pp. 6-7.
12. Scott Boxer interview, transcript, pp. 18-19.

13. York International Corporation 1995 Annual Report, pp. 21-22.
14. David Simpson, "Totally Focused on HVAC&R Growth," *Appliance* magazine, April 1994, p. y-4.
15. Ross Wix notes, June 15, 1996.
16. David Simpson, "Leading with Technology," *Appliance* magazine, April 1994, p. y-11.
17. Bill Napp, interviewed by the author, April 23, 1996. Transcript, p. 11.
18. Chuck Russ, interviewed by the author, April 25, 1996. Transcript, p. 8.
19. York Makes Showing in EPA Energy Star Program," *Western HVAC News* (July 1995).
20. "York International Tries Again for Shareholder OK," *Central Penn Business Journal* (April 28, 1995), p. 4.
21. "York International Makes $133 million Purchase," *The York Dispatch* (February 13, 1995), p. 1; York Acquires Evcon," *Contracting Business* (April 1995), p. 16.
22. "Spring Garden Township Company Can Expand," *York Daily Record* (July 13, 1995), p. 1.
23. "Frick Purchases Refrigeration Units of Danish Company," *Air Conditioning & Refrigeration News* (June 12, 1995), p. 21.
24. "York, Frick Company Announce Acquisitions," *York Insight* (Winter 1995), p. 20.
25. "York International Subsidiary Buys Firm," *York Daily Record* (August 7, 1995), p. 1.
26. James A. Bledsoe, "America Needs the Seawolf Submarine," Letter to *The York Dispatch* (August 3, 1995).
27. Marlo A. Palmieri,"Seawolf Sub Not Filled With Pork," Letter to

York Daily Record (August 3, 1995).
28. Terry Bowman, interviewed by the author, May 3, 1996. Transcript, p. 9.
29. John McDonald, interviewed by the author, January 30, 1996. Transcript, pp. 12-13.
30. Chuck O'Neal, interviewed by the author, April 23, 1996. Transcript, p. 8.
31. Kloster interview, p. 5.
32. "Driven by Quality, York Nearing 100% ISO Certification," *York Insight* (Summer 1995), p. 6.
33. "Standing Tall," *York Insight* (Summer 1995), pp. 4-5.
34. Pokelwaldt interview, transcript, p. 5.
35. Peter Spellar, interviewed by the author, January 30, 1996. Transcript, p. 25.
36. "Unitary Products Moving Toward R-410A," *York Insight* (Spring 1995), p. 15.
37. Kloster interview, p. 6-8.
38. Annual letter to shareholders, Robert Pokelwaldt, 1996 Annual Report, http://www.york.com/ 96report/stockholders.html.
39. "York Firm Challenged to Cool Off Olympians," Harrisburg Sunday Patriot News (August 6, 1995), p. 13.
40. Mike Ricci, interviewed by Jon VanZile, November 11, 1997. Transcript, p. 8.
41. Joseph Smith interview, transcript, p. 15.
42. Ricci interview, p. 14.
43. Ricci interview, p. 4.
44. "Olympic Sponsorship," York Insight, Volume 5, Iss. 3, Summer 1996, Special Olympic Review, p. 10.
45. Spellar interview, transcript, p. 9.
46. Pokelwaldt interview, transcript, p. 5.

INDEX